DYNAMIC
CHESS

DYNAMIC
CHESS

THE MODERN STYLE
OF AGGRESSIVE PLAY

by

R. N. COLES

REVISED AND ENLARGED EDITION

DOVER PUBLICATIONS, INC.

NEW YORK

This Dover edition, first published in 1966, is
a revised and enlarged version of the work originally
published by Sir Isaac Pitman & Sons, Ltd., London,
in 1956.
This edition is published by special arrangement
with Sir Isaac Pitman & Sons, Ltd., Pitman House,
Parker Street, Kingsway, London, W.C. 2.

Standard Book Number: 486-21676-4
Library of Congress Catalog Card Number: 66-20504

Manufactured in the United States of America
Dover Publications, Inc.
180 Varick Street
New York, N.Y. 10014

INTRODUCTION TO THE
DOVER EDITION

I N preparing this edition of a book originally written over ten years ago, I realized that the second part had to be brought up to date, not only in order to review the most recent period of Russian chess but also to examine the play of masters whose impact on the chess scene has been relatively recent.

The plan of the original edition, however, has again been followed, namely to give adequate attention to all of the most prominent Russian masters of the period and at the same time to give a suitable number of games from each decade.

An extra chapter which was added for the German edition has been retained and slightly enlarged, and I hope this new edition will prove to give as balanced a view of the whole period as did the previous one.

Fetcham, England   R. N. COLES
September, 1965

PREFACE

WHEN that most fascinating of chess writers, Richard Réti, showed in both his *Modern Ideas in Chess* and his *Masters of the Chessboard* that the development of chess ideas could be seen to follow a continuous pattern, he hinted, without being able to view the matter through the perspective of time, that in his own day evolution of ideas was giving place to a revolution in ideas. Had he, the chronicler of the Hypermodern Revolution, not died prematurely in 1929, we might well have had a later and more profound judgment upon the events of the revolution in which he himself took no small part.

As it is, the story has till now remained unwritten, and in this book I have endeavoured to go some of the way towards filling the gap. We are now able to view the Hypermodern Revolution as a stage between the old Classicism and the new Dynamism. Considered thus, its various features fall into place, and while some of the things which Réti and Nimzovitch thought important are indeed important, others on which they laid great stress can be seen to be in fact no more than side-issues.

The book is concluded with a considerable selection of the most modern examples of the new Dynamism, and though, as always when dealing with contemporary matters, some of the emphasis may later prove to have been misplaced, there is certainly no doubt that the Russian masters follow the Hypermoderns with the same pattern of continuous development as Réti himself noted in earlier generations. I hope that the juxtaposition of the ideas of the two periods will help to illuminate the scene both forwards and backwards, and by indicating the direction in which ideas are moving thereby make them easier of comprehension.

R. N. C.

TEDDINGTON, 1954.

CONTENTS

PART I—THE HYPERMODERN REVOLUTION

PART II—THE RUSSIANS

LIST OF GAMES

(Games marked with an asterisk are quoted in the annotations)

xiii

LIST OF GAMES

PART I
The Hypermodern Revolution

CHAPTER I

The Four Elements

THE birth of the dynamic idea in chess theory is comparatively recent, dating back no further than the second decade of the twentieth century. It now dominates the entire strategical and tactical conception of the game, and has infused chess with new and vigorous life.

The seeds of the idea can actually be traced back to Steinitz, but while much of Steinitz's theory and practice was understood and adopted in his own day, the dynamic features of his play were generally regarded as no more than unnecessary eccentricities of style.

To obtain a clear picture of the dynamic revolution in chess theory, it is necessary to examine the background against which it took place. By the turn of the century the theory of the game had been so explored that it appeared as if a final definition could be reached; pre-eminence seemed no longer to depend on greater knowledge of theory, but partly on greater adherence to it and partly on superior technique in applying it. Everything could be reduced to a logical basis once the four basic elements were appreciated.

From the earliest times *the element of material* had been understood, and an advantage in that element was recognized as conferring a probable winning advantage upon the player who possessed it.

Paul Morphy, in the mid-nineteenth century, threw emphasis on *the element of time* when he showed that an advantage in time could also confer winning chances, since it enabled its possessor to

Diagram 1
THOMPSON–MORPHY
(New York, 1857)

strike first with the heavier force; with this Morphy combined the conception of control of the central area, since occupation of that area provided the attack with the greater mobility and the greater

3

coherence, while denying those same factors to the opposition. The application of these two factors to actual play is now common practice even with beginners, and one example is sufficient to illustrate it. In the first tournament game Morphy ever played, he reached the position in Diagram 1, where, as Black he has already gained an advantage in time in that he has castled while his opponent's King is still in the centre. White now played 1 P×P, and if Morphy, like his contemporaries, had simply continued with 1 ..., B×P; 2 Kt×B, R×Kt, White could have played 3 P–Q4 with a fair game. But Morphy exploited the position by first seizing the centre with 1 ..., P–Q4; 2 B–Kt3 and then, still not yielding his time advantage by recapturing the Pawn, played 2 ..., P–K5; 3 P×P, P×P; 4 Kt–Kt1 (if Kt×P, B×P), Kt–K4; 5 B–K3, Kt–Q6*ch*; 6 K–K2, B×B; 7 P×B, Q–R5; 8 Kt×P, Q×Kt; 9 Q×Kt, Q×KtP*ch* and won.

Siegbert Tarrasch, towards the end of the nineteenth century, emphasized *the element of space*, showing that an advantage in space could also become a winning factor, because a cramped defence could not move from point to point with the same efficiency as the more mobile attack. The practical application of this principle is inevitably slower and more difficult than the exploitation of an advantage in time; a good example is seen in the position in Diagram 2.

Diagram 2

RICHTER–TARRASCH
(Nürnberg, 1888)

1 ...	P–KKt4
2 B–Q2	B–Kt5
3 Kt–Q4	P–QB4
4 Kt–K2	Kt–Kt4

Threatening 5 ..., B×Kt; 6 R×B, Kt–Q5; winning.

5 B–B3	QR–Q1
6 Kt–Q2	Kt–Q5
7 B×Kt	P×B

Now he threatens 8 ..., B–Kt5; 9 QR–Q1, KR–K1; winning.

8 P–QR3	P–QB4
9 Kt–KKt3	P–KR4
10 P–KB3	B–Q2
11 R–K2	P–Kt4

The scope of White's Knights is steadily limited.

12 QR–K1	B–KB1

If KR–K1, White would before long succeed in exchanging one pair of Rooks, and it is a principle of the use of an advantage in space that exchanges are avoided. If 12 ..., B–Q3; White could have effectively answered 13 Kt–K4.

13 Kt(3)–K4   R–KKt1

Threatening P–B4.

14 Kt–QKt3   R–B1
15 Kt(4)–Q2   P–B4
16 R–K5   B–Q3
17 R(5)–K2

If 17 R–Q5, R–Kt3; and the White Rook is in chancery.

17 ...   R–QR1

Threatening P–R4–QR5. But White reacts stubbornly.

18 Kt–R5   R(R)–Kt1

Not B–B2; 19 Kt–Kt7, B–Kt3; 20 Kt–Q6*ch*, and the absolute bind on White's position is broken.

19 Kt(5)–Kt3   P–R5
20 K–R1   R–KKt3
21 K–Kt1   B–K3
22 R–B2   R–QR1
23 R(2)–K2

The point of Black's recent manœuvres is now clear. If 23 Kt–R5, B–B2; 24 Kt–Kt7, B–KB5; 25 Kt–B1, R–QB1; with a strong threat of P–B5.

23 ...   P–R4
24 Kt–Kt1   P–R5
25 Kt(3)–Q2   P–QB5

Having completely cramped White's game, Black easily forces a break-in.

26 Kt–B1   R–QB1
27 K–R1   P–B6
28 P×P   P×P

The white Knight on QKt1 is now immobilized, and its position prevents White from bringing his Rooks across to meet the threat of an impending passed pawn on the Queen's side. A simple example of self-interference being forced upon the defence by an advantage in space.

29 Kt–K3   P–QKt5
30 Kt–B4

If 30 P×P, B×KtP; and the black QR pawn can only be stopped at the cost of a piece.

30 ...   B×Kt
31 P×B   R×P
32 R–K3   P×P
33 Kt×BP   B–Kt5
Resigns

Finally, there was what Capablanca termed *the element of position*, which was determined largely by the shape of the pawn structure, and the influence that structure had upon various pieces or squares.

Even before Tarrasch's day, Wilhelm Steinitz had evolved his theory of strong and weak squares. It had been recognized for some considerable time that pawns which were isolated or backward were sources of weakness; but though such a pawn was weak because it could only be defended by pieces, the fact that it could be so defended meant that it was not always an advisable target for attack, or at least not until almost all the pieces had been exchanged. Steinitz showed that the square in front of such a pawn was also weak, for it consti-

Diagram 3

STEINITZ–BLACKBURNE

(London, 1876)

tuted what he termed a "hole," namely a square amongst the hostile pawn skeleton from which an occupying piece could not be driven by pawns; more often the hole was to be found among a group of associated pawns, and Steinitz showed in actual play that occupation of such a hole was a long step forward to victory. A classic example occurred in the first game of his 1876 match with Blackburne. In the position in Diagram 3 Black has played P–Kt3 to drive off the offensive Knight, but in doing so he has created

two holes, one on his KR3 and one on his KB3. The occupation of these weak squares by Steinitz and the consequent victory were secured by Steinitz as follows—

1 Kt×B*ch*	Q×Kt	6 ...	Kt–B2
2 B–K3	Kt(1)–Kt2	7 Q–Q2	P–QR4
3 O–O–O	P–QB4		
4 P–Q4			

Aiming to secure access to Black's KB3 along the long diagonal.

4 ...	KP×P
5 P×P	P–B5
6 P–Q5	

Leaving his own KP backward and a hole on his K5. Here, though it was not realized at the time, was the germ of the dynamic idea— accepting a weakness in order to gain in strength.

Denying White any entry on the Queen's side, but he can do nothing about the more serious King's flank, and in a few moves White establishes himself on the two vital squares.

8 B–Q4	P–B3

This rids him of his hole on KB3, but the weakness of the square persists owing to the advance of the KKt pawn.

9 Q–R6	P–Kt5
10 P–Kt5	P–B4

If he tries to keep the diagonal

blocked by Kt(Kt)–K1, then 11 P–KR4, Q–Kt2; 12 Q × Q*ch*, K × Q; 13 P–R5, forcing the Black King's position open.

| 11 | B–B6 | Q–B2 |
| 12 | P×P | P×P |

The same continuation follows after 12 ..., Kt×P; 13 B×Kt, P × B.

13 P–Kt6

A quiet little combination to round off the earlier play. If Black replies P × P, then 14 Kt–Kt5, and there is no defence.

| 13 | ... | Q×KtP |
| 14 | B×Kt | Q×Q*ch* |

To try and avoid the loss of a piece with Q × B is fatal after 15 KR–Kt1, R–B2; 16 B × P.

15 B×Q and wins.

CHAPTER II

The Classical Style

TARRASCH, who absorbed much, but not all, of Steinitz's theories, expounded his conception of the game in simple terms, and his modified theory, which was part Morphy, part Steinitz and part Tarrasch, became the foundation of the classical style of chess play. Steinitz had often sacrificed time or space or both in his manœuvrings for strong and weak squares. Tarrasch denied the need to indulge in such eccentricities; to do so was in his view merely to make an already difficult game more difficult, and his opinion found ready and general acceptance. Thereby the classical style forgot, if it ever knew, the dynamic principle.

Briefly, the classic style consisted of a logical development of forces, avoiding any weakness in the pawn skeleton, while keeping an eye open for any weakness in the hostile pawn formation which could be made the object of attack. The centre was occupied by pawns as quickly as possible, or as much of it as could be secured before the enemy could prevent it, space was gained when it could be done without creating a weakness and time was gained if any opportunity for gaining it should arise. It was a style based upon the accumulation of small advantages.

Certain tactical factors, originating mostly from Steinitz, were accepted as contributing to the chance of later being able to gain an advantage, and of these the chief were first the possession of two Bishops against two Knights or Knight and Bishop in any position except a tightly closed one—an example was seen in Diagram 2—and secondly, the majority of pawns on the Queen's side because in the endgame, after King's side castling by both parties, this majority yielded the remoter passed pawn which was usually a winning endgame factor.

All this was seen to be so essentially logical that it was readily accepted as forming the only correct basis for sound play. If, as so often happened, no appreciable advantage could be obtained in any of

8

the four elements, then it became a question of tactical manœuvring in order to create or expose some slight weakness. On this the player then fastened, and to its exploitation he developed his entire game. From that point the strategy was clear cut; the best games of the classical style are marked by this extreme simplicity of fundamental strategy.

In the following game, as an example, Black saddles White during the opening stages with a backward Queen's pawn, and the whole conduct of his game thereafter is conditioned by this over-riding factor.

GAME I

FRENCH DEFENCE

Paulsen   Tarrasch

Nürnberg Tournament, 1888

1	P–K4	P–K3
2	P–Q4	P–Q4
3	P–K5	P–QB4

The struggle for occupation of the centre by pawns starts at once.

4	P–QB3	Kt–QB3
5	Kt–B3	Q–Kt3
6	B–Q3	P×P

After this White is able to maintain his centre pawns, but only with some loss of time, showing that 6 B–K2 would have been better. His Q pawn, however, becomes permanently backward.

7	P×P	B–Q2

Not Kt×P; 8 Kt×Kt, Q×Kt; 9 B–Kt5*ch*. But now the threat to the Q pawn is very real.

8	B–K2	KKt–K2
9	P–QKt3	Kt–B4
10	B–Kt2	B–Kt5*ch*

11 K–B1

The price White has to pay for the defence of his centre pawns is loss of the right to castle, since a Knight on either Q2 or QB3 would cut off one of the defences of the Q pawn.

11 ... B–K2

The Bishop has performed one task and now retires in order to solidify Black's game. White's Kt–Kt5 is prevented, while his P–KKt4 can now be answered with Kt–R5.

12 P–Kt3 P–QR4

Threatening to destroy White's Q side with P–R5, thus revealing another weakness which has sprung from the defence of the Q pawn.

13	P–QR4	R–QB1
14	B–Kt5	Kt–Kt5

Avoiding the dangers of O–O; 15 B–Q3, with concealed pressure on Black's KR pawn.

15 B×B*ch*

Black now has the initiative, for if White plays the natural looking Kt–B3, Black continues B×B; 16

9

Kt × B, Kt–B7 threatening Kt–K6*ch*, though Nimzovitch later regarded this line as preferable.

15 ...   K × B
16 Kt–B3   Kt–B3

From this point on White is made to feel the weakness of his Q pawn. Here Black makes use of it to clear the QB file for his Rooks.

17 Kt–QKt5   Kt–R2
18 Kt × Kt   Q × Kt
19 Q–Q3

Black threatened with Q–R3*ch* to put pressure on the white squares which would have left White deplorably short of moves.

19 ...   Q–R3

At the cost of doubling his Rook's pawns (so notoriously weakening that most players would hardly have considered it) he exposes the white QKt pawn to attack and asserts his control over the only open file (gain of space).

20 Q × Q   P × Q
21 K–Kt2   R–B7
22 B–B1

Not B–R3 because of B × B; 23 R × B, Kt–K6*ch*; 24 K–R3, R × P.

22 ...   R–QKt1
23 R–QKt1   R–B6
24 B–Q2   R(6) × P
25 R × R   R × R
26 B × P   R–Kt7

Black has eliminated his weakness in the Q side pawns and now

threatens Kt–K6*ch* again. The text move is stronger than R–R6 at once, when White could reply 27 R–QKt1 with an open file for his own Rook. If now 27 R–QB1, Kt–K6*ch*; 28 K–Kt1, Kt–B5.

27 B–Q2   B–Kt5

Not Kt × QP, hoping for 28 Kt × Kt, R × B because White would reply 28 B–B3, winning.

28 B–B4   P–KR3

Preparing P–Kt4 with a general restriction of White's game.

29 P–Kt4   Kt–K2
30 R–R1   Kt–B3
31 B–B1   R–B7
32 B–B3   R–B5

The renewed threat to the Q pawn now restricts White still further.

33 B–Kt2   B–B6
34 B × B   R × B
35 R–QKt1

He has no way of avoiding the forking of two pawns by R–B5.

35 ...   K–B2
36 P–Kt5

Fighting against the threatened slow death, he tries to free his game. A possible continuation would be 36 ..., P–KR4; 37 P–Kt6, P × P; 38 Kt–Kt5, Kt × QP; 39 R–Q1, R–B5; 40 R × Kt, R × R; 41 Kt × P*ch* winning, so it can be seen that White's bid for freedom is not entirely without teeth.

36 ...   R–B5

37 P×P	P×P
38 P–R5	

The doomed pawn is to be given up in the best possible way. If now 38 ..., Kt×RP; 39 R–R1, K–Kt3; 40 R–Kt1*ch*, K–R2 and Black's King is out of the game for the time being. As it is, White threatens R–Kt6.

38 ...	R–R5
39 K–Kt3	R×RP
40 K–Kt4	R–R6
41 R–Q1	

To free his Knight from the defence of the Q pawn, and so allow his King to advance on the weakened black pawns.

41 ...	R–Kt6
42 P–R4	Kt–K2
43 Kt–K1	Kt–B4

Now the K side pawns are supported and the threat to White's Q pawn in no way diminished.

44 Kt–Q3	P–QR4

Not Kt×P; 45 Kt–B5, R–Kt4; 46 Kt×RP*ch*.

45 Kt–B5	R–QB6
46 R–QKt1	

Faced with an impending loss owing to the advance of the QR pawn, he gives up any further attempt to hold the Q pawn and plays solely for a desperate counter-attack.

46 ...	Kt×QP

47 Kt–R6*ch*	K–Q1
48 R–Kt8*ch*	R–B1

Not K–K2; 49 R–Kt7*ch*, K–B1; 50 Kt–B7, threatening 51 R–Kt8*ch*, K–Kt2; 52 Kt–K8*ch*, K–Kt3; 53 P–R5*ch*, K–R2; 54 Kt–B6*ch*, K–Kt2; 55 R–Kt8*mate*.

49 R–Kt7	K–K1
50 Kt–B7*ch*	K–B1
51 Kt–Kt5	

Conceding that Black's defences have held, for if 51 K–R5, then Kt–B4; 52 Kt–Kt5, R–B5 threatening R×P*mate*.

51 ...	Kt×Kt
52 R×Kt	R–R1
53 P–B4	P–R5
54 R–Kt1	P–R6
55 P–B5	P–R7
56 R–QR1	R–R5*ch*
57 K–R5	K–Kt2
58 P×P	P×P
59 R–Kt1*ch*	K–R1
60 R–QR1	K–R2

Showing the neat timing of his previous move.

61 R–KKt1	

A last desperate trap.

61 ...	P–R8=Q
62 R–Kt7*ch*	K–R1

Which Black avoids. K×R would be stalemate.

Resigns

Tarrasch's impact on his contemporaries was even greater than that of Steinitz, but whereas the effect of Steinitz had been stimulating, the effect of Tarrasch was enervating. Steinitz made chess players think; Tarrasch tended to save them thinking by producing a plain and straightforward system of play which expounded the methods to be adopted from the beginning to the end of the game; its very completeness made it appear to be the last and final word on the game.

To say that chess became automatic would be putting it too strongly; it still called for the application of the highest mental qualities; imagination still blossomed in sacrificial conceptions of great beauty; but the fire to find something beyond what had already been discovered was gone. If chess was not quite automatic, it was nevertheless possible to make many moves in the game almost automatically; if it was a question of occupying the centre, of seizing an open file, or of creating a strong outpost, these things were done without question. The result was inevitably the growth of a dogma.

The dominance which this dogma had established over the chess

Diagram 4

CAPABLANCA–JANOWSKI

(San Sebastian, 1911)

masters of the day was shown when Capablanca in his first international tournament reached the position in Diagram 4. At this point his instinct told him that P–Kt3 was the correct move, in spite of the resulting holes on KB3 and KR3, in order to bring pressure to bear on the black Q pawn, but as he himself admitted, he was "afraid of being criticized for creating such a formation of pawns on the King's side" and of "doing what poor players so often do." No clearer evidence of the force of the dogma in the early twentieth century could be asked for. Capablanca instead played B–K2–B3, a manœuvre which caused him endless trouble later.

Actually, reaction against the barrenness and insufficiency of the dogma was already making itself apparent when Capablanca appeared on the scene to give a further lease of life to the classical style. Once his position in the chess world had been established, Capablanca had no hesitation in repudiating some of the more objectionable features of the dogma, but his style was none the less strictly modelled on the approved lines, and indeed he perfected that style, playing it with a new precision and a new refinement of technique. It was one of Tarrasch's principles that no inferior move should ever be made because it must inevitably lead to an inferior game, and no one could expect to survive in an inferior position except such strange geniuses as Steinitz and Lasker, and then only through weak play by the opponent. Consequently at the very worst the position should always be equal at least, and if in practice some of the masters of the classical style occasionally failed to keep the draw in hand, that merely proved that no one was perfect. "Keeping the draw in hand" as a policy later came to be regarded with some scorn, but Capablanca subscribed wholeheartedly to it, and when Lasker resigned to him in their world championship match in 1921 after losing 4 and drawing 10 games, Capablanca proudly claimed that at no time in the whole match had he been in an inferior position.

His divergence from the dogma of Tarrasch was chiefly a matter of interpretation. As part of the time element Tarrasch laid down that no piece should be moved twice until development was complete; Capablanca, as White against Blanco at Havana in 1913, played 1 P–K4, P–K3; 2 P–Q4, P–Q4; 3 Kt–QB3, P×P; 4 Kt×P, Kt–Q2; 5 Kt–KB3, KKt–B3; 6 Kt×Kt*ch*, Kt×Kt; 7 Kt–K5. The last move infringed Tarrasch's time rule, but Capablanca proved that since Black could not make use of the offered time because of positional difficulties, he was not in fact breaking the spirit of the rule. As part of the space element Tarrasch insisted on the early occupation of open files; a game Kaufmann and Fahndrich played against Capablanca and Réti in Vienna in 1914, where the black forces were, as Réti admits, largely conducted by Capablanca, went as follows: 1 P–K4, P–K3; 2 P–Q4, P–Q4; 3 Kt–QB3, Kt–KB3; 4 P×P, P×P; 5 B–Q3, P–B4; 6 P×P, B×P; 7 Kt–B3, O–O; 8 O–O, Kt–B3; 9 B–KKt5, B–K3; 10 Kt–K2, P–KR3; 11 B–R4, B–KKt5; 12 Kt–B3, Kt–Q5; 13 B–K2, Kt×B*ch*; 14 Q×Kt. Now Capablanca surprised Réti by rejecting 14 ..., R–K1, because he recognized that he would still have to face the awkward pin of his Knight; in place of R–K1 Capablanca found a series of moves which not only relieved the pin but created a weakening of the white pawn structure, and was therefore still in accordance with classical theory; these moves were 14 ..., B–Q5; 15 Q–Q3, KB×Kt; 16 Q×B, Kt–K5; 17 Q–Q4, P–KKt4; 18 Kt–K5, B–B4; 19 P–KB3 (if

B–Kt3, Kt × B; 20 BP × Kt, B × P; 21 Kt–Kt4, P–B4; 22 Kt–K3, B–K5; or worse 22 Kt × P*ch*, K–Kt2 trapping the Knight), P × B; 20 P × Kt, B × P.

Capablanca's most important rectification of classical theory was his discovery of the minority attack. It had been accepted for years without question that once a majority of pawns on the Queen's side had been established, an important advantage had been gained. Capablanca showed that if the player with the minority of pawns advanced those pawns and forced their exchange for hostile pawns, then the majority of three pawns to two was converted into a majority of one to nil, which was in fact giving the opponent an isolated pawn. Whenever this could be done, the proud majority, normally such an asset, became a liability. There were two prerequisites, first, that the pawn exchanges could be pushed to the very end, and secondly, that some pieces still remained on the board. The original theory of the Queen's side majority had been that, *after all the pieces had been exchanged*, the majority produced a remoter passed pawn which was usually a winner. Therefore the player with the minority must act early, *before the exchange of pieces*, when the isolated pawn, as like as not, would hold the germs of loss.

Refinements like these enabled Capablanca to play with an accuracy of purpose and a judgment of position which few of his contemporaries could match, but in essence he still followed the simple strategies of the classical style. In the following game, for instance, he gains time, converts it to a gain of space (occupation of open files), proceeds to the invasion of the seventh rank, then to full occupation of the rank, and so to a direct assault on the King—a procedure as straightforward and simple as anyone could desire.

GAME 2

QUEEN'S GAMBIT DECLINED

Nimzovitch   Capablanca

New York Tournament, 1927

	White	Black
1	P–QB4	Kt–KB3
2	K t–KB3	P–K3
3	P– Q4	P–Q4
4	P–K3	B–K2
5	QKt–Q2	

In preference to the old Kt–B3, so that he can recapture with the Knight on QB4 and so make a strong point of his K5.

5	...	O–O
6	B–Q3	P–B4
7	QP × P	Kt–R3

Black too will recapture with the Knight and make a strong point of his own K5. Note that 7 ..., QKt–Q2 is less accurate because of 8 P–B6.

8 O–O   Kt×P
9 B–K2   P–QKt3
10 P×P

Giving up hope of working the Knight via QB4 to K5 with any effect.

10 ...   Kt×P
11 Kt–Kt3   B–Kt2
12 Kt×Kt   B×Kt
13 Q–R4   Q–B3

Delaying the development of White's Q side, and so gaining time.

14 B–R6   B×B
15 Q×B   Kt–Kt5
16 Q–K2   KR–Q1

Showing his gain of time in the occupation of the open file.

17 P–QR3   Kt–Q6
18 Kt–K1   Kt×Kt
19 R×Kt   QR–B1
20 R–Kt1   Q–K4

White is now ready to free his game by P–QKt4, so Black must invade the White position at once. If, however, 20 ..., Q–B4 to enter at QB7, White replies 21 P–K4. The text move is a finesse to gain time to bring the Queen to Q4. If White now replies 21 P–QKt4, Black plays B–Q3; 22 P–Kt3, Q–K5 and the entry square QB7 is again under control.

21 P–KKt3

Missing his chance of keeping the black Queen off the white diagonals, which he could have achieved by 21 P–K4. Now Black breaks in.

21 ...   Q–Q4
22 P–QKt4   B–B1
23 B–Kt2   Q–R7
24 R–R1   Q–Kt6
25 B–Q4

A last effort to keep Black out by 25 QR–B1 would fail owing to the weakness of the Q side after 25 ..., P–QR4.

25 ...   R–B7
26 Q–R6

Defence was better by 26 Q–Q1 so that if 26 ..., P–K4; 27 R–K2.

26 ...   P–K4

Control of the seventh rank is now worth a pawn.

27 B×KP   R(1)–Q7
28 Q–Kt7

If 28 R–KB1, Q×KP; 29 B–B4 (not 29 P×Q, R–Kt7ch; 30 K–R1, R×Pch; 31 K–Kt1, R(B)–Kt7 mate), R×P; 30 B×Q, R–Kt7ch; etc. While if 28 Q–B1, Q–Q4; 29 B–B4, Q–B6 and the KBP is still vulnerable.

28 ...   R×P
29 P–Kt4   Q–K3
30 B–Kt3   R×P

A most attractive forcing of the rank. If now 31 B×R, Q×KtPch; 32 K–R1, Q–R6 and mates.

31	Q–B3	R(R)–Kt7*ch*
32	Q×R	R×Q*ch*
33	K×R	Q×KtP
34	QR–Q1	P–KR4
35	R–Q4	Q–Kt4
36	K–R2	P–R4
37	R–K2	P×P
38	P×P	B–K2
39	R–K4	B–B3
40	R–KB2	Q–Q4
	Resigns	

He is reduced to an utterly negative position. One Rook must stay on the KB file to prevent P–KKt4. The Bishop must stay on its present diagonal, otherwise B–K4*ch* follows. And what of the remaining Rook? If 41 R(4)–B4, B–K4; 42 R×P, B×B*ch*; 43 K×B, Q×R; 44 R×Q, K×R with a won ending, while if 41 R–K8*ch*, K–R2; 42 R–QB8, Q–K5 and more white pawns fall.

It may be noticed in both these games that the successful carrying out of the simple strategical idea depended at one point upon the exercise of high tactical imagination. In Game 1 Tarrasch's 19th move would not have occurred to many a lesser player, nor in Game 2 would Capablanca's 20th and 21st moves. Indeed, Capablanca's tactical manœuvre could have been defeated by accurate play. It was natural that, except among the very top flight of players, a game accurately played in the classical style tended increasingly to end in a draw. If Capablanca had not come along, the classical style would have perished through its own sterility even earlier; as it was, Capablanca himself was forecasting by the late 1920s that the day was not far distant when accurate technique would become the common property of every master player, enabling him to draw with every other master merely by applying it properly, and in this he was admitting that even in his hands the classical style was sterile and had no future. For all his improvements to the Tarrasch doctrine he found himself led into the same cul-de-sac as the rigid dogma had led so many before him.

It was against this background that the dynamic revolution took place, and in fact seems now to have been almost inevitable.

CHAPTER III

Birth of the Dynamic Idea

ALTHOUGH Capablanca's great virtuosity temporarily reprieved the classical style, the signs of reaction were apparent even before he came upon the scene. The principle of keeping the draw in hand and the consequent difficulty of forcing a win created among the chess-loving public a distaste for the methods employed, with their lack of breath-taking risks brilliantly overcome and their tendency to produce an ever-increasing number of dull draws; even many of the won games were won in a manner which excited little enthusiasm in the breasts of the amateurs, on whose support the chess masters depended for the cash prizes for which they competed.

The tournament promoters who had to find the cash prizes were the first to sense the need for a change, and just after the turn of the century they introduced "Gambit tournaments" in which the masters were forced to undertake the hazards they normally tended to avoid. This certainly produced some brilliant games and improvements in openings grown dusty with lack of use.

This nostalgic harking back to the glories of a former age struck a chord among a certain small group of masters, who saw in the revival of the gambits and sacrifices of former days an escape from the rather dreary monotony of the classical style. But this, the Romantic school, because it looked backward rather than forward for a new spirit in chess, was, like the pre-Raphaelites in the world of art, escapist rather than the herald of a new era.

Nevertheless, new forces were at work. A younger generation of masters, gifted with a natural ability to find their way through more complicated positions than those normally associated with the classical style, realized that it was in its essential simplicity that the sterility of the classical style lay. They had been given an inkling of this by Lasker, who in such games as the following had departed from the simple strategies of the true classical style by adopting a double strategy, attacking simultaneously the black Q pawn and the black

17

King's position. An attack on either of these two points alone could not have succeeded, the defensive resources being adequate, and a game conducted against only one of them would inevitably have ended in a draw. By alternating his attacks, a conception which Nimzovitch later developed, Lasker succeeds in forcing the issue.

GAME 3

RUY LOPEZ

Lasker	*Salve*

St. Petersburg Tournament, 1909

1	P–K4	P–K4
2	Kt–KB3	Kt–QB3
3	B–Kt5	P–Q3
4	P–Q4	B–Q2
5	Kt–B3	Kt–B3
6	O–O	B–K2
7	B–Kt5	

Tarrasch preferred the development of this Bishop in fianchetto, as its exchange for Black's KB, which normally soon follows the text move, eases Black's cramped game.

7	...	P×P
8	Kt×P	O–O
9	KB×Kt	P×B
10	Q–Q3	R–K1
11	QR–K1	P–B4
12	Kt–Kt3	Kt–Kt5

Forcing the desired exchange of Bishops, since if the white Bishop retires, Black plays Kt–K4. But Lasker is now able to put the black Knight rather out of play.

13	B×B	R×B
14	P–B4	R–Kt1

15	P–KR3	Kt–R3

If Kt–B3; 16 P–K5 and the Knight has to retire to K1, for if 16 ..., Kt–R4; 17 P–Kt4.

16	P–B5

A move that Tarrasch would never have made, since it leaves his KP backward and gives Black a strong square on his K4. In return Black must yield White a strong square on K6 (to prevent P–B6) and White's mobility in front of the black King is greatly increased. Lasker in fact jettisons the idea of keeping the draw in hand and here plays in dynamic style.

16	...	P–KB3
17	Kt–Q5	R–K1
18	P–B4	Kt–B2
19	Q–QB3	

Defending his QKtP and so freeing his other Knight for action.

19	...	R–K4
20	Kt–Q2	P–B3

After this Lasker has a weak black Q pawn as a target, but Black has reckoned that as it cannot be attacked by a white Knight, his own Knight's position can ensure its security.

21	Kt–B4	Q–Kt3

22 P–QKt3	QR–K1
23 Q–Kt3	K–R1

To allow the defence of his KKtP against White's next move.

24 Kt–R5	R–KKt1
25 R–B4	Q–Q1
26 Kt–B3	

If 26 R–Kt4, Q–KB1 and White is no nearer a successful attack on the KtP. Now if 26 ..., R–K1; 27 R–Kt4 wins, but Black is not quite so gullible.

26 ...	R–K2
27 R–R4	Q–K1

Diagram 5

Now Lasker must be careful how he presses his attack, for he has the burden of his weak KP to carry. In fact, few players but Lasker could have seen how to advance farther either against the weak black Q pawn or against Black's cramped K side. The promising line is Kt–B4, threatening Kt–Kt6*ch*, but Black will simply answer Kt–R3 since he no longer needs to defend his Q pawn.

Lasker therefore plays his Queen to a square where she will still be attacking the Q pawn after he has played Kt–B4.

28 Q–B2	R–B1
29 Q–Q2	Q–Kt1

To free his Knight.

30 K–R1	R(1)–K1
31 R–Kt4	

To weaken Black's attack on his K pawn and so make R–Q1 possible, continuing the pressure on the Q pawn.

31 ...	R–Kt1

Here Kt–R3 would be answered by 32 Kt × BP, so that if P × Kt; 33 Q × Kt, winning a pawn.

32 R–Q1	Q–Kt5

If Q–K1; 33 Q–Q3, Q–Kt1; 34 Kt–B4, R(1)–K1; 35 R–R4, and if R × P; 36 Kt–Kt6*ch*, winning the exchange. But now White switches his attack quickly back to the K side.

33 Q–KB2	Q–B6
34 Q–R4	Kt–R3
35 R–B4	Kt–B2
36 K–R2	R(1)–K1
37 Q–Kt3	R–KKt1
38 R–R4	

Against the likely looking 38 R–Kt4 Black can play 38 ..., Kt–R3; 39 R–R4, P–Q4; 40 BP × P, P × P; 41 R × P, B–B3 with new-found freedom for his Bishop; but after the text move 38 ..., P–Q4 would be answered by 39 BP×P, P×P; 40 Kt–B4 and, Black's Knight not being on R3, he has an extra threat and a winning one in Kt–Kt6ch. The text move now threatens Kt–B4–Kt6ch, and Black's natural answer of Kt–R3 would now cost him his Q pawn.

38 ...	P–Kt4
39 P×P e.p.	R×KtP
40 Q–B2	P–B4

Ridding himself of the KB pawn which has now become a still more serious weakness.

41 Kt–B4	R–B3
42 Kt–K2	Q–Kt7
43 R–Q2	Q–R8
44 Kt–Kt3	K–Kt1

The threat was 45 P×P, B×P; 46 Kt×B, R×Kt; 47 R×Pch, K×R; 48 Q–R4ch.

45 P×P	B×P
46 Kt–Q4	

Lasker could still try 46 Kt×B, R×Kt; 47 R×RP, but the text move is more decisive because more exchanges are forced and Black's centre is broken open.

46 ...	P×Kt
47 Kt×B	K–B1
48 Q×P	Q×Q
49 Kt×Q	Kt–K4
50 R–R5	

Preparatory to breaking the centre with P–B5.

50 ...	R(2)–KB2

51 P–B5	P×P

A pawn is bound to go, for if Kt–Q2; 52 Kt×P, Kt×P (P×P; 53 Kt×P); 53 R(5)–Q5, Kt–Kt2; 54 Kt×P. Black hopes by exchanging Knights to retain some of the drawing chances which exist when a pawn down in a Rook ending.

52 R×Kt	P×Kt
53 R×P	R–B7
54 R–Q8ch	K–Kt2
55 R–QR5	R–B7
56 P–R3	P–B4
57 R–QB8	R–Kt7
58 R–Kt5	R(2)–B7

Black's Rooks look aggressive, but Lasker easily answers the threat to his KKtP.

59 R–Kt7ch	K–Kt3
60 R–B6ch	R–B3

If K–Kt4; 61 R×Pch, K–Kt3 (K–B5; 62 R–B7ch); 62 R–B6ch, K–Kt4; 63 R–Kt7ch, K–R4; 64 R×Pch, and White has won two pawns.

61 R×BP	R–R3
62 P–QR4	R–KB3
63 R–B3	

Freeing the other Rook.

63 ...	P–QR3
64 R–Kt3ch	K–R3
65 R(3)–Kt7	Resigns

It is White after all who has the doubled Rooks on the seventh rank, and Black has no way of saving his KR pawn.

It was small wonder that play of this kind excited the attention of the younger school, who were looking for some way out of the existing impasse. Clearly if simplification could be avoided and complications successfully created, the situation would offer scope of the nature they sought.

The first impetus towards a more complicated style of play came from Julius Breyer, who instead of selecting openings where the objectives were small but clear-cut from the outset, not only to himself but also to his opponent, preferred to build up a position full of dynamic energy—"malignant energy" Tartakover called it— which could be released at will at a suitable target and at a suitable moment. In the early part of the game, during which this energy was being created and stored, Breyer often made moves which were in direct conflict with the tenets of the classical style but which were found later to fit perfectly into his scheme of play when the pent-up energy was finally released.

GAME 4

SEMI-SLAV DEFENCE

Asztalos   *Breyer*

Debrecen Tournament,
1913

1 P–Q4   P–Q4
2 P–QB4   P–QB3
3 P–K3   Kt–B3
4 Kt–KB3   P–K3

Breyer has already arrived at a situation where he has avoided committing himself to the natural early P–QB4.

5 Kt–B3   Kt–K5
6 Kt×Kt   P×Kt
7 Kt–Q2   P–KB4
8 P–B3   B–Q3

Threatening Q–R5*ch* to which P–Kt3 is not now an answer. White's

best line is 9 Q–K2, but he allows himself to be stampeded into a line which preserves for Black his strong point on K5. Breyer was a master of the subtle tensions which exist even in such simple positions.

9 P–B4   P–B4

Threatening to establish a passed K pawn.

10 Kt–Kt3   Kt–Q2
11 B–K2   Q–R5*ch*

Weakening the white squares on White's K side, and therefore preferable to the immediate Q–K2. The white squares and the long diagonal will later be happy hunting grounds for Black.

12 P–Kt3   Q–K2
13 O–O   P–KKt4

At once attacking the weakened

flank. It is not apparent that the QB can join in the assault, and Breyer's solution of this problem reveals what energy he has seen to be stored in that apparently inactive piece.

14 B–R5*ch*	K–B1
15 P×KtP	Q×P
16 R–B2	R–KKt1
17 R–Kt2	

The threat was B × P.

17 ...	K–K2
18 B–K2	P–Kt3
19 P–QR4	

Hoping to show up a Black weakness by playing P–R5.

19 ...	P–QR4
20 P×P	P×P
21 Q–K1	Kt–K4
22 Kt×RP	R×Kt

Drawing off the defending Queen

for just long enough to allow his attack to mature.

23 Q×R	Kt–B6*ch*
24 K–R1	

Naturally not 24 B×Kt, P×B; 25 R–KB2, B×P.

24 ...	Q–R4

Now B × P is again threatened.

25 Q–K1	B×P
26 B×Kt	

Necessary since R × B allows 27 Q × P*mate*.

26 ...	P×B
27 R×B	P–B7

A splendid move after which the QB comes into its own.

28 Q×P	Q–Q8*ch*
29 Q–Kt1	B–Kt2*ch*
30 R–Kt2	B×R*mate*

GAME 5

SEMI-SLAV DEFENCE
Breyer   *Esser*
Budapest Tournament,
1917

1 P–Q4	P–Q4
2 P–QB4	P–K3
3 Kt–QB3	P–QB3
4 P–K3	

A quiet move, in keeping with Breyer's style of storing energy rather than releasing it prematurely with consequent exchanges and simplification.

4 ...	Kt–B3
5 B–Q3	B–Q3
6 P–B4	

With a firm grip on the black squares in the centre which effectively stops Black's natural freeing move of P–K4. The hole created on K4 is safe from occupation for the time being, and White can still play P–K4 himself when his position has been adequately prepared.

6 ...	O–O
7 Kt–B3	P×P

Expecting to free his pieces by 8 B×P, P–QKt4; 9 B–Kt3, P–Kt5;

10 Kt–K2, B–R3. But the move gives up the fight for the centre and it was better to play QKt–Q2 and P–B4.

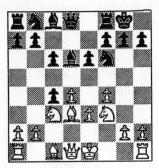

Diagram 6

8 B–Kt1

Since Black's last move has secured the centre for White, Breyer can safely launch an attack on the flank against the black King. The text move is none the less a highly original conception, for in addition to sacrificing a pawn he shuts in his QR. However, if 8 B–B2, his Queen would have no square on the diagonal QKt1–KR7, and Breyer is more concerned with building up energy than aimlessly developing his pieces.

8 ...	P–QKt4
9 P–K4	B–K2
10 Kt–Kt5	P–KR3
11 P–KR4	

The dynamic energy of White's position begins to make itself felt. If now 11 ..., P × Kt; 12 RP × P, Kt–Q2; 13 Q–R5. At the same time

White threatens 12 P–K5, Kt–Q4; 13 Q–B2, P–Kt3; 14 P–R5, breaking open Black's position.

| 11 ... | P–Kt3 |
| 12 P–K5 | P × Kt |

Expecting to emerge with a satisfactory game after 13 P × Kt, B × P; 14 RP × P, B × QP; but with a subtle sacrifice White retains his pressure.

| 13 RP × P | Kt–Q4 |
| 14 K–B1 | |

Another highly original and non-classical move which has the effect of energizing his whole position by avoiding either a pin of his QKt or a check on QKt4 at a vital moment later. If, for example, he were to try 14 Q–Kt4 at once, Black answers 14 ..., K–Kt2 so as to meet 15 Q–R3 with R–R1; then White has no better line than 15 R–R7*ch*, K × R; 16 Q–R5*ch*, K–Kt2 (or K–Kt1; 17 B × P, P × B; 18 Q × P*ch* with only a draw by perpetual check); 17 Q–R6*ch*, K–Kt1; 18 Kt–K4, Kt–Q2; 19 Kt–B6*ch*, Kt(2) × Kt; 20 KP × Kt, Kt × P(3); 21 P × Kt, B–Kt5*ch* (the saving check); 22 K–B1, Q × P and White's attack gets nowhere. He now plans to answer 14 ..., B–Kt5 with 15 Kt × Kt, BP × Kt; 16 B–K3, K–Kt2; 17 R–R7*ch*, K × R; 18 Q–R5*ch*, K–Kt2; 19 Q–R6*ch*, K–Kt1; 20 B × P, P × B; 21 Q × P*ch*, K–R1; 22 K–K2 winning.

14 ...	Kt×Kt
15 P×Kt	B–Kt2
16 Q–Kt4	K–Kt2
17 R–R7ch	K×R
18 Q–R5ch	K–Kt2
19 Q–R6ch	K–Kt1
20 B×P	P×B
21 Q×Pch	K–R1
22 Q–R6ch	K–Kt1
23 P–Kt6	

Revealing a further point to his 14th move. Black cannot now play 23 ..., B–R5ch and 24 ..., Q–K2 defending his second rank.

23 ...	R–B2

Not R–B4; 24 Q–R7ch, K–B1; 25 Q–R8mate.

24 P×Rch	K×P
25 Q–R5ch	K–Kt2
26 P–B5	

The energy inherent in his so far undeveloped pieces now becomes apparent.

26 ...	P×P
27 B–R6ch	K–R2
28 B–B4dis. ch	K–Kt2
29 Q–R6ch	K–Kt1
30 Q–Kt6ch	K–R1
31 K–K2	

The final blow.

31 ...	B–R5
32 R–R1	*Resigns*

There is no defence against 33 B–Kt5.

Successes like those obtained in the two preceding games served to convince Breyer that the hitherto accepted range of openings was inadequate to produce the complicated type of position in which he felt at home. Owing to his premature death in 1921 he did not live to see the astonishing developments of the next few years, but the following game shows him experimenting on these lines. His very odd opening moves are none the less in keeping with his idea of dynamic play, for though, contrary to Tarrasch's teaching, he gives up both time and space, his game thereby acquires a certain extra hidden energy.

GAME 6
BREYER DEFENCE
Euwe *Breyer*
Vienna Tournament, 1921

1 P–K4	Kt–QB3
2 Kt–QB3	Kt–B3

Later, Nimzovitch used to answer

1 P–K4 by developing his QKt, while Alekhin tried developing his KKt, but Breyer's line, with the development of both Knights before moving a pawn, is peculiarly his own.

3 P–Q4	P–K4
4 P×P	

Kt–B3 would lead into a fairly

simple version of the Four Knights' Game, but naturally White hopes for more.

4 ...	QKt×P
5 P–B4	Kt–B3
6 P–K5	Kt–KKt1

Although White has now gained in both time and space, he will have some difficulty in holding on to his advanced post on K5. This idea, that too early an advance creates weaknesses, was typical of the dynamic line of thought.

7 B–QB4	P–Q3
8 Kt–B3	

Clearly after 8 P×P, B×P Black's position is eased and White's advanced KB pawn becomes more of a hindrance than a help.

8 ...	B–Kt5
9 O–O	Q–Q2
10 Q–K1	O–O–O
11 Kt–KKt5	P×P

The first surprising release of energy. If now 12 Kt×BP, Q–Q5 ch; 13 K–R1, Q×B; 14 Kt×KR, and Black virtually has two pieces for his Rook. The best line for White was the simple 12 B–Kt3.

12 K–R1	P–B3

In return for the sacrifice of the exchange it is Black who has the strong point on K4, a surprising turn after his opening moves.

13 Kt–B7	Kt–R4

14 Kt×QR	Kt×B
15 Q–K4	Kt–Q3
16 Q–Kt4	B–K2

The threat was 17 P×P, P×P; 18 R×B

17 P×P	P×P
18 Kt×P	

Somewhat more promising was 18 Kt–B6, P×Kt; 19 Q–R5.

18 ...	Kt×Kt
19 R–B8ch	B×R
20 Q×Bch	Q–Q1

If Kt–Q1, White recovers his piece with 21 B–Kt5, P–KR3; 22 B×Kt, Q×B; 23 Q×P, Kt–B3; 24 Kt–K4. Breyer has calculated the defence very exactly, and the energy soon to be shown by his QKt tips the scale.

21 Q×P	Kt–B3
22 B–Kt5	R–Kt1
23 Q–R6	

Not 23 Q×Kt, R×B.

23 ...	R–Kt3
24 Q–R4	Kt–Q3
25 R–B1	Kt–B4
26 Q×B	Kt×Q
27 B×Q	Kt(5)–K6

The deciding blow.

28 R–B3	K×B
29 P–KR3	R–Kt6

Preventing P–KKt4, after which White has no resource left.

30 R×R	Kt×Rch
Resigns	

These and other irregular and highly bizarre reactions by Breyer and his associates against the classical dogma, led Tartakover to dub them "Hypermoderns," a term which later attained a stature which Tartakover himself never expected for it. And in the Hypermodern movement the name of Julius Breyer must always rank high, for he was one of its greatest pioneers and probably had a clearer idea than any of his contemporaries as to the true nature of dynamic chess.

CHAPTER IV

New Ideas on the Centre

INDEPENDENTLY of Breyer, and working from a different viewpoint, Aron Nimzovitch had meanwhile been having doubts about Tarrasch's theory of the centre and its control. To Tarrasch it was logical and therefore correct to occupy the centre with pawns, since nothing else could so effectively restrict the centralized activity of the opponent's pieces.

In the French Defence, for example, after 1 P–K4, P–K3; 2 P–Q4, P–Q4; 3 P–K5, P–QB4 Tarrasch as White made every effort to maintain his pawns on Q4 and K5 in order to cramp Black and leave him with the "bad" Bishop, that is, a Bishop whose scope was limited by its own pawns. He had in fact imposed upon the chess world the belief that strong central pawns were essential for central control, and White's problem in this particular opening was the maintenance at all costs of the pawn at the base of the chain on which the forward pawn depended. Equally, when playing Black, he did all he could to attack the white Q pawn, as illustrated in Game 1.

Nimzovitch realized that Tarrasch had simplified and diluted the original Steinitzian practice, and that some of the old master's deeper conceptions had been omitted altogether. He found that Steinitz had conceived the idea of a strong central square which he had controlled but not necessarily occupied continuously. Steinitz's view, as Nimzovitch understood it, was that when a strong square had been established, like White's K5 in the following game, it became a nerve-centre for the radiation of attacks and threats, and therefore all pieces were developed so as to be brought into relation with the strong square. When a large number of pieces were developed so that they all defended the strong square, that square was, as Nimzovitch put it, "over-protected." He affirmed that from the over-protected square all these pieces could quickly exert their maximum influence. The following example from Steinitz's play illustrates Nimzovitch's point.

GAME 7

FRENCH DEFENCE

Steinitz   *Weiss*

Vienna Tournament, 1882

1 P–K4	P–K3
2 P–K5	P–QB4
3 P–KB4	P–Q4
4 P×P*e.p.*	

Although the advanced pawn is exchanged, Steinitz has every intention of retaining a strong control over his K5.

4 ...	B×P
5 P–KKt3	B–Q2
6 Kt–KB3	B–B3
7 B–Kt2	Kt–B3
8 O–O	QKt–Q2
9 P–Q3	O–O
10 QKt–Q2	

Both players have a solid position, and if anything Black is better developed. Steinitz now proceeds to apply the principle of over-protection, and prefers the text move to the natural looking Kt–B3 because the Knight can now be brought via QB4 into relationship with the strong square K5.

10 ...	Kt–Kt3
11 Q–K2	Q–B2
12 P–Kt3	B–K2

So that after White's B–QKt2 (again over-protecting the strong square) his K side pawns will not be doubled by an exchange. But in fact the move only weakens his counter to the strong square.

13 B–Kt2	P–QR4
14 P–QR4	Kt(B)–Q4
15 Kt–B4	Kt–Kt5
16 QR–K1	

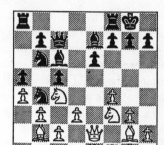

Diagram 7

Steinitz now has one pawn and five pieces bearing on K5, a striking example of over-protection.

16 ...	Kt(3)–Q4
17 Kt(3)–K5	B–B3
18 Q–B2	B–K1
19 P–KKt4	

A flank movement follows the establishment of the strong centre.

19 ...	R–Q1
20 P–Kt5	B–K2
21 Kt–Kt4	

Against P–B3.

21 ...	Kt–QB3
22 Q–R4	

The over-protecting pieces now spring into life.

22 ...	Kt–Q5

23 B–K4	P–B4

Already he has no satisfactory defence. If P–KKt3; 24 Kt–B6*ch*, B × Kt; 25 P × B, threatening KB × Kt and Q–R6. While if P–R3; 24 Kt × P*ch*, P × Kt; 25 Q × P, and wins easily.

24 P × P*e.p.*	Kt × P(3)
25 Kt × Kt*ch*	B × Kt
26 Q × P*ch*	K–B2
27 B–Kt2	R–KKt1
28 Kt–K5*ch*	K–B1
29 R–B2	P–QKt4

30 P × P	B × P
31 B–KR3	R–K1
32 R–K4	B–B3
33 R × Kt	

The attack plays itself, even to the sacrificial opportunities.

33 ...	P × R
34 B–R3*ch*	B–K2

35 B × P and mates next move.

White has Kt–Kt6 or Q × R or even, if the KKtP advances, Q–B7. The power of the strong square is in evidence to the very last.

Consequently, Nimzovitch himself threw overboard the idea that the only way to secure control in the centre was by pawn occupation, and in the following game he revived the Steinitzian conception of control without pawns.

GAME 8

FRENCH DEFENCE

Nimzovitch	*Salve*

Karlsbad Tournament, 1911

1 P–K4	P–K3
2 P–Q4	P–Q4
3 P–K5	P–QB4
4 P–QB3	Kt–QB3
5 Kt–KB3	Q–Kt3
6 B–Q3	

As in Game 1, B–K2 was preferable.

6 ...	B–Q2

Better was 6 ..., P × P; 7 P × P and only then 7 ..., B–Q2 forcing White's Bishop to retire to K2. The transposition allows White at once to explore his new ideas about the centre.

7 P × P

Surprisingly exchanging off the pawn which Tarrasch regarded as the corner-stone of White's game.

7 ...	B × P
8 O–O	P–B3

Undermining White's last central pawn, after which Tarrasch would undoubtedly have regarded White as having failed in his object. Nimzovitch, however, has recognized that what causes Black's bad Bishop in this opening is not the white pawn centre but the pawn on Black's K3. As long, therefore, as he can prevent this pawn advancing, whether he does so by a pawn or a piece or merely by pressure on K5, Black still has a difficult game.

9 P–QKt4

To allow the development of his QB, which is necessary for the protection and over-protection of the square K5.

9 ...	B–K2
10 B–KB4	P×P
11 Kt×P	Kt×Kt
12 B×Kt	

Diagram 8

The white pawn centre has completely evaporated, but the effect is to give the white pieces more scope than usual, unencumbered by their own pawns. White's problem is now to resist Black's efforts to force P–K4. An immediate attempt by 12 ..., B–KB3 would fail because of 13 Q–R5*ch*, P–Kt3; 14 B×P*ch*, P×B; 15 Q×P*ch*, K–K2; 16 B×B*ch*, Kt×B; 17 Q–Kt7*ch*.

12 ...	Kt–B3
13 Kt–Q2	

Preparing for further over-protection of the square K5. If 13 Q–B2, Black could sacrifice a pawn to force the advance of his K pawn by 13 ..., O–O; 14 B×Kt, B×B; 15 B×P *ch*, K–R1; 16 B–Kt6, P–K4.

13 ...	O–O
14 Kt–B3	B–Q3
15 Q–K2	

Further over-protection. The less consistent 15 B–Q4 fails because of 15 ..., Q–B2; 16 Q–K2, Kt–Kt5; 17 P–KR3, P–K4.

15 ...	QR–B1
16 B–Q4	Q–B2
17 Kt–K5	

The squares Q4 and K5 are as firmly occupied by pieces as, in Tarrasch's theory, they had to be by pawns. Black's QB is still a bad Bishop, and he makes an abortive attempt to bring it into play on the other flank.

17 ...	B–K1
18 QR–K1	B×Kt
19 B×B	Q–B3
20 B–Q4	

Restricting Black's bad Bishop once more to the defence of the K pawn.

20 ...	B–Q2
21 Q–B2	R–KB2

To answer 22 B×Kt with P×B, when this Rook will defend the KR pawn.

22 R–K3	P–QKt3

23 R–Kt3	K–R1

Still reserving the right to answer B × Kt with P × B, but now White is moving from his successful control of the centre to a direct K side attack.

24 B × RP	

A small combination which wins a pawn. If 24 ..., Kt × B; 25 Q–Kt6, R–K2; 26 B × P*ch*. Now at last Black can advance his K pawn, but it is too late.

24 ...	P–K4
25 B–Kt6	R–K2

26 R–K1	Q–Q3
27 B–K3	P–Q5
28 B–Kt5	R × P
29 R × R	P × R
30 Q × P	K–Kt1
31 P–QR3	K–B1
32 B–R4	B–K1
33 B–B5	Q–Q5
34 Q × Q	P × Q
35 R × R	K × R
36 B–Q3	K–Q3
37 B × Kt	P × B
38 P–KR4	*Resigns*

This conception of control rather than occupation of the centre found rapid acceptance among the members of the Hypermodern school, and in the following game Richard Réti, one of the foremost Hypermoderns, exploits the white colour-complex K4, Q5, QB4 and QB6 with exemplary skill.

GAME 9
RUY LOPEZ

Réti   *Spielmann*

Berlin Tournament, 1919

1 P–K4	P–K4
2 Kt–KB3	Kt–QB3
3 B–Kt5	P–Q3
4 P–Q4	B–Kt5

Spielmann was one of the foremost Romantics, but it is being over-romantic to try and turn a very defensive variation into an attacking one.

5 P–Q5	P–QR3
6 B–R4	P–QKt4
7 P × Kt	P × B

Diagram 9

8 P–B4

A move which is readily comprehensible in the modern school of thought, but which would have seemed quite meaningless to earlier

31

generations. The complex of white central squares is now completely dominated by White.

8 ...	Kt–K2
9 Q×RP	B×Kt
10 P×B	Kt–Kt3
11 B–K3	B–K2
12 Kt–B3	

The square Q5 is to become a strong outpost for White.

12 ...	O–O
13 O–O–O	P–B4
14 Kt–Q5	P–B5
15 B–Q2	B–R5
16 B–R5	R–B2
17 P–B5	

With the threat of 18 P×P, Q×P; 19 Kt×QBP, while if 17 ..., P×P; 18 Kt×QBP at once.

17 ...	R–QB1
18 K–Kt1	B–K2

White's game is now full of energy while Black's has become suddenly sterile. The time is ripe for a combinative finish.

19 B×P	R×B
20 Kt×B*ch*	QR×Kt
21 P×P	R–K1

If it is true that two united passed pawns on the sixth rank are worth a Rook, then White already has a material advantage.

22 Q–B4	R(1)–B1
23 R–Q3	Q–B1
24 R–Kt3	K–R1
25 R–Q1	

White is now all ready to play P–Q7 followed either by P–B7 or R–Kt7. Black tries a desperately ingenious defence in vain.

25 ...	R–Q2
26 Q–Q5	R–R2
27 Q–B5	R–Q2
28 Q–Kt6	*Resigns*

For P–Q7 can no longer be effectively prevented.

Nimzovitch's conception that central pawns were not necessary for central control was something radically new in chess theory, but it accorded well with the ideas of the Hypermodern school, and Breyer toyed with the idea in his defence in Game 6.

Réti took the argument a step further. When Blackburne, in the position in Diagram 3, played P–KKt3 he not only created weaknesses on KB3 and KR3 but he made his KKt3 an object of attack for the hostile KR pawn when it advanced to its 5th rank. Equally then, when central pawns were moved, weak squares and points of attack must be similarly created. After 1 P–Q4, P–Q4 White automatically weakened his K4 and so did Black, and an example of the resulting struggle by each side to secure control of those squares was seen in Game 2. Moreover, Black's P–Q4 created a target on Q5 which White's 2 P–QB4 at once set about attacking.

From this the next step was quite logical, although at the time it had all the appearance of something bizarre. If the centre could be controlled without pawns and without pawn advances, an opening move which at once created weaknesses could be avoided, and the advance of the central pawns could be deferred until it could be seen how best the hostile position could be undermined and attacked.

Thus a whole range of new openings and defences was introduced. Réti as White played 1 Kt–KB3 (preventing Black's P–K4), followed by 2 P–B4 (disputing control of Q5). Pressure on the centre was then reinforced by the fianchetto development of the Bishops, and only when Black had committed himself beyond repair in the centre did White continue with either P–Q4 or P–K4 or both, thus physically disputing the centre only when the opponent was not in a position to react against any weaknesses Réti might be creating on his own side.

The advantage of this new range of openings was that a more complicated type of middle game resulted. Breyer had already shown that by avoiding opening lines which were too clear-cut it was possible to arrive at a position of much greater dynamic energy than resulted from normal openings. It was hoped that the same dynamic energy would be found in these Hypermodern openings with their avoidance of an immediate head-on clash. Certainly, the resulting middle game with its complicated pattern of pressures and veiled attacks was of the type in which the skill of the young Hypermodern masters found full scope.

What was later to be seen more clearly was that whereas Breyer kept the need for dynamic energy in the forefront and let the opening more or less take care of itself, the emphasis was now on the new theory of the centre with a not unreasonable hope that dynamic energy would automatically follow, though in point of fact this was not always the case, especially after the first flush when the new range of openings came to be more fully analysed.

In the following early example of Réti's System, Black is determined in spite of White's first move to force P–K4, but against the new theory of the centre this avails him little.

33

GAME 10

RÉTI SYSTEM

Réti   *Gruber*

Vienna Tournament, 1923

1	Kt–KB3	Kt–KB3
2	P–B4	P–Q3
3	P–KKt3	B–B4
4	B–Kt2	P–B3
5	P–Kt3	Q–B1
6	P–KR3	

It is essential for the successful conduct of this opening that pressure on the centre be maintained until the moment is ripe for its occupation. Therefore White protects his KB against exchange after B–R6.

6 ...		P–K4
7 B–Kt2		

Diagram 10

The initial deployment against the centre is completed. White now has to decide whether to strike at Black's K pawn with P–Q4 or to play against the slightly weakened squares Q5 and KB5. Since Black could answer P–Q4 with P–K5 followed

by P–Q4, Réti chooses the latter course.

7 ...	Kt–R3
8 Kt–B3	P–R3
9 P–Q3	B–K2
10 Q–Q2	Kt–B2
11 Kt–Q1	O–O
12 Kt–K3	

Pressure against the squares Q5 and KB5 begins.

12 ...	B–R2
13 O–O	Kt–Q2

Since the square Q4 seems to be satisfactorily under control, he prepares with P–KB4 to establish control of KB4 also.

14 Kt–R2

A sudden switch to an attack on the square K5 by the threat of P–KB4, thus showing how flexible the situation is when central commitments have not been made.

14 ...	Kt–K3
15 P–B4	P×P
16 P×P	

Now the success of White's opening is apparent; he has destroyed Black's centre, secured the long diagonal against the black King and also has an open KKt file which in combination with the diagonal is a dire threat to the square KKt7. The immediate threat is P–B5 and later P–B6.

16 ...	P–KB4
17 K–R1	Kt–B3

18 R–KKt1

White is now quite prepared to sacrifice his KB pawn for the attack on KKt7.

18 ...   Kt–R4
19 B–KB3   Kt(4)×P
20 Kt–Q5

This square comes into White's scheme after all. If now 20 ..., P × Kt; White wins by 21 Q × Kt, Kt × Q; 22 R × P*ch*, K–R1; 23 R × KB*dis. ch*, K–Kt1; 24 R–Kt1*ch*.

20 ...   Kt × Kt
21 P × Kt   B–Kt4

Here if P × P, then 22 B × QP, pinning the vital Knight which defends the KKt pawn.

22 P × Kt   Q × P

Naturally 22 ..., B × Q allows 23 R × P*ch* with an early mate, and so White has won a piece.

23 Q–B3   B–B3
24 Q–Q2   K–R1
25 R–Kt2   R–B2
26 QR–KKt1   B–K4
27 P–Q4

The pawn comes up into the centre at last, and in so doing decides the issue.

27 ...   B–B3
28 P–Q5   *Resigns*

For if 28 ..., P × P; 29 B × P, White wins the exchange, and if 28 ..., Q–K2; 29 P × P, P × P; 30 B × P, and White has the advantage in every sector.

More usually Black took immediate advantage of the opportunity to play P–Q4, but this similarly yielded White various opportunities for attack. In the first of the following two games White misses the crucial moment for the central pawn advance—timing is all-important in these situations—but fortunately gets a second chance; in the second game he plays more exactly.

GAME 11

RÉTI SYSTEM

Réti   Yates

New York Tournament,
1924

1 Kt–KB3   P–Q4
2 P–B4   P–K3

If P × P White can play either P–K3 or Kt–R3, using in the event of the latter move the manœuvre employed by Capablanca in Game 2 to recover the pawn and establish a strong square on K5. However, 2 ..., P–QB3 was generally preferred to P–K3 because the black QB is not then shut in.

3 P–KKt3   Kt–KB3

4 B–Kt2	B–Q3
5 P–Kt3	O–O
6 O–O	R–K1
7 B–Kt2	QKt–Q2

Now once again White has to decide whether to attack the occupied square Q5 or the weakened squares QB5 and K5. By temporizing he misses his moment.

8 P–Q3	P–B3
9 QKt–Q2	P–K4

Eliminating a weak square and freeing his game considerably.

10 P×P	P×P

White's only chance of attack on Q5 is now P–K4 which would be met by P–Q5. So he is compelled to combine occupation of the open file with an elaborate attack on K5 as his only remaining option.

11 R–B1	Kt–B1
12 R–B2	B–Q2
13 Q–R1	Kt–Kt3
14 R(1)–B1	B–B3

Better was Q–K2, for the fight is now for the black squares which the text move does nothing to promote. Nimzovitch even recommended P–QKt4 in order to exploit the Q side.

15 Kt–B1	Q–Q2
16 Kt–K3	P–KR3

Another inconsequent move. P–Q5 would have prevented White from continuing his attack on the black squares, which he is now able to force to a successful conclusion.

17 P–Q4	P–K5
18 Kt–K5	B×Kt

White threatened to win material on Black's QB3.

19 P×B	Kt–R2
20 P–B4	P×P e.p.
21 P×P	Kt–Kt4
22 P–B4	

White now holds all the central black squares, while Black's hold on the white squares depends largely on a weak isolated pawn.

22 ...	Kt–R6ch
23 K–R1	P–Q5

Giving up a pawn which would be lost anyway when White shifts his Rooks on to the Q file. But any hopes of play on the long diagonal are soon seen to be unfounded.

24 B×P	QR–Q1
25 R×B	

The end of Black's play on the long diagonal, and a clever exchanging combination to bring about a won ending.

25 ...	P×R
26 B×BP	Kt–B7ch
27 K–Kt2	Q×QB
28 Q×Q	R×Q
29 B×R	Kt–K5
30 P–K6	

The fact that Black's KB pawn is pinned makes this move decisive.

30 ...	R–Q7ch
31 K–B3	Resigns

In the next game Réti times his central advance more accurately, but an additional interest in the opening arises from the fact that he thereby arrives at a position which a later generation reached by much more direct and less roundabout methods from the Catalan Opening, sometimes because of its close association called the Réti–Catalan. Thus the indirect methods of approach which seemed implicit in Réti's view of the centre were later discarded for that same direct approach which in the Hypermodern opinion was to be deplored because of the weaknesses it created. To this extent the fears of the Hypermoderns were found to be exaggerated, but to the extent that these new openings produced more dynamic middle game positions, their inventions have persisted if often in a more direct form.

GAME 12

CATALAN OPENING

Réti   Bogolyubov

New York Tournament,

1924

1	Kt–KB3	Kt–KB3
2	P–B4	P–K3
3	P–KKt3	P–Q4
4	B–Kt2	B–Q3
5	O–O	O–O
6	P–Kt3	R–K1
7	B–Kt2	QKt–Q2
8	P–Q4	

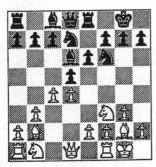

Diagram 11

Not making the same mistake as in the previous game. The squares QB5 and K5 are now definitely weak for Black, and the option of an attack on Q5 remains.

8 ...   P–B3

A position reached in later years from the Catalan Opening 1 P–Q4, P–Q4; 2 P–QB4, P–K3; 3 P–KKt3, with the continuation 3 ..., Kt–KB3; 4 B–Kt2, P–B3; 5 Kt–KB3, B–Q3; 6 O–O, O–O; 7 P–Kt3, QKt–Q2; 8 B–Kt2, R–K1. Thus apparently bizarre ideas become part and parcel of more normal opening methods of play.

9 QKt–Q2   Kt–K5

Giving up all attempts to control more than the white squares, since an attack on the black squares by P–K4 would leave him with a weak isolated pawn after 10 BP×P, BP×P; 11 P×P, Kt×P; 12 Kt×Kt, B×Kt; 13 B×B, R×B; 14 Kt–B4, R–K1; 15 Kt–K3, B–K3; 16 Q–Q4.

10 Kt×Kt	P×Kt
11 Kt–K5	P–KB4

Not Kt–B3; 12 Q–B2, and the advanced pawn falls.

12 P–B3	P×P
13 B×P	

Typically reserving the K pawn for the attack on the central white squares, which when it comes will incidentally open the KB file.

13 ...	Q–B2
14 Kt×Kt	B×Kt
15 P–K4	P–K4

Black, in preventing P–K5, counters White's attack on the white squares with his own attack on the black squares.

16 P–B5

With this move White ensures that he will emerge with the better pawn position.

16 ...	B–KB1
17 Q–B2	

Not only attacking Black's KB pawn but, through the defence of his own QB pawn, Black's K pawn also.

17 ...   KP×P

Not BP×P; 18 B×P, with a double attack on the K pawn and the KR pawn.

18 P×P

Whereas White's advanced pawn can be easily defended, Black's cannot.

18 ...	QR–Q1
19 B–R5	

A combination which will force Black to open the KB file where the issue will be decided.

19 ...	R–K4
20 B×P	R×KBP

Not R–Q4; 21 Q–B4, K–R1; 22 B–Kt4, and White has won a pawn.

21 R×R	B×R
22 Q×B	R×B
23 R–KB1	R–Q1

The only defence of his Bishop, for if B–K2; 24 Q–B7*ch*, K–R1; 25 Q–B8*ch*, and if Q–K2; 24 B–B7*ch*, K–R1; 25 B–Q5 (cutting off the Rook), Q–B3; 26 Q–B8, winning.

24 B–B7*ch*	K–R1
25 B–K8	*Resigns*

For he can no longer doubly defend his Bishop, whereas after 25 B–B4, Q–K2 Black could have held out. If 25 ..., B–K2; 26 Q–B8*ch* and mates.

It came almost as a shock to the Hypermodern masters to find that the novel opening systems which they had evolved over the years and finally with much labour brought to the hard test of competitive play were immediately adopted by a still younger generation who played them as to the manner born.

GAME 13

RÉTI SYSTEM

Euwe   *Loman*

Rotterdam Tournament,
1924

1	Kt–KB3	P–Q4
2	P–B4	P–Q5

Trying to gain space in the classical manner, and so restrict White's later attempts to find a suitable moment for his own central advance. But as Breyer showed in Game 6, and as the Hypermoderns were to show in many other novel openings, the farther a pawn advances the more difficult it becomes to defend. Here, moreover, Black at once submits to White control of the white central squares.

3 P–QKt4

The fianchetto in a more extended form than usual, which has the merit of taking the sting out of Black's natural supporting move of P–QB4.

3	...	P–KKt3
4	B–Kt2	B–Kt2
5	Kt–R3	P–K4
6	Kt–B2	

Preventing P–K5 by the threat to the Q pawn.

6	...	B–Kt5

7	P–K3	Kt–K2

Not P–K5; 8 Kt(2)×P, P×Kt; 9 Kt–K6, B×Kt; 10 B×B, with advantage. While if P–Q6; 8 Kt–R3, Kt–K2; 9 Q–R4*ch*, Kt–Q2; 10 B×QP, with advantage. Thus Black's centre becomes weakened.

8	P×P	P×P
9	P–KR3	B×Kt

The only move to save the Q pawn.

10	Q×B	P–QB3
11	P–KR4	

The centre is already sufficiently stabilized to permit a flank attack.

11	...	O–O
12	P–R5	R–K1
13	O–O–O	P–R4

An attempt at counter-attack which comes too late.

14	P×KtP	KRP×P
15	Q–R3	P×P
16	Kt×QP	

This sacrifice to open the long diagonal settles the issue. If Black now tries to avoid the mate on his KR1 by playing 16 ..., K–B1 then 17 Q–R7, B×Kt; 18 Q–R6*ch*, K–Kt1; 19 Q–R8*ch*, and the result is the same.

16	...	B×Kt
17	Q–R8*ch*	*Resigns*

The new ideas on the centre were similarly applied in defence. The next chapter is concerned with the various Indian defences against the Queen's Pawn Opening, but new defences against 1 P–K4 similarly appeared. Breyer in Game 6 and Euwe in the preceding game had both shown that the conception of holding back the central pawns and inducing the opponent to advance too far could be turned to good account. Tartakover summed it up by saying that the owner of the advanced pawn "had his initiative to defend." In no opening was the theme more clearly exemplified than in the novel and bizarre defence introduced by Alekhin and named after him. The defence had a considerable vogue for some twenty years, but like some of the other Hypermodern openings the emphasis was on the new ideas of the centre rather than on dynamic positions, and the latter did not always necessarily follow the former. It is significant that Alekhin himself, who was much more alive than the other Hypermoderns to dynamic requirements, did not repeat the experiment again in spite of his success in the following game.

GAME 14

ALEKHIN DEFENCE

A. Steiner   *Alekhin*

Budapest Tournament, 1921

1 P–K4	Kt–KB3
2 P–K5	Kt–Q4
3 P–Q4	

After 3 P–QB4, Kt–Kt3; 4 P–Q4, Black still starts his counter-play against White's centre by P–Q3. Alternatively White sometimes tried 3 P–QB4, Kt–Kt3; 4 P–B5, Kt–Q4; 5 Kt–QB3, Kt × Kt; 6 KtP × Kt, and still Black's P–Q3 gave him adequate play against White's apparent gain in space.

3 ...	P–Q3
4 B–Kt5	

Hoping to delay the advance of the black K pawn, but the strategical requirements of the position demanded support for his centre black squares with Kt–KB3 or P–KB4.

4 ...	P × P
5 P × P	Kt–QB3
6 B–Kt5	B–B4

With pressure on the black centre squares and control of the white squares, Black is prepared to put up with a doubled pawn.

7 Kt–KB3	Kt–Kt5
8 Kt–R3	Q × Q*ch*
9 R × Q	

Preferring to give up a pawn rather than play 9 K × Q, O–O–O*ch*; 10 K–B1, P–B3 and Black will control the centre squares of both colours. As the subsequent play shows, he had good reason for supposing that Black might not be able to hold his extra pawn.

9 ...	Kt×P*ch*
10 Kt×Kt	B×Kt
11 R–QB1	B–K5
12 Kt–Q4	B×P
13 R–KKt1	O–O–O
14 Kt×Kt	B×Kt
15 B×B	P×B
16 R×P	

Black has held his pawn, but the gain takes a great deal of exploiting.

16 ...	R–Q4
17 B–B4	P–K3
18 K–K2	B–B4
19 P–Kt4	

Not 19 R × KtP, K–Kt2 trapping the other Rook.

19 ...	B×KtP
20 R×KtP	R–Q2
21 B–K3	P–QR4
22 R–B4	P–R4
23 R–R4	B–B6
24 R–Kt5	R–Q4
25 P–B4	P–KB3

A most ingenious defence to avoid losing his extra pawn.

26 R(5)×P	R×R
27 R×R	P×P
28 P×P	B×P
29 R–R7	

There was more hope in the quick and immediate advance of his KR pawn.

29 ...	R–Kt4
30 K–B3	R–Kt7

31 R–R5	

Every simplification reduces Black's winning chances. If 31 P–KR4, R × P and Black has a dangerous passed QR pawn. But the ending is still a technical win for Black.

31 ...	B×P
32 R×P	B–Q3
33 K–K4	K–Q2
34 B–Q4	R–Q7
35 B–K3	R–K7
36 K–Q3	R–K8
37 B–Q4	R–QB8
38 B–K3	R–Q8*ch*
39 K–K4	R–K8
40 K–Q3	P–K4
41 B–B2	R–KB8
42 B–K3	K–K3
43 K–K4	R–KR8
44 B–B2	R–R7
45 B–K3	R–R5*ch*
46 K–Q3	B–Kt5
47 R–R7	P–B4
48 P–R3	P–B5*ch*
49 K–K2	B–Q3
50 R–R8	R–R7*ch*
51 K–Q1	R–R6
52 K–Q2	K–Q4
53 R–Q8	P–B6*ch*
54 K–K2	

He must hold on to his Bishop, and if 54 K–Q3, either P–K5*ch*; 55 K–K2, P–B7 is a winning line, or even more cleverly, as Alekhin pointed out, 54 ..., P–B7; 55 R–QB8, B–K2; 56 R × P, B–Kt4;

41

57 R–K2, P–K5ch; 58 K–Q2,
R × B; 59 R × R, K–Q5 and he has
won a piece.

54 ...	K–K5
55 R × B	R × Bch
56 K–B2	

Not 56 K–Q1, R–Q6ch; 57
R × R, K × R; 58 P–R4, P–B7ch;
59 K–B1, K–B6; 60 P–R5, P–K5
and wins.

56 ...	R–Q6
57 R–QB6	R–Q7ch

58 K–K1	K–Q6
59 R–Q6ch	K–B7
60 R–K6	R–Q4
61 K–K2	K–Kt6
62 R–QB6	P–B7
Resigns	

For if 63 R–Kt6ch, K × P; 64
R–R6ch, K–Kt7; 65 R–Kt6ch, K–
B8; 66 R–Kt8, R–Q7ch; 67 K–K1,
R–Q5; 68 K–K2, R–K5ch; 69
K–Q3, K–Q8; 70 R–QB8, R–Q5
ch; 71 K–K3, P–B8 = Qch.

As a matter of fact, this very idea of inducing White to overplay
his hand by making a premature central advance had been introduced
ten years earlier by Nimzovitch in his own particular variation of the
Sicilian Defence. The following game is therefore a parallel to the
previous one.

GAME 15

SICILIAN DEFENCE

Yates   Nimzovitch

London Tournament, 1927

1 P–K4	P–QB4
2 Kt–KB3	Kt–KB3
3 P–K5	

Accepting the invitation.

3 ...	Kt–Q4
4 B–B4	Kt–Kt3
5 B–K2	Kt–B3
6 P–B3	P–Q4
7 P–Q4	P × P
8 P × P	B–B4

White has maintained his hold on
the black squares, but Black starts
playing on the white squares.

9 O–O	P–K3
10 Kt–B3	B–K2
11 Kt–K1	Kt–Q2

Preventing 12 P–B4, which would
now be answered by Kt × QP; 13
Q × Kt, B–B4 winning the Queen.

12 B–Kt4	B–Kt3
13 P–B4	Kt × QP
14 Kt × P	

The point of White's 12th move.
If now P × Kt; 15 B × Ktch, Q × B;
16 Q × Kt, with impunity.

14 ...	Kt–QB3
15 Kt × B	Q–Kt3ch

Seizing his opportunity of exerting
some pressure on the black as well as
the white central squares.

42

| 16 K–R1 | Kt×Kt |
| 17 Q–R4 | |

Better was Q–K2 and B–K3, contesting the centre.

| 17 ... | P–KR4 |
| 18 B–R3 | |

A sad necessity, for if B–B3, then 18 ..., Kt–B4 with strong central control plus a side threat of P–R5 and Kt–Kt6ch.

18 ...	B–B4
19 Q–R3	Q–Kt4
20 K–Kt1	Kt–QKt3
21 Q–KB3	Kt(3)–Q4
22 P–QKt3	Q–Kt3ch

Black has succeeded in occupying his Q4. It is notable that his long-range checks cross the central squares and cannot be effectively met by interposition.

| 23 R–B2 | R–QB1 |
| 24 B–Q2 | R–R3 |

Here is the flank attack which so often springs from a secure centre, though Nimzovitch himself felt that at this point he fell between two stools through not being in a position to throw everything into the attack, but having part of his forces deployed for strategic play in the centre.

| 25 R–Q1 | B×B |
| 26 Q×B | Kt–B4 |

27 Q–Q3	R–Kt3
28 Kt–B3	R–Kt5
29 P–KR3	R–Kt6
30 P–QR4	Kt–R5
31 K–B1	

Unpinning the Rook against the threat of Kt×Ktch.

31 ...	R–B3
32 P–R5	Q–Q1
33 K–Kt1	Kt–B4
34 K–R2	P–R3
35 Q–Kt1	

Threatening Kt–Q4 followed by Kt×Kt and K×R, but Black has now rearranged his forces for the final attack.

35 ...	Q–K2
36 Kt–Q4	Q–R5
37 B–K1	

Not 37 Kt×R, R×RPch; 38 P×R, Q×Rch; 39 K–R1, Kt–Kt6 *mate*.

| 37 ... | Kt×P |
| 38 R×Kt | |

Now if 38 Kt×R, R×KtPch; 39 R×R, Q×Pch; 40 K–Kt1, Q×R*mate*.

38 ...	R×RPch
39 P×R	Q×Rch
40 K–Kt2	Kt–K6ch
Resigns	

Mate in two cannot be avoided.

Much more esoteric, and therefore much less generally popular, was the original defence against 1 P–K4 which Nimzovitch evolved, and which is named after him.

GAME 16

NIMZOVITCH DEFENCE

Brinckmann   Nimzovitch

Niendorf Tournament, 1927

1 P–K4   Kt–QB3
2 Kt–QB3

If 2 P–Q4, P–Q4; 3 P–K5, B–B4 with a fairly easy development.

2 ...   P–K3
3 P–Q4   P–Q4
4 P–K5

Now the game has transposed into a kind of French Defence in which Black has played Kt–QB3 instead of P–QB4. Since White has committed his centre pawns, even the Hypermoderns would not regard it as necessary to withhold P–QB4 any longer, but Nimzovitch has the idea that by not playing the move until later, several useful variations are denied to White.

4 ...   KKt–K2

If QKt–K2; 5 QKt–K2, P–QB4; 6 P–QB3, and if 4 ..., B–Kt5; 5 Q–Kt4.

5 Kt–B3   P–QKt3

One of the advantages of the system is that Black solves the age-old problem of the bad Bishop in the French Defence.

6 Kt–K2

Making it easier for Black, but if 6 B–K2, P–QR4 followed by 7 ..., B–R3.

6 ...   B–R3
7 Kt–Kt3   B × B
8 K × B

Now, for all Black's holding back his QB pawn, White's French Defence finds itself deprived of its best attacking piece.

8 ...   P–KR4

A positional manœuvre on the flank which bears the true Nimzovitch hallmark. He secures a grip on some more of the white squares, and at the same time prevents White from getting some purchase on the black squares with Kt–R5.

9 B–Kt5

Threatening 10 Kt–R4, P–Kt3 (to defend the KR pawn); 11 B–B6, with a powerful hold on the black squares.

9 ...   Q–B1
10 Q–Q3

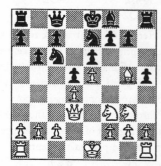

Diagram 12

Not 10 Kt–R4, Q–R3*ch*; 11 K–Kt1, Q–R5 with the Q pawn in exchange for the KR pawn, a centre pawn being almost always worth more than a flank pawn. At this point White's extra space would have convinced Tarrasch that Black had a thoroughly bad game, but like Breyer, Nimzovitch recognizes that it is preferable to have a cramped position dynamic with potential energy rather than a non-dynamic position which is free.

| 10 ... | Kt–Kt3 |
| 11 P–B3 | P–R5 |

Now White can no longer enforce his hold on the black squares with either Kt–R4 or P–KR4. This further advance of a flank pawn in order to pursue a strategical motif originating in the centre is quite noteworthy.

12 Kt–K2	B–K2
13 P–KR3	B×B
14 Kt×B	QKt–K2
15 K–Kt1	P–KB3

At last Black makes his effort to secure the centre.

| 16 Kt–B3 | Q–Q2 |

Preparing P–QB4 which would at the moment be answered by 17 Q–Kt5ch.

| 17 K–R2 | P–QB4 |
| 18 P–B4 | |

Black is threatening Q–B2 winning the centre, and if 18 KP × P, Q–B2 ch; 19 K–Kt1, KtP × P and White's KR is shut in. So he meets the threat to his own black squares with counter-play against the white squares.

| 18 ... | Q–B2 |
| 19 P×QP | P–B5 |

Nimzovitch pointed out that if P × KP; 20 Q–Kt5ch, K–B1; 21 Kt–Kt5, P × P*dis. ch* 22 P–B4, Kt × BP; 23 KR–KB1, Kt × QP; 24 Kt × P*ch*, winning.

20 Q–B2	P×QP
21 KR–K1	O–O
22 Kt–B3	P×P
23 Kt×KP	Kt×Kt
24 P×Kt	

And here Nimzovitch thought there were chances of a draw by 24 R × Kt, Kt–B3; 25 Kt × P, Q–Q3; 26 Q × P, Kt × R; 27 P × Kt, Q × P *ch*; 28 P–B4, Q–K3; 29 P–B5, Q–K4*ch*; 30 K–R1, R–B2; 31 QR–Q1, though the chances appear somewhat slender. Certainly after the text move the passed black Q pawn becomes a terror.

24 ...	P–Q5
25 Kt–Kt5	Q–B4
26 Kt–Q6	P–Q6

If P–QKt4 to hold the QB pawn, then 27 QR–Q1, P–Q6 (against Q–K4); 28 R × P, R × P; 29 R–Q2, and the worst is over for White.

27 Q×P*ch*	Q×Q
28 Kt×Q	R×P
29 QR–Q1	R–QB1
30 Kt–K3	

Not 30 Kt–Q6, R(1)–B7 with complete control of the valuable 7th rank.

30 ...	R–Q1
31 Kt–B4	Kt–B4
32 P–R4	

Not 32 Kt–Q6, Kt×Kt; 33 R×P, Kt–Kt2; 34 R×R*ch*, Kt×R; 35 P–K6, Kt×P; 36 R×Kt, R×P with a won ending. While if 32 P–K6, R–K7; 33 R×P, R(7)×R; 34 R×R*ch*, K–R2 and the threat of Kt–Kt6 and R–R8*mate* cannot be avoided. The text move is designed to maintain the Knight against the threat of P–QKt4.

32 ...	K–B2
33 R–K4	R–K7
34 R–B4	K–K3
35 R–Kt4	P–Q7
36 R–Kt6*ch*	K–B2
37 R–Kt4	P–R3

The move that forces the Knight to give way at last by the threat of P–QKt4. If 38 Kt×P, Black plays R–K8 at once.

38 R–B4	K–K3
39 Kt–Q6	Kt–K6
Resigns	

Nimzovitch was a great believer in the weakness of the doubled pawn, and this had a considerable effect upon his development of new opening variations. He admitted that there was little wrong with a formation of pawns on QB2, QB3 and Q3, except that it entirely lacked dynamic potentialities; induce it to adopt the position QB2, QB3 and Q4 and its weakness is evident. Moreover, if the opponent's pawn stood on Q4, it was almost axiomatic with the Hypermoderns that one should have the opportunity of attacking it with P–QB4. But if the doubled pawn formation was QB2, QB3 and Q4, the advance P–QB4 was very difficult since P–QKt3 in preparation was no longer available. Consequently Nimzovitch always strove to impose this particular pawn weakness on his opponents in the belief that he thereby reduced the dynamic potentialities of their positions; the idea of reducing one's opponents' dynamism rather than increasing one's own was much more negative than Breyer's view of the matter, and it possibly explains in part why Nimzovitch never quite reached the heights of success attained by more dynamic players.

For years the accepted opening moves of the French Defence had been 1 P–K4, P–K3; 2 P–Q4, P–Q4; 3 Kt–QB3, Kt–KB3. Long years before Winawer used to play 3 ..., B–Kt5, but that was because he had a fad that Knights were better than Bishops. When Steinitz and Tarrasch proved the contrary, everyone forgot the move 3 ..., B–Kt5. But now it was revived for two reasons—first, it gave Black the chance of imposing the "doubled pawn complex" on

White, which was regarded as well worth the exchange of Bishop for Knight, and secondly it avoided the loss of time with the KKt when White advanced P–K5 and thereby gave added energy to the defence. The Winawer variation is in fact one of the great legacies of the Hypermoderns, and has virtually replaced the older variations entirely.

The following game is a splendid example of Hypermodern play since it emphasizes the white pawn weakness and the weakness of the whole associated colour complex, and ends with a remarkable alternating attack.

GAME 17

FRENCH DEFENCE

Mannheimer   Nimzovitch

Frankfurt Tournament, 1930

1 P–K4	P–K3
2 P–Q4	P–Q4
3 Kt–QB3	B–Kt5
4 P×P	P×P
5 Kt–B3	Kt–K2

In accordance with the Hypermodern preference for asymmetrical rather than symmetrical developments, and also to follow with B–KB4 obtaining strong pressure on the white squares.

6 B–Q3	QKt–B3
7 P–KR3	B–KB4
8 B×B	Kt×B
9 O–O	B×Kt
10 P×B	O–O
11 Q–Q3	Kt–Q3

Controlling both QB5 and K5, and preventing the undoubling of White's QB pawns..

12 Kt–Kt5	P–KKt3
13 B–B4	Q–B3

14 B–Q2

Much more to the point was B × Kt, removing Black's strong piece.

14 ...	P–KR3
15 Kt–B3	K–R2
16 Kt–R2	Q–R1

A strange move with a defensive purpose. If Q–Kt2; 17 Kt–Kt4, P–KR4; 18 B–R6.

17 Q–K3	Q–Kt2
18 Q–B3	Kt–K5
19 B–B1	P–B4

Black's central control is now apparent. He occupies most of the white squares, and his pressure on the black squares with his Queen prevents White's P–B4.

20 Q–Q3   Kt–R4

Again preventing P–QB4.

21 P–KB4	Q–Q2
22 Kt–B3	Q–B3
23 Kt–K5	Q–K3

Not Q × P; 24 Q × Q, Kt × Q; 25 B–Q2, winning a piece.

24 R–Kt1	P–Kt3
25 K–R2	Kt–B5

47

Diagram 13

All the white squares are now occupied, so he proceeds to develop a King's side attack.

26	B–K3	P–KKt4
27	P–Kt3	R–B3
28	QR–K1	R–KKt1
29	B–B1	P–Kt4

The King's side attack will not of itself prove sufficient, so he prepares the Lasker method of alternating this with an attack on the Queen's side, foreseeing that the barrier of white QB pawns will prevent White from being able rapidly to switch defences from side to side.

| 30 | Kt–B3 | P–KKt5 |
| 31 | P×P | R×P |

32	Kt–Kt1	R(3)–Kt3
33	R–B3	Q–Kt1
34	Kt–K2	P–KR4
35	K–Kt2	

Against P–R5, which would bring the attack to a successful conclusion.

35	...	P–R5
36	R–R1	R–KR3
37	R–R3	Q–Kt3

His King's side attack has reached its maximum force, so he moves over to his alternating attack.

| 38 | B–K3 | Q–R3 |
| 39 | B–B2 | |

He has no time for 39 Kt–B1, because then 39 ..., P×P; 40 R×R*ch*, Q×R with disaster for White on the KR file.

| 39 | ... | Q×P |

There is a kind of delightful impudence about the closing stages.

40	B–K1	P–R4
41	K–B1	Q–Kt8
42	Kt–Kt1	P–R5
43	K–K2	P–R6
44	R–B1	P–R7
	Resigns	

CHAPTER V

The Indian Legacy

IT was, however, with the Indian defences that the Hypermodern masters wrote their most important chapter in the books of theory and practice. A wholly new vista of opening strategy was opened up, a legacy of which subsequent generations have made full use. The name Indian was given to these openings because, like the Réti System, they frequently made use of the fianchettoed Bishop, a development which had been a favourite with Indian players brought up in the slower and more indirect school of Oriental chess.

Apart from the Dutch Defence there was at the time no regular asymmetrical defence against 1 P–Q4. Yet Hypermodern theory held that by 1 ..., P–Q4 in reply Black must inevitably be creating a weakness which could be attacked. They could point, for example, to the game Rubinstein–Salve from the Lodz tournament of 1908, where the opening ran 1 P–Q4, P–Q4; 2 P–QB4, P–K3; 3 Kt–QB3, P–QB4; 4 BP×P, KP×P; 5 Kt–B3, Kt–KB3; 6 P–KKt3, and White's pressure on the weak black Q pawn ultimately brought victory.

In fact, it was in their view even more important for Black to avoid early commitments than for White, since White had the initiative of the first move; the Réti System, avoiding early commitments for White, was later found to pursue a largely illusory objective, since Black lacked the initiative to take advantage of early commitments, and White could quite safely commit himself to the same opening by the more direct methods of the Catalan Opening.

Irregular defences to 1 P–Q4 had of course been played before, not with the substratum of new strategical theory now available, but merely to avoid the book lines. Thus Capablanca, at a time when he feared his lack of knowledge of the openings might lead him into lines that he would unwittingly find were disadvantageous to him, had played as Black: 1 P–Q4, Kt–KB3; 2 P–QB4, P–Q3; 3 Kt–QB3, QKt–Q2; 4 P–K4, P–K4. This now became known as the Old

Indian Defence in contradistinction to the new Indian defences which the Hypermoderns were evolving.

One of the first of these defences to attain any considerable stature and form was the Queen's Indian Defence, where Black's system was based on 1 ..., Kt–KB3, 2 ..., P–K3 and 3 ..., P–QKt3. Now Black can at a suitable moment decide whether to play P–B4 or P–Q4 or some other line, the point being that he reserves options according to White's play. What did soon become apparent was that Black was a move in arrears as compared with the Réti System, and therefore had a sterner struggle before him to contest the centre. Generally he could hope for no more than a share of the spoils, the white squares for example in the Queen's Indian Defence, while White secured control over the black squares. This meant that an even greater degree of caution had to be exercised in timing any central advance than was the case with the white pieces in the Réti System, and often the central advance had to be withheld altogether as in the following game.

GAME 18

QUEEN'S INDIAN DEFENCE

Przepiorka   Nimzovitch

Kecskemét Tournament,

1927

1 P–Q4	Kt–KB3
2 Kt–KB3	

For a time this replaced P–QB4 as White's 2nd move in order to forestall a gambit discovered in Budapest in 1917, which ran 1 P–Q4, Kt–KB3; 2 P–QB4, P–K4 with the continuation 3 P×P, Kt–Kt5 and White could only maintain his extra pawn at considerable risk. Later the Budapest Defence was less feared and 2 P–QB4 came back into general use.

2 ...	P–K3
3 P–B4	P–QKt3
4 Kt–B3	B–Kt2

Preventing P–K4. The strategical outline of the struggle for the centre is already clear.

5 Q–B2	B–Kt5
6 P–QR3	B×Kt*ch*
7 Q×B	P–Q3
8 P–KKt3	

White is not going to surrender control of his K4 without a fight.

8 ...	QKt–Q2
9 B–Kt2	Q–K2
10 O–O	O–O
11 P–QKt4	Kt–K5
12 Q–B2	P–KB4

Now Black has successfully won his share of the centre.

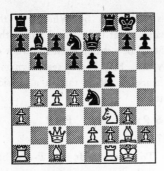

Diagram 14

| 13 | Kt–Kt5 | Kt(2)–B3 |
| 14 | Kt×Kt | |

If 14 P–B3, Kt×Kt; 15 B×Kt, P–K4; and Black, whose grip on the white squares has been weakened, attacks White's hold on the black squares.

14	...	B×Kt
15	B×B	Kt×B
16	P–B3	

Now he contests the white squares and Black will be hard put to it. But by exchanging the Bishop which defends his King he gives Black a chance.

| 16 | ... | Kt–B3 |
| 17 | B–Kt2 | R–B2 |

One of Nimzovitch's "mysterious" Rook moves. He doubles Rooks on a closed file as a means of deterring White from completing his attack on the centre by P–K4.

18	QR–B1	QR–KB1
19	Q–Q3	P–KR4
20	P–K4	

Playing into Black's hands. A quiet move such as K–R1 was required.

20	...	P×P
21	P×P	Kt–Kt5
22	P–R3	

Black threatened P–R5, breaking open the position, but this does not help.

22	...	Kt–B7
23	Q–K2	Kt×Pch
24	K–R1	Q–Kt4
25	R×R	R×R
26	Q–Kt2	Kt–B7ch
27	K–Kt1	Q–K6
	Resigns	

The following game is a variant of the same idea, but Nimzovitch's handling of the middle game is much more dynamic than his usual style.

GAME 19

QUEEN'S INDIAN DEFENCE

Vidmar *Nimzovitch*

New York Tournament, 1927

| 1 | P–Q4 | Kt–KB3 |
| 2 | Kt–KB3 | P–K3 |

| 3 | P–B4 | B–Kt5ch |

It is a characteristic of many of the Indian defences that they can quickly transpose one into another. The text move introduces Bogolyubov's form of Indian Defence, but by his later P–QKt3 Nimzovitch

turns the opening back into normal
Queen's Indian lines.

4 B–Q2	Q–K2
5 Kt–B3	O–O
6 P–K3	P–Q3
7 B–K2	

If 7 B–Q3, P–K4 with a threat to
open the K file.

7 ...	P–QKt3

Now that White has developed his
KB so quietly, Black plays to seize
control of his K5.

8 O–O	B–Kt2
9 Q–B2	QKt–Q2
10 QR–Q1	KB×Kt
11 B×B	Kt–K5
12 B–K1	P–KB4
13 Q–Kt3	

Defending his K pawn in readiness
for P–B3, and at the same time
exerting a veiled pressure on Black's
K pawn.

13 ...	P–B4

Defending his own K pawn in
turn by preventing P–B5, and striking also at the black squares in
typical style.

14 Kt–Q2	Kt×Kt
15 R×Kt	P–K4

Dynamic play, allowing a central
hole in the conviction that it will lead
White nowhere. If now 16 P–Q5,
the black Bishop eventually goes back
to QB1 and re-enters the game on the
other flank. More dangerous still to
Black is the opening of the Q file and

its occupation by White; by the
standards of the classical school this
should be a strong point in favour of
White, but Black sees dynamic
chances to offset this in a K side
attack.

16 P×KP	P×P
17 P–B3	

To answer P–B5 with P–K4, but
now the KB pawn is itself a point of
attack.

17 ...	P–KKt4
18 B–B2	

Preparing to double his Rooks, for
18 Q–Q3, QR–Q1; 19 Q–Q6,
Q–Kt2 does not lead to anything
very definite.

18 ...	Kt–B3
19 KR–Q1	QR–K1
20 Q–R4	B–R1
21 R–Q6	

It is curious how impotent are the
doubled Rooks on the open file.

21 ...	Q–KKt2
22 B–B1	

Against P–Kt5 and the opening of
the KKt file, but it is part of the
Hypermodern strategy to have more
than one string to one's bow.

22 ...	P–K5
23 B–K1	

Not 23 B–K2, P×P; 24 B×P,
Kt–K5.

23 ...	P×P
24 B–B3	Q–K2

25 R(6)–Q3

Now not 25 B×Kt because of Q×P*ch*; 26 K–R1, P×P*ch*; 27 B×P, Q–K8*ch* and mates.

25 ...	P×P
26 B×P	B×B
27 B×Kt	

If 27 K×B, then Q–K5*ch* gives a winning attack.

27 ...	Q–K5

Triumph on the white squares.

28 R(1)–Q2	B–R6
29 B–B3	Q–Kt5*ch*
Resigns	

Later the fianchetto of White's KB became accepted as the best line against the Queen's Indian Defence, but Black's resources were still adequate. By judicious simplification he could ensure at least equality, the standard line being 1 P–Q4, Kt–KB3; 2 P–QB4, P–K3; 3 Kt–KB3, P–QKt3; 4 P–KKt3, B–Kt2; 5 B–Kt2, B–K2; 6 O–O, O–O; 7 Kt–B3, Kt–K5. This line, however, led to evenly balanced positions which allowed only of slight subtleties, and certainly not to the dynamic positions for which modern players seek. Consequently, the Queen's Indian Defence suffered a diminution of favour. The following game is an early example of the White fianchetto.

GAME 20

QUEEN'S INDIAN DEFENCE

Sämisch	Nimzovitch

Copenhagen Tournament, 1923

1 P–Q4	Kt–KB3
2 P–QB4	P–K3
3 Kt–KB3	P–QKt3
4 P–KKt3	B–Kt2
5 B–Kt2	B–K2
6 Kt–B3	O–O
7 O–O	P–Q4

Later Kt–K5 was preferred, but the text move equally ensures control over his K5, though with some reduction of force along the diagonal.

8 Kt–K5	P–B3
9 P×P	

This exchange merely eases Black's game, which is a little cramped.

9 ...	BP×P
10 B–B4	P–QR3

Preparing to make a strong outpost square of his QB5 by continuing with P–QKt4 and then bringing a Knight to occupy the outpost.

11 R–B1	P–QKt4
12 Q–Kt3	Kt–B3
13 Kt×Kt	

Forestalling Black's plan of Kt–QR4–B5.

13 ...	B×Kt
14 P–KR3	

White now had nothing better than to simplify with 14 Kt–K4, Kt × Kt; 15 R × B.

14 ...	Q–Q2
15 K–R2	Kt–R4
16 B–Q2	P–B4

Against P–K4 and preparing for attack. White is now driven back in all quarters.

17 Q–Q1	P–Kt5
18 Kt–Kt1	B–QKt4

The Bishop gains the freedom of the white squares again, while P–K4 for White is yet once more delayed.

19 R–Kt1	B–Q3
20 P–K4	BP × P

But for this surprise, giving up the Knight, White might have proved once again that the Queen's Indian Defence holds few terrors for him. But the sacrifice turns the tables; for his piece Black gets two pawns and entry into the 7th rank.

21 Q × Kt	R × P
22 Q–Kt5	R(1)–KB1
23 K–R1	R(1)–B4

24 Q–K3	B–Q6

Cutting off the White Queen's escape to QKt3, and thus threatening to win the piece by R–K7.

25 QR–K1	P–R3
Resigns	

Diagram 15

One of the most extraordinary dénouements on record to any sacrificial combination. White cannot now move a piece without loss, and he can only stall in other ways for a few moves by 26 P–R3, P–QR4; 27 P × P, P × P; 28 P–Kt3, K–R2; 29 P–Kt4, R(4)–B6; 30 B × R, R–R7*mate*.

Mention has already been made in the introductory paragraph to Game 17 of Nimzovitch's predilection for doubled pawns in his opponent's game, because of the consequent diminution of dynamic potentialities. This somewhat negative view of dynamic play was in fact expanded by Nimzovitch into a complete theory of the game, in which the doubled pawn was merely one item.

He differentiated between those reactions on the part of an opponent which could be regarded as inevitable, such as Black's P–QB4 in Game 8 after 1 P–K4, P–K3; 2 P–Q4, P–Q4; 3 P–K5, and those which could be forestalled or at least deprived of their sting by suitable preventive and prophylactic measures, such as Black's P–K4 in the same game. His mysterious Rook moves in Game 18 are another example of this reduction of the opponent's dynamic power.

From such examples he worked out a complete theory of what he termed the "Blockade," the essence of which was that preventive measures could and should be taken against hostile expansion, in other words hostile dynamic possibilities, before one's own attack was launched. The Blockade might be applied only to one or two points or it might be extended over the whole of the board; in the latter case it might also be associated with the control of extra space, but it could equally well be applied when the opponent controlled more space. It has at times been misinterpreted as equivalent to Tarrasch's cramping tactics in the play from Diagram 2, but the essential difference is that Tarrasch's manœuvres were attacking manœuvres whereas Nimzovitch's Blockade manœuvres are the defensive manœuvres prior to the launching of an attack.

In no game was the theory of the Blockade better exemplified than in the next game, where the preventive moves which set up the Blockade are made by the Queen in a remarkably original manœuvre.

The game illustrates another form of Indian defence which Nimzovitch made so peculiarly his own that it has since been known as the Nimzovitch Indian, usually contracted to Nimzo-Indian, Defence; and this in spite of the fact that the Queen's Indian Defence was equally his own. The Nimzo-Indian Defence differs from the Queen's Indian Defence in that a fianchetto of the QB is by no means an essential though sometimes a concomitant feature. An alternative name that has been applied to it is the Middle Indian Defence.

GAME 21

NIMZO-INDIAN DEFENCE

Johner	*Nimzovitch*

Dresden Tournament, 1926

1 P–Q4	Kt–KB3
2 P–QB4	P–K3
3 Kt–QB3	B–Kt5

White's P–K4 is prevented not by P–Q4 but by the pin of the Kt.

4 P–K3	O–O
5 B–Q3	P–B4

Now the advance is prevented by striking at the black squares, so that if White finally succeeds in forcing P–K4 (that is, assuming he still decides to make the effort), then Black will have compensating control of White's Q4.

| 6 Kt–B3 | Kt–B3 |
| 7 O–O | B×Kt |

Played not so much from fear of P–K4 as to create weaknesses in White's pawn skeleton which can be usefully exploited and which will reduce White's dynamic chances.

| 8 P×B | P–Q3 |

Now if 9 P–K4, P–K4; 10 P–Q5, Kt–QR4; and Black's doubled pawns have been weakened by the advance of the Q pawn.

| 9 Kt–Q2 | P–QKt3 |

With an option of attacking White's pawn on QB4 by Kt–QR4 and B–R3, a line which White forestalls at the cost of allowing Black more room for central action.

| 10 Kt–Kt3 | P–K4 |
| 11 P–B4 | |

If 11 P–Q5, Black gains further ground by P–K5; 12 B–K2, Kt–K4.

| 11 ... | P–K5 |
| 12 B–K2 | Q–Q2 |

Since the centre is secure, there is a danger that White will feel free to start a K side attack by P–KKt4, and the text move is the first stage of an elaborate blockade manœuvre to prevent this.

13 P–KR3	Kt–K2
14 Q–K1	P–KR4
15 B–Q2	

15 Q–R4 fails because of the hole at KKt3 which Black could then exploit by 15 ..., Kt–B4; 16 Q–Kt5, Kt–R2; 17 Q×RP, Kt–Kt6.

Diagram 16

| 15 ... | Q–B4 |

Threatening Q–R2 and P–R5, putting an end to all White's K side hopes—blockade play at its best.

| 16 K–R2 | Q–R2 |
| 17 P–QR4 | Kt–B4 |

Having minimized White's dynamic possibilities, Black now turns to attack by threatening 18 ..., Kt–Kt5ch; 19 P×Kt, P×Pdis. ch; 20 K–Kt1, P–Kt6.

| 18 P–Kt3 | P–R4 |

Creating a hole on QKt4 and a weak backward pawn on QKt3,

neither of which will prove of value to White. At the same time he prevents P–R5, "rolling up" the black Q side pawns, for after P–R5 and P × P White might exert serious pressure on the weak backward pawn, since he would also have the QR file available for manœuvre. The text move is therefore the lesser evil.

19	R–KKt1	Kt–R3
20	B–KB1	B–Q2
21	B–B1	QR–B1

Threatening B–K3 and P × P, winning the white QB pawn. White is thus forced to block the centre completely and permit Black to proceed on the flank.

22	P–Q5	K–R1
23	Kt–Q2	R–KKt1
24	B–KKt2	P–KKt4
25	Kt–B1	R–Kt2
26	R–R2	Kt–B4
27	B–R1	R(1)–KKt1
28	Q–Q1	P × P
29	KP × P	B–B1
30	Q–Kt3	B–R3

Alternating the original threat against the doubled pawn with his threats against the King. If now 31 Q × P, then Black demolishes White's centre pawns. And that the K side attack is no mean one is shown by the following variation given by Nimzovitch himself: 31 B–Q2, R–Kt3; 32 B–K1, Kt–Kt5ch; 33 P × Kt, P × P*dis. ch*; 34 K–Kt2, B × P; 35 Q × B, P–K6; 36 Kt × P (against

Q–R6*mate*), Kt × Kt*ch*; winning the Queen.

31	R–K2	Kt–R5
32	R–K3	

Not 32 Kt–Q2 continuing the attack on the K pawn because of 32 ..., B–B1; 33 Kt × P, Q–B4; 34 Kt–B2, Q × P*ch*; 35 Kt × Q, Kt–Kt5*mate*.

32	...	B–B1
33	Q–B2	

He has no time to play Q × P now.

33	...	B × P
34	B × P	

If 34 K × B, Q–B4*ch*; 35 K–R2, Kt–Kt5*ch*; 36 K–R3, Kt–B7*dbl. ch*; 37 K–R2, Q–R6*mate*.

34	...	B–B4
35	B × B	Kt × B
36	R–K2	P–R5

Now White's defences crumble.

37	R(1)–Kt2	P × P*ch*
38	K–Kt1	Q–R6
39	Kt–K3	Kt–R5
40	K–B1	R–K1
	Resigns	

The threat is 41 ..., Kt × R; 42 R × Kt, Q–R8*ch*; 43 R–Kt1 (if K–K2, Q × R revealing the point of Black's 40th move), P–Kt7*ch*; 44 K–B2, Kt–K5*ch*; and White has to let his Rook go. 41 K–K1 is no answer because of 41 ..., Kt–B6*ch*; 42 K–Q1, Q–R8*ch* and mates.

In the following example the emphasis is all on the doubled pawn complex.

GAME 22

NIMZO-INDIAN DEFENCE

Mattison   *Nimzovitch*

Karlsbad Tournament, 1929

1 P–Q4	Kt–KB3
2 P–QB4	P–K3
3 Kt–QB3	B–Kt5
4 Kt–B3	B × Kt*ch*
5 P × B	P–Q3
6 Q–B2	Q–K2

White is contesting the white squares strongly, so Black prepares to play P–K4 and contest the black squares.

7 B–R3

Forestalling Black's intention, and preparing to play P–B5, thus getting rid of his doubled pawn.

7 ...	P–B4
8 P–Kt3	P–QKt3
9 B–KKt2	B–Kt2
10 O–O	O–O
11 Kt–R4	

This attempt to dispute Black's hold on the white squares merely displaces the Knight without in any way helping him on the white squares.

11 ...	B × B
12 K × B	Q–Kt2*ch*
13 K–Kt1	Q–R3

The attack on the doubled pawn now begins.

14 Q–Kt3	Kt–B3
15 KR–Q1	Kt–QR4
16 Q–Kt5	Q × Q
17 P × Q	Kt–B5

The occupation of the square is effective even though the pawn is no longer there. Black's play on the white squares is evidence of the success of his opening strategy.

18 B–B1	P–QR3
19 P × RP	R × P
20 P × P	KtP × P
21 Kt–Kt2	Kt–Q4
22 R–Q3	KR–R1

Now White must lose material.

23 P–K4	Kt–K4
Resigns	

For if 24 R–Q1 (R–Q2, Kt–B6 *ch*), Kt × P; 25 R–B1 and the KP or the QRP must fall.

So serious did the doubled pawn complex in this opening appear to be that new lines were developed to forestall this particular weakness. In the following example Nimzovitch as Black still succeeds in finding a Q side weakness to exploit.

GAME 23

NIMZO-INDIAN DEFENCE

Bogolyubov   Nimzovitch

San Remo Tournament, 1930

1 P–Q4	Kt–KB3
2 P–QB4	P–K3
3 Kt–QB3	B–Kt5
4 Q–Kt3	P–B4
5 P×P	Kt–B3

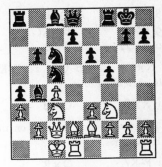

Diagram 17

Not only maintaining the pin which allows him to dispute the white central squares, but also putting pressure on the black squares.

6 Kt–B3	Kt–K5
7 B–Q2	Kt×QBP
8 Q–B2	P–B4

Success on the white squares once again.

9 P–K3	O–O
10 B–K2	P–QKt3
11 O–O–O	

Partly from fear of the very strong diagonal attack on his King if he castles on the other side, and partly to bring pressure on to Black's backward Q pawn. The backward pawn, however, is once again found to be not so weak, and the attack which develops against the white King shows that P–QR3 first would have been better.

11 ...	P–QR4
12 P–QR3	P–R5

Fastening on to the hole on QKt6 which is a genuine weakness. White cannot reply 13 P×B because of 13 ..., Kt×P; 14 Q–Kt1, Kt–Kt6*mate*, nor can he avoid this by interpolating 13 K–Kt1, B–Kt2 because after 14 P×B, Kt×P; 15 Q–B1, Kt–Kt6 the Queen is trapped.

13 Kt–QKt5	B×B*ch*
14 Kt×B	Kt–R4

Against P–QKt4.

15 B–B3	P–Q4

Getting rid of his weakness and reinforcing his attack. If now 16 Kt–Q4, B–R3; 17 P×P, B–Q6.

16 P×P	B–R3

The weakness on the white squares has spread not only to QKt6 but also to QKt4. If now 17 P×P, Black still wins by 17 ..., B×Kt; 18 B×R, B–Q6. So White plays to get a Rook for two pieces.

17 Kt–B4	B×Kt

18	P×P	Q–B2	
19	B×R	B×Kt	
20	B–Q5	B×B	

Not 20 ..., B–Q6; 21 P–K7 *dis. ch*, leading to mate.

21	R×B	Q–B3

Still maintaining the play on the white squares.

22	P–K7	Q×R
23	P×R=Q*ch*	K×Q
24	R–Q1	Q–K4
25	P–R3	P–R4
26	P–KKt4	RP×P
27	P×P	Kt(R)–Kt6*ch*
28	K–Kt1	P×P
29	R–Kt1	Q–Q4
30	R–Q1	

Not 30 R×P, Q–R8*ch* and mates.

30	...	Q–K5

After the exchange of Queens, the ending would be easy for Black.

31	R–Kt1	Kt–Q7*ch*

By inserting this move first Black now forces the attack home.

32	K–B1	Q–Q4
33	Q–R7	

Making a flight square for the King, since 33 R×P leads to 33 ..., Kt(4)–Kt6*ch*; 34 K–Q1, Q–R8*ch*, while 33 P–Kt4 fails against 33 ..., Kt(4)–Kt6*ch*; 34 K–Kt2, Kt–B5*ch*; 35 K–R2, Kt–Q5; 36 Q×P, P–QKt4; 37 Q–R7, Kt–R4*dis. ch*; 38 K–R1, Kt(5)–Kt6*ch*; 39 K–Kt2, Q–Q7*ch*; 40 K–Kt1, Q–Q6*ch*; 41 K–Kt2, Kt–B5*ch*; 42 K–R2, Q–B7*mate*. But now the Queen is cut off and the attack still succeeds.

33	...	Kt(7)–K5
34	Q–R8*ch*	K–B2
35	K–Kt1	Q–Q6*ch*
	Resigns	

For after 36 K–R2 he is mated by 36 ..., Kt–B6*ch*; 37 P×Kt (K–R1, Kt–Kt6*mate*), Q–B7*ch*; 38 K–R1, Kt–Kt6*mate*.

Even in his own day critics were not missing to query Nimzovitch's negative theory of dynamics, and they took the Nimzo-Indian Defence and White's doubled pawn as a typical example. To reduce one's opponent's dynamism was not necessarily to increase one's own, nor was it in keeping with the teaching of Breyer. Sämisch, for example, held that White's doubled QB pawns in the Nimzo-Indian Defence could be endured because the resulting position was sufficiently full of dynamic energy to compensate for the weakness; he actually used to invite the doubling of the pawns at the outset. This view, though it commanded only lukewarm support at the time, came to be warmly endorsed by a later generation.

GAME 24

NIMZO-INDIAN DEFENCE

Sämisch   Grünfeld

Karlsbad Tournament, 1929

1 P–Q4	Kt–KB3
2 P–QB4	P–K3
3 Kt–QB3	B–Kt5
4 P–QR3	B×Kt*ch*
5 P×B	P–Q3
6 P–B3	

Cutting across Black's normal play on the white squares with the idea of establishing a dynamic position in the centre.

6 ...	O–O
7 P–K4	P–K4

Denied access to the white squares, he has perforce to make what he can of the black.

8 B–Q3	Kt–B3

Inviting P–Q5 when the weakness of the doubled pawns would be emphasized and his own access to the black squares would be increased. White resists the bait.

9 Kt–K2	Kt–Q2
10 O–O	P–QKt3
11 B–K3	B–R3
12 Kt–Kt3	Kt–R4
13 Q–K2	Q–K1

(See Diagram 18)

14 P–B4

The energy in White's centre begins to make itself felt.

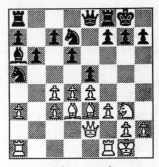

Diagram 18

14 ...	P–KB3
15 R–B3	K–R1
16 QR–KB1	Q–B2

Forcing White at last to admit the threat to his doubled pawn.

17 BP×P	QP×P
18 P–Q5	Kt–Kt2

At once shifting his ground on to the weakened black squares.

19 Kt–B5	Kt–Q3
20 R–R3	P–Kt3

Taking steps against White's outpost so as to weaken the force of the attack before continuing his manœuvres against the Q side, but the move gives White further weaknesses to exploit.

21 Kt–R6	Q–Kt2
22 P–Kt4	P–KKt4

He is once more forced to concede the outpost square and has a weak KB pawn into the bargain.

23 R–R5	Kt–B4

24 B×Kt   P×B

Preventing any frontal attack on his doubled pawns and leaving Black also with doubled pawns. He has thus emerged with the advantage of a K side initiative.

25 R–B3   Q–K2
26 R(3)–R3   B–B1
27 Q–KB2   Kt–K1
28 R–B3   Kt–Kt2
29 R(5)–R3

Not 29 R×KtP, B–Q2 and the Rook is trapped.

29 ...   B–Q2
30 R(R)–Kt3

Preparing the advance of his KR pawn.

30 ...   B–K1
31 P–KR4   P×P
32 R–Kt2   P–R6

The pawn cannot be held, and giving it up this way interferes with White's build-up against the KB pawn with Q×P and R(2)–KB2.

33 R×RP   B–Kt3
34 R–B3   QR–Kt1

Having established his defensive position, he prepares a counter-initiative on the Q side.

35 Q–R4   R–Kt6
36 R(2)–KB2   R×BP

Black has won the doubled pawn after all, but at the cost of allowing White a devastating attack. On the other hand White's finish was not easy to foresee, and R–Kt3 to hold the square KB3 was a negative manœuvre hardly likely to appeal to the younger and more dynamic of the Hypermoderns.

37 P–Kt5   Kt–K1
38 P×P   Q–Q1

If Q–Q3; 39 P–B7, Kt–Kt2; 40 R–B6, with increasing pressure.

39 Kt–Kt4   R×B

A desperate attempt to break the force of the attack, but if Q–Q3; 40 Q–Kt5 still wins the K pawn.

40 R×R   B×P
41 R–K3   Kt–Q3
42 Kt×P   B–B4

Hoping to win the dangerous white KB pawn at last, but a drastic finish follows. Black no doubt thought the Bishop was taboo because of the resulting fork.

43 R×B   Kt×R
44 Kt–Kt6*ch*   K–Kt1
45 R–K7

A beautiful move. If now Kt×Q; 46 R–Kt7*mate*. If P×Kt; 46 Q–R7*mate*. And if Kt×R; 46 P×Kt, Q–K1; 47 P×R=Q*ch*, winning easily.

45 ...   R–B2
46 R×R   K×R
47 Kt–K5*ch*   K–B1
48 Q×P   *Resigns*

For if Q×BP (against 49 Q–R8 *mate*), then 49 Kt–Q7*ch*.

While the Queen's Indian and Nimzo-Indian defences can be readily recognized as kindred systems with their emphasis on white square control and particularly White's K4, the King's Indian Defence was based on an entirely different strategy.

The advance of a centre pawn was regarded by the Hypermoderns not only as weakening the squares on each side of it but also as creating a point in itself which could be attacked. In the Réti System White had the option of choosing which weakness he would make his target, but when the same principles were applied in defence, it was usually only possible due to White's extra move for Black to realize one or other of these objectives; either the weak squares or the advanced pawn could be attacked, but hardly ever both. The Queen's Indian and Nimzo-Indian defences concentrated on the weak squares; the King's Indian Defence had to strike at the white pawn on Q4.

In practice the defence ran into considerable difficulties. Whereas in the Queen's Indian the development of the first two pieces—the KKt and QB—brought pressure at once on to the objective, the development in the King's Indian Defence of Black's KKt and KB brought no pressure of any forcible kind on to the centre squares, so that White obtained a fairly free run in the centre in the early stages. For this reason the defence did not attain any great popularity until considerably later. Of course, if White overstepped the bounds of prudence in the centre, then Black might well set up a successful reaction as he did in the Alekhin Defence. The following game is just such an example.

GAME 25

KING'S INDIAN DEFENCE

Colle   *Euwe*

Antwerp–Rotterdam Match, 1926

1 P–Q4	Kt–KB3
2 P–QB4	P–KKt3
3 Kt–QB3	B–Kt2
4 P–K4	P–Q3
5 P–B4	

The Four Pawns Variation, for all its Tarrasch-like gain of space, does not give the benefits which might be expected from it.

5 ...	O–O
6 Kt–B3	P–B4

(See Diagram 19)

The attack on the black squares and White's Q pawn begins to take shape.

7 P–Q5	P–K3

Diagram 19

8 B–Q3	P×P
9 BP×P	

Not KP × P because of R–K1*ch*.

9 ...	Q–Kt3
10 B–B2	

He cannot castle because of P–B5 *dis. ch* and if 10 Kt–QR4, then 10 ..., Q–B2; 11 O–O, P–B5; 12 B–B2, P–QKt4 with good counter-pressure on the Q side.

10 ...	P–B5

11 Q–K2	R–K1
12 B–R4	B–Q2
13 B×B	QKt×B
14 Kt–Q2	Kt×KP

Black's development is already so far ahead that he can indulge in combinative measures.

15 Kt(3)×Kt	QR–B1
16 K–B1	

Not 16 Kt×BP, Q–Kt5*ch*.

16 ...	P–B4
17 Kt×BP	QR×Kt
18 Kt–B6*ch*	

If 18 Q×R, R×Kt; 19 Q–B8*ch*, Kt–B1; 20 Q–B2, Q–Kt4*ch*; 21 K–Kt1, B–Q5*ch*.

18 ...	Kt×Kt
19 Q×R	Kt–Kt5

Resigns

For again after 20 Q–B2 comes Q–Kt4*ch*. And the pawn White so forcibly advanced on his 5th move still stands in utter idleness.

When, however, White played more quietly to control the centre by fianchettoing his own K Bishop, not only could Black find less to strike at but White was himself well placed to launch a Q side attack as in the following game.

GAME 26
KING'S INDIAN DEFENCE

Rubinstein　　　　*Réti*

London Tournament, 1922

1 P–Q4	Kt–KB3
2 Kt–KB3	P–Q3
3 P–B4	QKt–Q2

4 Kt–B3	P–K4
5 P–KKt3	P–KKt3

That Black has played P–K4 to attack the white pawn on Q5 before fianchettoing his K Bishop is merely a transposition of moves. The underlying strategy remains unaltered, but on this occasion White reacts in similar style by regarding Black's advance of the K pawn as weakening the central white squares, and he accordingly sets about taking advantage of this in Hypermodern style by the fianchetto of his own K Bishop, a recipe which has been widely adopted in the treatment of the King's Indian Defence.

6 B–Kt2	B–Kt2
7 O–O	O–O
8 P–K4	P–Kt3

Seizing the moment to counter White's play on the white squares, while the diagonal is blocked.

9 P–KR3

To retain the two Bishops after B–K3, which could at the moment be answered by Kt–Kt5.

9 ...	B–Kt2
10 P–Q5	

Defending his K pawn and occupying all the weak white squares, but now Black can begin to play on the black squares, which is the original theme of his defence. Moreover, the pawn skeleton is such that the advance P–KB4 will be effective.

10 ...	Kt–R4
11 Kt–K1	Q–K1

Not yet P–KB4 because of 12 P×P, P×P; 13 Q×Kt.

12 B–B3	Kt(4)–B3

For the moment the attempt is defeated.

13 B–K3	K–R1
14 Kt–Q3	Kt–B4

15 B–Kt2	Kt–R4
16 B–B3	Kt–B3
17 P–QKt4	Kt×Kt
18 Q×Kt	Kt–Kt1

At last he will be able to advance the KB pawn, but meanwhile White has prepared an advance on the other wing.

19 P–B5	P–B4
20 P–B6	B–B1
21 K–R2	Q–K2
22 B–Kt2	P–B5
23 B–Q2	Q–B3
24 Kt–Kt5	B–QR3
25 P–QR4	R–B2
26 P–R5	QR–KB1

He cannot force the blocking of the Q side by B×Kt; 27 Q×B, P–QR3; 28 Q–Q3, P–QKt4; because White has the ingenious move 28 P×KtP, P×Q; 29 R×R, P×P; 30 R–Kt8, and the passed Q side pawns amply compensate for his material inferiority.

27 P×KtP	B×Kt
28 Q×B	RP×P
29 R–R3	P×P*ch*
30 P×P	Q×R

Not quite sound, and he has nothing better than Q–K2; 31 R×R, when the game is still no more than equal.

31 B×Q	R×B
32 B–K3	B–R3
33 P–Kt4	

Of course not 33 B×B, R(1)–B7 *mate*. But he could disprove Black's

30th move with 33 B–Kt1, R–Q8; 34 R–R2, R(1)–B8; 35 B–B2, winning.

33 ...   B×B
34 R×B   P–Kt4

Preparing to bring his Knight to KR5.

35 Q–R6   Kt–K2
36 R–K2   Kt–Kt3
37 Q–Kt7   R(8)–B2

38 R–R2   K–Kt2
39 R–R7   R–B7*ch*

Not Kt–R5 threatening 40 ..., R–B7*ch*; 41 K–Kt1, R–B8*ch*; 42 R(1)–B7*ch*, K–Kt3; 43 R–Kt7*mate*, because of 40 Q×BP, R×Q; 41 R×R*ch*, winning. Black therefore has nothing better than the text move, accepting the draw by perpetual check.

Since Black appeared to obtain adequate chances if he could force the move P–KB4, a further line was introduced, known as the Lasker Variation, in which White set out from the start with the Nimzovitch view that Black's P–KB4 was by no means inevitable and that Blockade measures could be taken against it before it occurred. Since this involved the advance P–KKt4 by White, the associated strategy was a K side attack by White instead of the usual Q side advance, and in fact White often castled on the Q side, leaving Black to try and attack there. As with almost all Blockade manœuvres, Black's dynamism was effectively reduced but White's little if at all enhanced, with the result that a not very vigorous game resulted; the following is an excellent example of the line, handled by no less a Blockade expert than Nimzovitch himself.

GAME 27

KING'S INDIAN DEFENCE

Nimzovitch   Tartakover

Karlsbad Tournament, 1929

1 P–Q4   Kt–KB3
2 P–QB4   P–KKt3
3 P–B3   B–Kt2
4 P–K4   P–Q3
5 Kt–B3   O–O
6 B–K3   QKt–Q2

Twenty years were to pass before the Russians discovered how Black could retain dynamic chances in this variation. This they achieved by aiming at P–KB4 before White could put a bind on the position, thus: 6 ..., P–K4; 7 P–Q5, Kt–R4; 8 P–KKt4, Kt–B5; 9 KKt–K2, P–KB4. After this discovery the Lasker variation no longer has much point.

7 Kt–R3   P–K4
8 P–Q5   P–QR4
9 Kt–B2   P–Kt3

10 Q–B2	Kt–B4
11 B–Kt5	B–Q2
12 P–KKt4	

The themic move of the variation. White's centre, and in particular his K4, is well supported, Black's P–KB4 is indefinitely postponed, and a K side assault on Black is now imminent.

12 ...	Q–B1
13 P–KR4	K–R1

Against the opening of the KKt file. At no time can Black revitalize his game by a sacrifice on KKt5, since the opening of a sector there would only benefit White. Thus if now 13 ..., Kt×KtP; 14 P×Kt, P–KB3 (against B–K7); 15 B–K3, B×P; 16 Kt×B, Q×Kt; 17 B–K2, and the black Queen must retreat, for if 17 ..., Q–Kt6ch; 18 K–Q2, and 19 QR–KKt1 is a grave threat.

14 P–R5	P×P
15 B×Kt	B×B
16 R×P	B–Kt2

White has succeeded in opening the KR file instead, and now threatens Q–Q2–R6.

17 Kt–R1	P–KB3

The threat now is 18 Q–R2, P–R3; 19 P–Kt5. It is still useless to play 17 ..., B×P; 18 P×B, Q×P because the Queen can do no damage after 19 Q–R2, P–R3 (Kt×P; 20 R–R4, Q–Kt3; 21

B–Q3); 20 B–K2, Q–B5; 21 Kt–Kt3 (threatening R–B5), Q–B3; 22 Kt–B5.

18 Q–R2	P–R3

Finally giving up all hopes for his fianchettoed Bishop except in a role of abject defence.

19 Kt–Kt3	K–R2
20 B–K2	R–KKt1
21 K–B2	

He is not even going to give Black the usual pleasure of at least hoping for a Q side attack against the castled King. Instead the monarch is to seek safety behind his own attacking forces.

21 ...	R–R1
22 R–R4	Q–K1
23 R–KKt1	B–KB1
24 K–Kt2	Kt–Kt2

Everything hastens to the defence against the impending attack.

25 Kt–R5	Q–Kt3
26 P–B4	Kt–Q1

P×P; 27 Q×P would only increase White's scope without in any way solving Black's defensive problems.

27 B–B3	

To free the QKt.

27 ...	Kt–B2
28 Kt–K2	B–K2
29 K–R1	K–Kt1
30 Kt(2)–Kt3	K–B1
31 Kt–B5	R–KKt1

Diagram 20

32 Q–Q2

Each side has now completed its respective preparations for attack and defence, and as so often happens when the principles of the Blockade are applied, White has succeeded in reducing Black's dynamic chances to nil, but at the same time has not greatly increased his own. He now indulges, as he can afford to, in some idle gestures on the other flank.

32 ...	R–B1
33 R–R2	K–K1
34 P–Kt3	K–Q1
35 P–R3	R–QR1
36 Q–B1	B–KB1

By continuing a non-committal defence with some move like R–QB1, Black could force White either to try and develop an alternative attack elsewhere or admit that he cannot break through. Instead, in an effort

to continue the flight of his King to the Q side which began on the 29th move, he blunders away the exchange. If it did nothing else, the Blockade theory strongly applied often made the task of the defence so wearying that accuracy failed.

37 Kt–R4	Q–R2
38 Kt×P	Q–R1
39 Kt×R	Q×Kt
40 P–Kt5	KP×P
41 P×P	Q–R2
42 Q×P	B×P
43 Q–B6*ch*	K–B1
44 Kt–B5	B×Kt
45 P×B	K–Kt2
46 Q–Kt6	R–R1

Of course 46 ..., Q×Q; 47 P × Q, would cost more material, but the awkward interdependence of Black's pieces costs him material in the end anyway.

47 Q×Q	R×Q
48 R–Kt6	K–B1
49 P–B6	R–R1

Not yet K–Q1 because of 50 R–Kt8*ch*, K–Q2; 51 B–Kt4*mate*. While if K–Q2; 50 B–Kt4*ch*, K–K1; 51 R–Kt8*ch*, B–B1; 52 R × R.

50 B–Kt4*ch*	K–Q1
51 B–K6	K–K1
52 B×Kt*ch*	K×B
53 R(2)×B	*Resigns*

It was in an attempt to give the player of the King's Indian Defence a better share of the centre that Grünfeld developed a variation which has since come to be regarded as a separate branch of the Indian defences. The opening moves of his variation ran 1 P–Q4, Kt–KB3; 2 P–QB4, P–KKt3; 3 Kt–QB3, P–Q4. Play on the black squares then followed quite logically with 4 P × P, Kt × P; 5 P–K4, Kt × Kt; 6 P × Kt, P–QB4; 7 Kt–B3, B–Kt2; 8 B–K2, O–O; 9 O–O, and a secondary feature of his strategy becomes apparent in that he can play P × P and after White's P × P he has a pawn majority on the Queen's wing in a situation where the minority attack can hardly be applied. It should be noted that Black only plays P–Q4 after White has played Kt–QB3, otherwise he cannot continue with Kt × Kt which is essential to the weakening of the long diagonal and to the preparation for the pawn majority; thus if, as in the following game, White defers the development of his QKt, Black must also defer the move P–Q4. The game well illustrates the strategic pressures of this variation, even the blunder arising directly out of them.

GAME 28

GRÜNFELD DEFENCE

Bogolyubov   Euwe

3rd Match Game, Holland, 1928

1	P–Q4	Kt–KB3
2	Kt–KB3	P–KKt3
3	P–B4	B–Kt2
4	Kt–B3	O–O
5	P–KKt3	

Anticipating an ordinary King's Indian Defence, but now Black switches to the Grünfeld line.

5	...	P–Q4
6	P × P	Kt × P
7	B–Kt2	

The usual P–K4 would only weaken the square KB3 now that he has played P–KKt3.

| 7 | ... | P–QB4 |

| 8 | O–O | Kt × Kt |
| 9 | P × Kt | Kt–B3 |

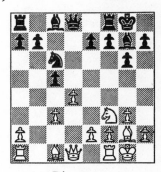

Diagram 21

10 P–K3

Already Black's pressure on his Q4 is severe enough to make him weaken KB3 after all. Of course 10 P–Q5 is met by B × P.

| 10 | ... | Q–R4 |
| 11 | Q–Kt3 | R–Kt1 |

Getting out of White's pressure on

the long diagonal and preparing both the development of his Q Bishop and the advance of his Q side pawns.

12 B–Q2   B–Kt5
13 QR–Q1

This attempt to reinforce his Q4 brings disaster because his previous attempt to bolster the square with P–K3 has weakened the square KB3 on which there is now a fatal pin.

13 ...   P×P
14 BP×P   Q–R4

and wins.

For material loss must now be accepted, quite apart from the fact that Black has satisfactorily created his Q side majority. White continued for a few more moves, but the advance of Black's Q side pawns soon settled the issue.

CHAPTER VI

Dynamics and Dynamite

THE conception of a dynamic revolution which had first been aired by Breyer, so far from being carried through by the Hypermoderns, had tended if anything to change direction in their hands. They became obsessed by the new ideas on the centre, and analytically distracted by the discovery of a tremendous new continent of opening theory. Nimzovitch, it is true, evolved his own dynamic theory, but it was a negative one and far removed from Breyer's original aspirations.

Nevertheless, the man to restore the old impetus and reset the compass was already there. Alexander Alekhin (1892–1946), to the extent that he restored the emphasis on dynamic chess, may be said to be the founder of modern chess play. Gifted with combinative power beyond anything seen since Anderssen's day, no player was better equipped to reveal the hidden subtleties of a dynamic position.

His genius, indeed, was so diverse that it is practically impossible to define any limits by which it can be said to be bounded. In whatever direction it led him, he seemed to soar above his fellows as an eagle above sparrows, and to range in fields where few if any were capable of following. From first to last his watchword seemed to be "Experiment"; ever introducing new moves, some good, some less good, he constantly staggered his opponents with some novel variation, and having displayed it left it to others to examine in detail while he moved on to something else. This ever fertile invention had one aim, to obtain dynamic positions by avoiding lines analysed to exhaustion. It was a method which no player of lesser invention or imagination could have long sustained; frequently it involved considerable hazards.

Long before the day of the Hypermodern revolution this urge to experiment, as a means of avoiding the dull academic play of the Classical school, had made itself apparent, as for example in the following game where he gave an old opening an entirely new twist on the sixth move. Since 1914, of course, the Chatard Attack has developed from an original novelty into an orthodox textbook variation.

GAME 29

FRENCH DEFENCE

Alekhin   *Fahrni*

Mannheim Tournament,
1914

1 P–K4	P–K3
2 P–Q4	P–Q4
3 Kt–QB3	Kt–KB3
4 B–Kt5	B–K2
5 P–K5	KKt–Q2
6 P–KR4	

The novelty. Sacrifice of a pawn for compensating attacking chances.

6 ...	B×B
7 P×B	Q×P
8 Kt–R3	Q–K2
9 Kt–B4	

Threatening 10 Kt(4)×QP, P×Kt; 11 Kt×P, Q–Kt4; 12 Kt×P*ch.*

9 ...	Kt–B1
10 Q–Kt4	

Now he not only threatens 11 Kt(4)×QP, P×Kt; 12 Q×B*ch*, but also Q×KtP.

10 ...	P–KB4
11 P×P*e.p.*	P×P
12 O–O–O	

Not 12 Kt(4)×QP because P×Kt discovers check, but now the threat is on again.

12 ...	P–B3
13 R–K1	K–Q1

If B–Q2; 14 Kt(4)×QP, BP×Kt; 15 Kt×P, Q–Q1; 16 Q–R5*ch*, Kt–Kt3; 17 Q×Kt*ch*, P×Q; 18

R×R*ch*, K–B2; 19 R×Q, P×Kt; 20 B–Q3, and wins.

14 R–R6	P–K4
15 Q–R4	QKt–Q2
16 B–Q3	P–K5
17 Q–Kt3	

Threatening entry at QB7 and KKt7, the first by 18 Kt(4)×P, P×Kt; 19 Kt×P, and the second, if Black tries to forestall the first with 17 ..., Q–Q3, by 18 B×P, P×B; 19 R×KP.

17 ...	Q–B2
18 B×P	P×B
19 Kt×P	R–KKt1

Diagram 22

20 Q–QR3

One of the typical quiet surprise moves which occur so often at the end of an Alekhin combination, and which suddenly reveal hidden dynamics. The pressure is switched to a new quarter by the threat of 21 Q–R5*ch*, P–Kt3; 22 Q–B3.

20 ...	Q–Kt2
21 Kt–Q6	Kt–QKt3

22 Kt–K8	Q–KB2	23 Q–Q6*ch*	Q–Q2

If Q–Q2; 23 Kt×P, Q–KB2; 24 Q–Q6*ch*, B–Q2; 25 R–K8*ch*, winning the queen.

Not B–Q2; 24 Q–B7*mate*.

24 Q×P*ch*	Resigns

To a player like Alekhin, whose imagination found itself parched amid the arid deserts of the Classical style, the Hypermodern revolution appeared like an oasis of fresh water, even though it was to become as far as he was concerned largely a mirage. He delighted in original situations, where combination and tactics might replace the dry science of positional strategy, and this was just what the new movement seemed to offer. In his own notes to a brilliant game against Reshevsky at Kemeri in 1937 he remarks, "I must confess that the final attack gave me much more pleasure than a scientifically correct but purely technical exploitation of positional advantages. Chess is not only knowledge and logic."

For a time Alekhin threw himself wholeheartedly into the Hypermodern movement. Game 14 showed him introducing one of the most Hypermodern of all openings, but, as already mentioned, he only played it the once. He explored the new ideas on the centre, and in particular the conception that a central pawn majority was even more to be desired than a flank majority. In the next game he exploits this theory in magnificent style, winning brilliantly against no less a master than the doyen of the Classical school. But once again it was an opening he adopted only the once, for unlike the true Indian defences which were based on a long-term strategy, the Blumenfeld Defence was a pseudo-Indian based on a tactical device, which had only to fail to leave Black's game devoid of either strategical or dynamic opportunities.

GAME 30

BLUMENFELD DEFENCE

Tarrasch   Alekhin

Pistyan Tournament, 1922

1 P–Q4	Kt–KB3
2 Kt–KB3	P–K3
3 P–B4	P–B4
4 P–Q5	P–QKt4

Sacrificing his QKt pawn, not as in the Evans Gambit to gain time, but to draw the white centre pawns away to a flank and so secure the central majority. Basically the whole conception is as old as Philidor, who always believed that victory could be obtained by the advance of a central pawn wedge.

5 P×KP

If 5 P×KtP, Kt×P and Black's theme is realized. Better than the text move, however, is 5 B–Kt5, after which White keeps a grip on the centre and Black's tactical idea has failed to come off, leaving him with no good long-term strategy to fall back on.

5 ...	BP×P
6 P×P	P–Q4

Diagram 23

The theme of the gambit is now clear. Black has his central majority.

7 P–K3	B–Q3
8 Kt–B3	O–O
9 B–K2	B–Kt2
10 P–QKt3	QKt–Q2
11 B–Kt2	Q–K2
12 O–O	QR–Q1
13 Q–B2	P–K4

Control and occupation of the centre has been easily carried out, and he can now proceed to a direct attack on the King.

14 KR–K1	P–K5

15 Kt–Q2	Kt–K4
16 Kt–Q1	Kt(3)–Kt5
17 KB×Kt	

Not 17 Kt–B1, Kt–B6*ch*; 18 P×Kt, P×P; 19 B–Q3, Q–R5; 20 Kt–Kt3, Q–R6. White hopes to be able to defend both KB2 and KR2 satisfactorily, but Black cleverly switches the attack to White's KKt2.

17 ...	Kt×B
18 Kt–B1	Q–Kt4
19 P–KR3	

Preparing to bring a Rook to KKt1.

19 ...	Kt–R3
20 K–R1	Kt–B4
21 Kt–R2	P–Q5

The theme of the central majority reappears in conjunction with pressure on the long diagonal, for if now 22 P×P, P–K6; 23 R–KKt1 (Kt×P, Kt×Kt; 24 P×Kt, Q–Kt6), Kt–Kt6*ch*; 24 P×Kt, Q×P; 25 Kt–KB3, B×Kt winning by force.

22 B–B1	P–Q6
23 Q–B4*ch*	K–R1
24 B–Kt2	Kt–Kt6*ch*
25 K–Kt1	B–Q4

The black pieces gain in energy in Breyer-like fashion.

26 Q–R4	Kt–K7*ch*
27 K–R1	R–B2

White is not allowed even the compensation of a passed QKt pawn.

28	Q–R6	P–R4
29	P–Kt6	Kt–Kt6*ch*
30	K–Kt1	P×P
31	Q×KtP	P–Q7
32	R–KB1	Kt×R
33	Kt×Kt	B–K3
34	K–R1	

If 34 Q–B6, to answer B×RP with 35 Q×KP, Black wins by 34 ..., R–B6; 35 Q×KP, B–Q4; 36 Q–Q3, Q×P*ch*; 37 K×Q, R–Kt6*dbl. ch*; 38 K–R2, R–Kt7*ch*; 39 K–R1, R–R7*dbl. ch*; 40 K–Kt1,

R–R8*mate*. A fine zigzag combination.

34	...	B×RP
35	P×B	R–B6
36	Kt–Kt3	P–R5
37	B–B6	

Despair.

37	...	Q×B
38	Kt×P	R×P*ch*
	Resigns	

For if 39 K–Kt1, B–R7*ch* wins the Queen, and if 39 K–Kt2, Q–B6 *ch* and mates.

But if he preferred not to repeat the risky experiment of playing the Blumenfeld Defence, Alekhin could not resist playing with dynamite. On more than one occasion he risked dangerous opening novelties, though never more than once for each; like Lasker, he relied on throwing an opponent off balance psychologically by presenting him with some absolutely new problem, and he anticipated as a consequence that he would have a game in which dynamic opportunities would abound. This is by no means every man's solution of how to gain dynamic chances, but it is certainly one aspect of Alekhin's great genius, and the next three games all show him in this particular mood.

GAME 31

TARRASCH DEFENCE

Pirc   *Alekhin*

Bled Tournament, 1931

1	P–Q4	P–Q4
2	P–QB4	P–K3
3	Kt–QB3	P–QB4
4	P×QP	BP×P

Sacrificing a pawn, and throwing White right off the normal positional lines in this opening.

5 Q–R4*ch*

Equally winning material and permitting more exchanges is the move Q × P, which is therefore preferable. A typical continuation could be 5 ..., Kt–QB3; 6 Q–Q1, P×P; 7 Q×P, B–K3; 8 Q×Q*ch*, R×Q; 9 P–K3, Kt–Kt5; 10 B–Kt5*ch*, K–K2; 11 K–K2, with advantage to White.

5	...	B–Q2
6	Q×QP	P×P
7	Q×QP	

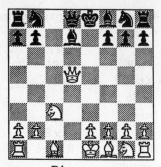

Diagram 24

Now it can be seen that Black has in effect given up a pawn for two tempi—one, the development of the KKt without loss of time, and second, the ability to bring his KB into play in a single move. Other things being equal, two tempi are insufficient compensation for a pawn, but when added to a dynamic position in the hands of an Alekhin and to some almost imperceptible error on White's part, the result is beautiful and startling.

7 ...	Kt–QB3
8 B–Kt5	Kt–B3
9 Q–Q2	P–KR3
10 B×Kt	Q×B
11 P–K3	O–O–O
12 O–O–O	

GAME 32
FRENCH DEFENCE
Alekhin   *Nimzovitch*
Bled Tournament, 1931

| 1 P–K4 | P–K3 |
| 2 P–Q4 | P–Q4 |

Alekhin recommended Kt–Q5 as keeping a slight edge for White. Now those two tempi are turned to brilliant account.

12 ...	B–KKt5
13 Kt–Q5	R×Kt
14 Q×R	B–QR6
15 Q–Kt3	

Not 15 P×B, Q–B6*ch*; 16 K–Kt1, R–Q1; 17 Q×R, Kt×Q; 18 R–B1, B–B4*ch*.

15 ...	B×R
16 Q×B(3)	Q×P
17 Q–Q3	B–Kt5
18 Kt–B3	B×Kt
19 Q–B5*ch*	K–Kt1
20 Q×B	Q–K8*ch*
21 K–B2	R–QB1
22 Q–Kt3*ch*	Kt–K4*dis. ch*
23 K–Kt3	Q–Q8*ch*
24 K–R3	R–B4
Resigns	

For if 25 P–Kt4, R–B6*ch*; 26 K–Kt2, Q–B8*mate*. Or if 25 P–Kt3, Q–B8*ch*; 26 K–R4 (K–Kt4, Q–B6 *ch*; 27 K–R3, R–R4*mate*), R–R4*ch*; 27 K×R (K–Kt4, Q–Q7*mate*), Q–R6*ch*; 28 K–Kt5, P–R3*ch*; 29 K–Kt6, Q–Kt5*ch* and mates.

| 3 Kt–QB3 | B–Kt5 |
| 4 Kt–K2 | |

Another Alekhin gambit, played to energize the position rather than follow positional lines with the normal P–K5.

4 ...	P×P
5 P–QR3	B×Kt*ch*

It was later regarded as safer to decline the gambit by B–K2.

6 Kt×B	P–KB4

Hardly sound Hypermodernism. Nimzovitch should have known better than to weaken his black squares to such an extent. The result is both summary and horrible.

7 P–B3	P×P
8 Q×P	Q×P
9 Q–Kt3	Kt–KB3

If Kt–K2, to save the KKt pawn,

GAME 33
SLAV DEFENCE

Alekhin	*Euwe*

6th Match Game, Haarlem, 1937

1 P–Q4	P–Q4
2 P–QB4	P–QB3
3 Kt–QB3	P×P
4 P–K4	P–K4

If P–QKt4; 5 P–QR4, P–K4; 6 P×KtP, P×QP; 7 B×P, B–QKt5; 8 R–R4, P–QR4; 9 P×P *e.p.* with advantage.

5 B×P	P×P
6 Kt–B3	

Yet another of Alekhin's sacrificial hazards, which would hardly bear repetition since Black could play 6 ..., P×Kt; 7 B×P*ch*, K–K2; 8 Q–Kt3, P×P; 9 B×P, Q–Kt3;

White gets a strong game by 10 B–K3, Q–B3; 11 O–O–O.

10 Q×KtP	Q–K4*ch*
11 B–K2	R–Kt1
12 Q–R6	R–Kt3
13 Q–R4	B–Q2

Not R×P; 14 B–KB4.

14 B–KKt5	B–B3
15 O–O–O	B×P
16 KR–K1	B–K5
17 B–R5	Kt×B
18 R–Q8*ch*	

Triumph of the black squares.

18 ...	K–B2
19 Q×Kt	*Resigns*

10 B×Kt, R×B; 11 Q×R, Q–Kt5*ch*; 12 Kt–Q2, Q×B, as Alekhin subsequently found in analysis. But as so often happens, the player who is surprised by novelty fails to find the best reply.

6 ...	P–QKt4
7 Kt×KtP	B–R3

Not P×Kt; 8 B–Q5.

8 Q–Kt3	Q–K2

If B×Kt; 9 B×P*ch*, K–Q2; 10 Kt×P, winning.

9 O–O	B×Kt
10 B×B	Kt–B3

And here not P×B; 11 Q–Q5.

11 B–QB4	QKt–Q2
12 Kt×P	R–QKt1
13 Q–B2	Q–B4
14 Kt–B5	

Not 14 Kt × P, hoping for Q × Kt;
15 B × P*ch* winning the Queen, because 14 ..., R–B1 gives Black the
advantage.

| 14 ... | Kt–K4 |
| 15 B–B4 | Kt–R4 |

Now White indulges in a sharp
exchanging combination which ensures the win.

| 16 B × P*ch* | K × B |
| 17 Q × Q | B × Q |

| 18 B × Kt | R–Kt4 |
| 19 B–Q6 | B–Kt3 |

The threat was 20 P–QR4, R–R4;
21 P–QKt4.

20 P–QKt4

Now the threat of P–QR4 wins
more material.

20 ...	R–Q1
21 QR–Q1	P–B4
22 P × P	B × P
23 R–Q5	*Resigns*

But it was in his more orthodox methods of building a dynamic
position that Alekhin signposted the way for others to follow. Even
in openings long since regarded as exhausted by analysis he would
seize on a new suggestion, either of his own or someone else's, burn
the midnight oil to see if it could be turned to good use, and then
spring upon an admiring world one more example of dynamic development. Even so skilled an attacking player as Spielmann confessed,
"I can comprehend Alekhin's combinations well enough, but where
he gets his attacking chances from and how he infuses life into the very
opening—that is beyond me." In the following game Alekhin adopts
a Russian suggestion for White's 13th move; already it was considered
that the position after 12 moves on either side was virtually exhausted,
so that Alekhin's ability to evolve a dashing sacrificial attack in only
four more moves is as astonishing as it is typical.

GAME 34

PILLSBURY ATTACK

Alekhin   Carlsson

Orebro Tournament, 1935

1 Kt–KB3	P–Q4
2 P–Q4	Kt–KB3
3 P–B4	P–K3
4 Kt–B3	B–K2
5 B–Kt5	QKt–Q2
6 P–K3	O–O

7 R–B1	P–B3
8 B–Q3	P × P
9 B × P	Kt–Q4
10 B × B	Q × B
11 O–O	Kt × Kt
12 R × Kt	P–K4

Black's last four moves constitute
the Capablanca Defence, a line which
effectively reduces the dynamic opportunities for both sides. Years of
exhaustive analysis had already gone

78

in the endeavour to find by what possible continuations either side could gain an advantage. Thus Alekhin's success in the present game is all the more remarkable.

13	Q–B2	P×P
14	P×P	Kt–B3
15	R–K1	Q–Q3
16	Kt–Kt5	P–KR3

(See Diagram 25)

17	Kt×P	R×Kt
18	Q–Kt6	Q–B1
19	R–B3	

This threat to recover his piece by R × Kt shows how suddenly Alekhin has conjured an attack out of a simple position.

| 19 ... | Kt–Q4 |

| 20 | R×R | Q×R |
| 21 | R–K8*ch* | |

Everything goes like clockwork. Even Capablanca was never more technically efficient.

21	...	Q–B1
22	R×Q*ch*	K×R
23	B×Kt	P×B
24	Q–Q6*ch*	*Resigns*

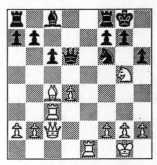

Diagram 25

No less easily did he find a means of developing a dynamic game against the drawish Caro-Kann Defence.

GAME 35
CARO-KANN DEFENCE
Alekhin   Tartakover
Kecskemét Tournament,
1927

1	P–K4	P–QB3
2	P–Q4	P–Q4
3	Kt–QB3	

Probably the most dynamic line for White. 3 P–K5 fails because Black does not thereby suffer a bad Bishop and White has to exchange

his K Bishop, which is his best attacking piece, while 3 P × P rids Black of the slight loss of time involved in his first move.

3	...	P×P
4	Kt×P	Kt–B3
5	Kt–Kt3	

The Classical school used to play 5 Kt × Kt*ch*, because it imposed on Black certain slight weaknesses in the pawn structure. Alekhin is more concerned with retaining dynamic chances.

79

5 ...   P–K4

Alekhin considered this "probably sufficient to equalize," but Black's KB4 is weakened and is excellently exploited by Alekhin. A safer alternative was 5 ..., P–K3 with play against the centre by P–B4 later.

6 Kt–B3	P×P
7 Kt×P	B–QB4
8 Q–K2*ch*	B–K2

If 8 ..., Q–K2 White at once occupies the weak square KB5 by 9 Q×Q*ch*, B×Q; 10 Kt(4)–B5. Thus Black has lost time, and 7 ..., B–K2 is seen to have been better.

9 B–K3	P–B4
10 Kt(4)–B5	O–O
11 Q–B4	R–K1
12 B–Q3	P–QKt3
13 O–O–O	B–R3

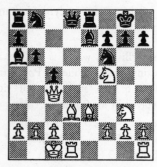

Diagram 26

White has now developed so dynamic a position that he can already indulge in a brilliant combinative attack.

14 Kt–R6*ch*	P×Kt
15 B×P*ch*	Kt×B

Not K–R1; 16 Q×KBP followed by Kt–B5 and mate cannot be avoided.

16 Q–Kt4*ch*	K–R1
17 R×Q	R×R
18 Q–K4	

The quiet move at the end of an Alekhin combination; Black now has insufficient compensation for his Queen. Equally if 17 ..., B×R; 18 Q–B3 wins material in a similar way.

18 ...	Kt–QB3
19 Q×Kt	B–KB1
20 Kt–B5	

The weakness of the key square still manifests itself.

20 ...	B–B5
21 B×RP	B–Q4
22 Q–B7	QR–B1
23 Q–B4	R–B3
24 B×B	R×B
25 Q–K5*ch*	Kt–B3
26 Kt–Q6	*Resigns*

Where Alekhin parted company with the Hypermoderns was that while he appreciated and understood their new views on the centre, he did not necessarily place the same emphasis on the advantages of withholding central pawn advances; there were in his view many occasions where the old classical method of advancing a central pawn early could do more to increase dynamic opportunities. In this way he shifted the emphasis back from the new views on the centre to Breyer's demand for dynamic chances at all costs. Even in the new Hypermodern openings themselves, the Indian defences, Alekhin as Black had no hesitation in advancing a central pawn if he felt it was better, and the following game is a typical example of this view.

GAME 36

NIMZO-INDIAN DEFENCE

Vidmar   Alekhin

San Remo Tournament, 1930

1	P–Q4	Kt–KB3
2	P–QB4	P–K3
3	Kt–QB3	B–Kt5
4	Q–B2	

This came to be regarded as the best move against the Nimzo-Indian Defence, preventing as it does the doubling of the QB pawn and countering the pressure on K4. It was only later, when the masters came round to Sämisch's view that White could stand the doubling of the pawns because of the increase in the dynamic energy of his position, that 4 P–K3 superseded Q–B2 as the most popular line.

4 ...		P–Q4

The days of restricted centres soon passed. The new defences remain but the play against the white squares is now conducted on quite classical and direct lines.

| 5 | P–QR3 | B × Kt*ch* |

6	Q × B	Kt–K5
7	Q–B2	Kt–QB3

Another of Alekhin's surprise opening novelties, in preference to the usual 7 ..., P–QB4; 8 P × BP, Kt–QB3.

8	P–K3	P–K4
9	P–B3	

Once more Alekhin's opponent is surprised by a novelty and fails to find the best line, which was 9 P × QP, Q × P; 10 B–QB4, Q–R4*ch*; 11 P–Kt4, Kt × KtP; 12 Q × Kt, Kt–B7*dbl. ch*; 13 K–K2, Q–K8*ch*; 14 K–B3, Kt × R; 15 B–Kt2. But White has set out to play the present opening positionally, and finding himself threatened with a welter of tactical considerations, makes a desperate effort to keep the opening on a positional plane.

9 ...		Kt–B3
10	P × QP	Q × P
11	B–B4	Q–Q3
12	P × P	Kt × P
13	B–Q2	O–O
14	B–Kt4	P–B4
15	R–Q1	

Not 15 B × P, Q × B; 16 B × P*ch*, R × B; 17 Q × Q, Kt–Q6*ch*.

15 ...	Q–B3
16 B–Q2	B–B4

An attractive method of completing his development, though Alekhin afterwards decided that he would have done better by 16 ..., Kt × B; 17 Q × Kt, B–K3; 18 Q–B2, Q–Kt4 with a powerful grip on the white squares.

17 Q × B	Kt × B
18 B–B1	KR–K1
19 K–B2	R–K3
20 Kt–R3	Kt–K5*ch*
21 K–K1	

Of course not 21 P × Kt, R–B3.

21 ...	Kt(K)–Q3
22 Q–Q3	Kt × KP
23 B × Kt	P–B5
24 Q–Q5	

If 24 Q–B3, Kt–B4. Now, although he comes out a pawn ahead, the additional exchange of Queens results in his having much reduced winning chances.

24 ...	R × B*ch*
25 K–B2	Q × Q
26 R × Q	R–Q6
27 R × R	P × R
28 R–Q1	Kt–B5
29 R × P	Kt × KtP
30 R–Kt3	Kt–B5
31 R × P	Kt × P
32 Kt–Kt5	P–QR4

Defence of the KBP by P–B3

would cost the QRP after 33 Kt–K6, P–QR4; 34 Kt–B7, R–QB1; 35 R–R7, Kt–B5; 36 K–K2, and the draw would be certain.

33 Kt × BP	P–R5
34 Kt–Q6	Kt–B7
35 R–Kt2	P–R6
36 R × Kt	P–R7
37 R × P	R × R*ch*

White has got rid of the pawn at the cost only of the exchange and not of a whole piece. Now Black has to start winning the game all over again.

38 K–Kt3	K–B1
39 P–R4	

If White sat tight, it is difficult to see any way in which Black could force the position. Even after such loosening moves as the text move, it is not obvious how the win is to be achieved and it says much for Alekhin's technical mastery that he is able to win this ending.

39 ...	K–K2
40 Kt–K4	P–R3
41 Kt–B2	K–K3
42 Kt–Q3	K–B4
43 Kt–B4	R–R5
44 Kt–Q3	R–QB5
45 Kt–B2	R–B3
46 Kt–R3	K–K4
47 P–R5	

This further loosening helps Black still more.

47 ...	R–B7
48 Kt–B4	R–Q7

49	Kt–R3	K–Q5	53 K–Kt4	R–B3
50	Kt–B4	K–K6	54 P–B5	R–B2
51	Kt–K6		55 P–Kt3	K–K5

If 51 Kt–R3, then R–R7; 52 Kt–B4, R–R4 winning the KR pawn.

51 ...   R–Q4

52 P–B4

Not 52 K–R4, R–K4; 53 Kt × P, R–KKt4; 54 Kt–K6, R × P winning.

52 ...   R–KB4

As a result of the initial loosening of his pawn skeleton White has found himself forced to let it disintegrate completely, and now the harvest begins to come in.

56	Kt–B5*ch*	K–Q5
57	Kt–Kt3*ch*	K–K4
	Resigns	

The leaders of the Hypermodern school believed, like all true revolutionaries, that because they had discovered something new in chess principles, all previous principles were thereby rendered obsolete. Their ideas were presented with all the extravagances and pretentiousness that was inevitable in such circumstances.

It was the task of those who followed to pare away the extravagances of the Hypermodern style, whilst retaining those elements which had something of value; and in this no master played a greater part than Alekhin. He recognized that the old ideas of the Classical school, though they might well need modifying in the light of new theory, nevertheless still had much of value to offer to the student of chess, and his style came to achieve a pleasing blend of the old and the new.

The two concluding games show Alekhin playing for a control of space more in the style of Tarrasch, but whereas Tarrasch's space control was often arid and devoid of tensions, Alekhin's play in both games retains a strong element of the dynamic chess, which is the true legacy of the Hypermodern revolution.

GAME 37

FRENCH DEFENCE

Alekhin   Nimzovitch

San Remo Tournament, 1930

1	P–K4	P–K3	
2	P–Q4	P–Q4	
3	Kt–QB3	B–Kt5	
4	P–K5	P–QB4	
5	B–Q2	Kt–K2	
6	Kt–Kt5	B × B*ch*	
7	Q × B	O–O	
8	P–QB3		

He treats the pawn chain in the

old Classical manner, in contrast to Nimzovitch's 7th move in Game 8.

| 8 ... | P–QKt3 |

With the idea of solving the problem of the bad Bishop in the same way as he did in Game 16, but Alekhin is alive to the plan.

9	P–KB4	B–R3
10	Kt–B3	Q–Q2
11	P–QR4	

Resolutely resisting the Bishop exchange.

| 11 ... | QKt–B3 |

Intending with Kt–R4 to get a good grip on the weak white squares. Kt–R4–Kt6, for example, is an immediate threat.

| 12 | P–QKt4 | P×KtP |
| 13 | P×P | B–Kt2 |

The plan for this Bishop has been defeated by simple and logical play.

| 14 | Kt–Q6 | P–B4 |
| 15 | P–R5 | Kt–B1 |

Not P×P; 16 P–Kt5, Kt–Q1; 17 R×P, with a great gain in space.

16	Kt×B	Q×Kt
17	P–R6	Q–KB2
18	B–Kt5	

It is White who is victorious on the white squares after all, in addition to which he can be the first to occupy the open QB file if he wishes.

18 ...	Kt(1)–K2
19	O–O	P–R3
20	KR–B1	KR–B1

| 21 | R–B2 | Q–K1 |

Allowing a pin on QB3 which in the end proves fatal, but if Kt–Q1; 22 R(1)–QB1, R×R; 23 R×R, R–B1; 24 R×R, Kt×R; 25 Q–B3, Kt–K2; 26 Q–B7, and wins easily.

22	R(1)–QB1	QR–Kt1
23	Q–K3	R–B2
24	R–B3	Q–Q2
25	R(1)–B2	K–B1
26	Q–B1	R(1)–B1
27	B–R4	

Although Black has adequately met the pin on his QB3, White threatens to force the Knight away by P–Kt5, whereupon a piece is lost on QB2. To meet this Black has started bringing his King over, but as the King would arrive too late, a pawn must now be given up to gain time.

27 ...	P–QKt4
28	B×P	K–K1
29	B–R4	K–Q1

The King has arrived, and now 30 P–Kt5, Kt–QKt1 would not win material on QB7.

| 30 | P–R4 | *Resigns* |

For he suddenly realizes he is in *Zugzwang*. Nothing can be moved except the K side pawns, and they will soon have no moves left. Then the only move will be Q–K1, after which P–QKt5 will force the issue on QB7 after all.

GAME 38

FRENCH DEFENCE

Alekhin   *Capablanca*

AVRO Tournament, Holland, 1938

1 P–K4	P–K3
2 P–Q4	P–Q4
3 Kt–Q2	

The Tarrasch Variation, which is intended to allow in the easiest manner the classical support of the pawn skeleton by P–QB3.

3 ...	Kt–KB3

Permitting White his intended easy and harmonious development. Much more resistant is 3 ..., P–QB4.

4 P–K5	KKt–Q2
5 B–Q3	P–QB4
6 P–QB3	Kt–QB3
7 Kt–K2	Q–Kt3
8 Kt–B3	

White's development is complete and Black must now decide on a course of action. Von Gottschall against Tarrasch at Dresden in 1892 tried 8 ..., B–K2; 9 O–O, O–O; 10 Kt–B4, K–R1; 11 B–B2, R–KKt1; but after 12 Q–Q3 White had a formidable attack. Capablanca here tries a more vigorous development of the black K Bishop but with no better result.

8 ...	P×P
9 P×P	B–Kt5*ch*

Diagram 27

10 K–B1

An example of Alekhin's blending of the old and the new. The Classical school did not like foregoing castling in this manner, but on the other hand they did believe in denying exchanges to the more cramped opponent. But whereas in this position they would probably have given more weight to the former factor, Alekhin with the dynamic ideas of modern chess in his mind prefers the latter consideration.

10 ...	B–K2
11 P–QR3	Kt–B1

Castling would invite an immediate attack by P–KR4, when White would develop threats faster than Black could summon up defences to meet them. He therefore brings the defensive units across first.

12 P–QKt4	B–Q2
13 B–K3	Kt–Q1

He is already moving on very cramped lines, but if Kt–Kt3 then 14 P–KR4 at once enforces a retreat or a weakness.

14 Kt–B3	P–QR4
15 Kt–QR4	Q–R2
16 P–Kt5	

After this move the whole of Black's Q side is tied up.

16 ...	P–QKt3

At least he can deny White an outpost square on his QB4.

17 P–Kt3	P–B4
18 K–Kt2	Kt–B2
19 Q–Q2	P–R3

Starting a fight for the black squares on the K side, but the weakening of the white squares offers White an alternative target.

20 P–R4	Kt–R2
21 P–R5	

Giving up control of his KKt5 to Black, so as to secure control of KKt6 for himself, once again the dynamic player's balancing of disadvantages and advantages. The decision has its justification in the fact that Black cannot make the fullest use of the black squares because P–Kt4 is now denied to him, owing to the reply P × Pe.p.

21 ...	Kt(B)–Kt4
22 Kt–R4	Kt–K5
23 Q–Kt2	

Persistently denying exchanges to a cramped opponent. Even 23 ..., B × Kt would now be a blunder because after 24 P × B the advanced black Knight has no escape from White's P–B3.

23 ...	K–B2
24 P–B3	Kt(5)–Kt4
25 P–Kt4	

Black's expedition has come home empty-handed, and now White begins to strengthen his operations on the white squares.

25 ...	P × P
26 B–Kt6ch	K–Kt1
27 P–B4	Kt–B6

Not Kt–K5; 28 B × Kt, P × B; 29 Kt–Kt6, winning the exchange, while other Knight moves will eventually lose the KKt pawn to White's Q–K2.

28 B × Ktch	R × B

Not K × B; 29 Q–B2ch, K–Kt1; 30 Kt–Kt6, again winning the exchange.

29 Kt–Kt6	B–Q1
30 QR–QB1	B–K1
31 K–Kt3	

Now the material begins to fall, first the KKt pawn and then the Knight which has no escape.

31 ...	Q–KB2
32 K × P	Kt–R5
33 Kt × Kt	Q × RPch
34 K–Kt3	Q–B2
35 Kt–KB3	*Resigns*

Black actually lost on time, but he has no compensation for the lost material, and White amongst other things is threatening Q–QB2 followed by Kt–Kt5.

PART II
The Russians

CHAPTER VII

The Russian School

WHEN Alekhin died in 1946 while still holding the World title, there followed a brief interregnum before a new champion succeeded to the title. It was scarcely a matter for surprise when the Hague–Moscow Championship tournament of 1948 was won by Mikhail Botvinnik ahead of Euwe, the surviving ex-champion, and other contenders. It had long been evident not only that Botvinnik would prove the strongest player in the world, but also that the Russian school of chess was likely to have by far the most significant influence on the future of chess, however strong might be the best players of the American and other schools.

The history of the Russian school really goes back to the years immediately following the Revolution of 1917, when for the first time the playing of chess was supported and financed by the State. The rich patron of chess had disappeared with the seventeenth and eighteenth centuries, but enough moneyed supporters had remained to finance the game through the nineteenth century. It was, however, becoming increasingly difficult by the twentieth century for all but a very few to devote sufficient time to the game to excel at it without drifting into grave pecuniary embarrassment, although the keen support of a multitude of amateur enthusiasts, each contributing his small mite either haphazard or through some national organization, has preserved the holding of master tournaments, if often on a decreasingly impressive scale. It is not without significance that in the areas where chess is not State-aided the greatest activity is to be found where commercial influences are most congenial.

The State aid in Russia, which made adequate funds available for a great increase in chess-playing, and later for the holding of master tournaments and matches on a large and impressive scale, was radically to alter the balance of national chess strengths. For a time the political repercussions of Russia's revolution seemed likely to have an opposite effect, when such masters as Alekhin and Bogolyubov felt obliged to transplant their genius into other countries. There remained, of course, many fine players, but they fell just short of the highest levels. When the first international tournament of the new Russia was held in Moscow in 1925, the best that any of the home players could do was to come equal 7th, and as if to rub salt in the wound the first prize was won by the ex-Russian master, Bogolyubov.

But constant nurturing of young chess talent proved its value in the long run, for it soon became evident that in Botvinnik Russia at last had a master of the highest class. In 1934 he drew a match with the most promising young master in central Europe, Salo Flohr, and in a small tournament at Leningrad he won first prize, while Euwe, one of the two foreign guests, could come no higher than sixth. Now at last the Russians had every justification for hoping that if another great master tournament were held a Russian master might have a good chance of winning. The Moscow tournament of 1935 quite erased the unhappy results of the 1925 tournament; the first and second prizes were shared by Botvinnik and Flohr, ahead of Lasker and Capablanca among others. At Moscow in 1936 Botvinnik was second to Capablanca, but ahead of Flohr and Lasker, while at Nottingham in 1936 Botvinnik and Capablanca shared first and second prizes ahead of Alekhin, Euwe, Flohr, Lasker, Reshevsky, Fine, and others.

A combination of events, political and otherwise, now reversed the process which had robbed the Russian school of much of its finest genius when it first came into existence. So far from losing masters, it now began to gain them. Among those who by 1946 were playing under the Russian flag was the Czech, Flohr (1st at Hastings 1932, 1933, and 1934, Margate 1936, Podebrady 1936, the Leningrad–Moscow tournament of 1939, the Kemeri–Riga tournament of 1939, and equal 1st at Sliac Kupele 1932, Hastings 1935, Moscow 1935, and Kemeri 1937), and the Estonian, Paul Keres (1st at Prague 1937, Semmering 1937, Margate 1939, Salzbrunn—or Szczavno Zdroj—1950, and Budapest 1952, and equal 1st at Margate 1937, Ostend 1937, the AVRO tournament of 1938, Buenos Aires 1939, and Salzburg 1943). With two such fine players and with Botvinnik himself as opponents, the still younger Russian masters were given the best and hardest schooling that could be demanded, and in the years following 1946 (after the Second World War) a host of new names, all of master strength, keep appearing in the Russian lists. A

Russian national championship in these years was stronger than most international tournaments, and this was indeed a new portent in chess history.

The Fédération Internationale des Échecs (F.I.D.É.), which had come into existence some twenty years earlier, was faced on Alekhin's death with arranging competitions for a successor. It not only did this, but also arranged a series of world-wide eliminating tournaments so that in every third year a challenger would emerge to play for the title. The first five Candidates' tournaments were all won by Russian masters (Budapest 1950 by Bronstein and Boleslavsky jointly, the former winning the play-off; Neuhausen–Zürich 1953 and Amsterdam 1956 by Smyslov; 1959 in Yugoslavia by Tal; 1962 at Curaçao by Petrosyan). The interzonals as a preliminary to each Candidates' tournament also fell to Russian masters (Saltsjöbaden 1948 to Bronstein, Saltsjöbaden 1952 to Kotov, Göteborg 1955 to Bronstein again, and Portorož 1958 to Tal); and it was not until the 1962 tournament at Stockholm that the young American genius, Fischer, broke the monopoly, while in 1964 at Amsterdam there was a quadruple tie between Smyslov, Spassky, Tal and another non-Russian in Larsen.

Smyslov in 1957, Tal in 1960 and Petrosyan in 1963 each went on from their success in the Candidates' tournament to wrest the title from Botvinnik, but the champion's strength was such that on the first two occasions he turned the tables in a return match. Petrosyan was perhaps fortunate that by 1964 Botvinnik was prevented by a change of rules from the usual return.

Among the masters of the Russian school are to be found many styles of play, ranging from the scientific strategic play of Smyslov (who has been likened to Capablanca) to the violent attacking play of Tal. To generalize is therefore dangerous, but by and large it can be said that certain factors, or at least attitudes of mind, are common to almost the whole school of Russian chess. Above all, they place the stress upon dynamic positions; for this reason Smyslov, for example, at his peak won and lost more games than Capablanca ever did. The classical conceptions of strategy had been widened and enlivened by the Hypermoderns, but as Alekhin proved, they had not been overturned; the weak points and the strong points still emerged as landmarks to guide the player in his conduct of the game. The dynamic chess now practised by the Russians shook even these time-honoured guides.

The search for a dynamic position led the Russians to play at times in a manner which would not only have horrified Tarrasch but would even have startled the Hypermoderns themselves.

In the Sicilian Defence, for example, even Staunton learned from experience that Black could scarcely risk P–K4, leaving his Q pawn backward, a line he tried but soon abandoned. All the teachings of Steinitz and Tarrasch confirmed this view. Yet the Russian masters time and again play that very manœuvre, a remarkable case of the wheel turning full circle. Their view is that the increase in dynamic energy in Black's game compensates for the weak pawn; they are, in fact, offering a gambit of something less than a pawn in order to secure strong play, and put that way it is a perfectly legitimate proposition. Again, when Sämisch as White in the Nimzo-Indian Defence had recommended years earlier a similar acceptance of a weakened pawn position in order to gain energy, he failed to win support against a view of strategy which followed Steinitz in believing that no temporary abstract initiative could offset a permanent structural weakness. Now the Russians almost invariably played Sämisch's variation; there could be no clearer sign of the times.

Their point of view can be summarized as follows: what had for generations been accepted as a weakness, such as a hole or an isolated pawn, was not weak *unless or until the opponent began to attack it*; a much smaller hostile weakness which could be attacked first was in fact the greater weakness. Thus the dynamic approach brought about a radical adjustment in the views on weakness and strength. It was no longer possible to measure one's weaknesses against those of one's opponent by the old methods, but it was necessary to assess also the potentialities and speeds of the relative attacks. This called for a new degree of acute positional judgment, and in this the Russian school has especially trained itself.

Possibly one should except such a player as Petrosyan from this generalization, deep and subtle as his thinking is; his undercover manœuvres are so delicate that, while they usually prevent an opponent from disturbing the balance of the game except to his own disadvantage, they are also very often insufficient to tip the balance his own way.

The constant search for positions of dynamic possibility led to a great heightening of interest in opening variations, an interest which had been greatly stimulated by the original Hypermodern movement. The new openings developed by the Hypermoderns were the Russians' especial hunting ground, but they developed new tactical chances in many of the old classical openings, or they gave to those openings new twists which increased their dynamic energy.

It is therefore small matter for wonder that never before had there been such an absorbing interest in opening variations. As had always been the case, certain lines became obsolescent, but the speed of change was now accelerated because of the number of masters all working in a similar direction, and the book lore of one year was half out-of-date a year later.

Since the Russians, irrespective of individual styles, were preoccupied with positions of dynamic energy, it became a question of projecting one's will-power into the little pieces of carved wood advancing and retreating on the chequered board, not simply at certain critical moments but all the time. There must be no relaxing either towards the end of a game or towards the end of a tournament. For this reason the Russians pay great attention to physical condition; it was neglect of this very factor which had toppled Alekhin from the heights in 1935, and only by strong self-discipline was he able to recover. The Russians exert the strongest self-discipline at all times, and it is noticeable that they play their best towards the end of a severe tournament when other competitors are beginning to weaken.

Tournament chess, in fact, has become so severe a strain that the Russian chess master approaches it like a boxer facing a championship fight. Not only does he train mentally, psychologically and physically, but he goes into battle supported by "seconds" who, like any boxer's seconds, keep him apprised of the opponent's foibles and weaknesses, and tender appropriate advice, massage his adjourned positions as carefully as any bruised tendon, and keep a watchful eye on any new ideas which are to be snapped up from other competitors or their seconds.

Against this massively organized chess play even the great genius of such a master as young Fischer (who actually romped home ahead of all the Russians in the 1962 Interzonal) seems to be blunted; David's victory against Goliath was perhaps an exception that proved a rule. In the subsequent Candidates' tournament the Russian pressure quite crushed poor Fischer, and there were some who suggested that Capablanca's dictum—that any master could draw with any other by the mere application of technique (see p. 16)—was in fact applied among the Russians until Fischer had been disposed of and only then did the struggle between them begin. There may be some truth in this which could perhaps justify Fischer's subsequent withdrawal from the international scene. However, by 1965 the tournament system of selecting a candidate has been superseded by a series of individual matches, thus removing Fischer's complaint, and it is to be hoped that on this basis a more mature Fischer and a Tal fully restored to health will revive the dynamism which seems to have been abandoned temporarily at this stage of international chess.

The Russian outlook, which accepts no dogma or hard and fast rules, is naturally flexible, and this is particularly demanded by the alert watch for tactical opportunities arising during the course of a game. At any moment the plan of campaign may have to be adjusted to suit the tactical needs of the position. In the following game, for example, White prepares the strategy of the minority attack, and there is little doubt that a player like Tarrasch or Capablanca would have carried that strategy through to its conclusion. But because Black squanders a certain amount of time, White realizes that a direct K side attack is also a possibility, and he accordingly changes from one strategy to another. Changing horses in midstream is a notoriously hazardous procedure, and it says much for White's very fine judgment of position that in the game under review he is able to do this with absolute success.

GAME 39

PILLSBURY ATTACK

Botvinnik   Keres

Russian Championship, 1952

1	P–Q4	Kt–KB3
2	P–QB4	P–K3
3	Kt–QB3	P–Q4
4	P×P	P×P

5	B–Kt5	B–K2

The Exchange Variation gives White the ideal pawn skeleton for a minority attack, though the exchange of pawns is played here at an earlier stage than usual.

6	P–K3	O–O
7	B–Q3	QKt–Q2
8	Q–B2	R–K1
9	KKt–K2	

An innocuous variant from the normal Kt–B3, which makes it easier to contest the squares K4 and KB5, but less easy to contest K5.

9 ...   Kt–B1
10 O–O

More aggressive, but at the same time leaving White fewer options, is the older move 10 O–O–O which leads to the so-called Chameleon Variation. A game Flohr–Asgeirsson at Folkestone 1933 continued 10 O–O–O, P–B3; 11 P–KR3, P–QKt4; 12 P–KKt4, P–QR4; 13 Kt–Kt3, P–R5; 14 K–Kt1, Q–R4; 15 QKt–K2, B–Q2; 16 Kt–B5, B×Kt; 17 B×B, Q–Kt3; 18 R–QB1, R–R3; 19 Kt–B4, P–Kt5; 20 Q–K2, Kt–K5; 21 B×B, R×B; 22 B×Kt, R×B; 23 Kt–Q3, Kt–Q2; 24 Kt×P, *Resigns.*

10 ...   P–B3
11 QR–Kt1

The strategical corollary of his opening. He prepares to launch the minority attack with P–QKt4, P–QR4 and P–Kt5.

11 ...   B–Q3

Threatening 12 ..., B×P*ch*; 13 K×B, Kt–Kt5*ch*; 14 K–Kt1, Q×B.

12 K–R1   Kt–Kt3

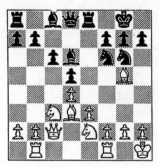

Diagram 28

13 P–B3

Already having doubts whether he need pursue his minority attack or whether he can try and take advantage of Black's dilatory play by a thrust in the centre.

13 ...   B–K2
14 QR–K1

He selects the latter.

14 ...   Kt–Q2
15 B×B   R×B
16 Kt–Kt3   Kt–B3

The Knight cannot be maintained here against the advance of the white K pawn, and Kt(2)–B1 was a better defence.

17 Q–B2   B–K3
18 Kt–B5   B×Kt
19 B×B   Q–Kt3
20 P–K4   P×P
21 P×P   R–Q1
22 P–K5

Lasker played the same manœuvre in Game 3, leaving one pawn back-

95

ward and weak, with a weak square in front of it, solely to obtain an advanced outpost which would cramp the opposition.

22 ...	Kt–Q4
23 Kt–K4	Kt–B1
24 Kt–Q6	Q–B2

Against Kt–B8.

25 B–K4

The alternation of pieces on strong central squares—here a Knight followed by a Bishop on K4, and a Bishop followed by a Knight on KB5—was a principle forcibly expounded by Nimzovitch.

| 25 ... | Kt–K3 |
| 26 Q–R4 | |

Provoking a weakening of the King's position before exchanging his Bishop.

26 ...	P–KKt3
27 B×Kt	P×B
28 R–B1	

Occupying the open file in the classical fashion of Tarrasch, though here primarily for tactical reasons, in order to secure a jumping-off point to bring the Rook into the K side attack. The fusing of old and new strategies and strategical teachings into a composite style of modern, vigorous and dynamic play is most striking.

28 ...	Q–Q2
29 R–QB3	R–KB1
30 Kt–B5	

And finally a combinative finish. The modern master must be fully equipped in every phase of play. If now 30 ..., P×Kt; 31 R–Kt3*ch*, Kt–Kt2; 32 Q–B6 and mates, or 30 ..., R(2)–K1; 31 Q–B6, arriving at a similar mate by a transposition of moves.

| 30 ... | R(1)–K1 |
| 31 Kt–R6*ch* | |

Stronger than the mere win of the exchange.

31 ...   K–B1

If K–Kt2; 32 Q–B6*ch*, K×Kt; 33 R–R3*mate*, and if K–R1; 32 Q–B6*ch*, Kt–Kt2; 33 Kt×P*ch*, K–Kt1; 34 Kt–R6*ch*, K–R1; 35 Q–B8*ch*.

32 Q–B6	Kt–Kt2
33 R(3)–B3	R–B1
34 Kt×P	R–K3
35 Q–Kt5	Kt–B4
36 Kt–R6	Q–Kt2

If K–K1; 37 R×Kt, P×R; 38 Q–Kt8*ch*, K–K2; 39 Kt×P*mate*.

| 37 P–KKt4 | *Resigns* |

The flexibility of outlook revealed in the preceding game was just one indication of the original and independent approach which marked Botvinnik's play, and to a large extent the play of most of the Russian masters. The next game reveals this still more clearly, for Botvinnik's opponent pursues strategies which not even the Hypermoderns dared to question, and yet Botvinnik's subtlety is such that these long-accepted *motifs* are on this occasion proved illusory.

GAME 40
ENGLISH OPENING
Botvinnik   Reshevsky
AVRO Tournament, Holland, 1938

1	P–QB4	P–K4
2	Kt–QB3	Kt–QB3
3	P–KKt3	P–KKt3
4	B–Kt2	B–Kt2
5	P–K3	

These White opening moves, both of pawns and pieces, were frequently played by Staunton both as White and Black. But by the time of Steinitz such a layout was suspect because of the apparent weakness of the white squares and of KB3 in particular. Botvinnik is concerned with dynamic possibilities rather than static weaknesses, and takes the view that a weakness is only a weakness if it can be attacked. Another point is that the first four moves have set the strategic pattern, White striving to control the white centre squares and Black the black centre squares, and with the text move White begins to contest the black squares also.

5	...	P–Q3
6	KKt–K2	KKt–K2
7	P–Q4	P×P
8	P×P	O–O
9	O–O	Kt–B4
10	P–Q5	

Thus far Black has succeeded, for White has now to surrender the black squares to the opponent.

10	...	Kt–K4
11	P–Kt3	P–QR4

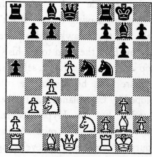

Diagram 29

In accordance with classical and Hypermodern theory he threatens P–R5, weakening White's Q side pawns and exploiting the long diagonal to White's Q side which he has forced White to open. He also creates a secure square on his QB4 for a Knight. That all this apparently sound strategy turns out a will-o'-the-wisp is proof of Botvinnik's supreme appreciation of the influence which tactical play can have upon strategical theory.

12	B–Kt2	Kt–Q2
13	P–QR3	

The tactical answer.

13	...	Kt–B4
14	P–QKt4	Kt–Q2

15	Q–Kt3	Kt–Q5	
16	Kt×Kt	B×Kt	
17	QR–Q1	B–Kt2	
18	KR–K1	P×P	
19	P×P	Kt–B3	

Already White has stabilized his position. He is adequately contesting the long diagonal, he holds the central open file and is ahead in development, having driven Black's Knight on to an awkward square. Black now feels the need to get his Q Bishop into the game, but in selecting the square KB4 he breaks the rule developed by Capablanca and further expounded by the Hypermoderns that development for its own sake has no purpose and every developing move must therefore serve the main strategy. It was better to play 19 ..., P–Kt3 with a view to B–QR3.

20	P–R3	P–R4

B–B4 at once would be met by P–Kt4, so he feels forced to weaken his position in the hope of improving it. P–Kt3 for B–QR3 was still a more promising line.

21	P–B5

Now White's long diagonal begins to emerge as a dominant factor.

21	...	B–B4
22	Kt–Kt5	B–Q2

The first admission of error, for if he tries to meet the threat of Kt–Q4 by Q–Q2, then 23 P–B6.

23	P–B6	P×P
24	P×P	B–B1

The final admission of error, for even B–K3 is denied him owing to the reply 25 R×B, P×R; 26 Kt–Q4, Q–K2; 27 Kt×P, Q–B2; 28 B×Kt, B×B; 29 B–Q5, K–R1; 30 Kt–B4, Q–Kt2; 31 Q–Q3, winning.

25	Kt×QP	

A little combination to clinch matters. Of course P×Kt is met by 26 P–B7.

25	...	B–K3
26	R×B	P×R
27	Kt–B5	

Putting paid to Black's pretensions on the long diagonal to White's Q side.

27	...	Q–K1
28	Kt×B	K×Kt
29	R–Q7ch	R–B2
30	B–K5	K–Kt1
31	R×P	R×R
32	B×R	R–R8ch
33	K–R2	R–R2
34	B–K5	R–KB2
35	P–B7	Kt–Q2
36	Q–B2	

The final stroke, queening the pawn, for if now 36 ..., Kt–Kt3 then 37 Q×Pch, K–B1; 38 B–Q6ch.

36	...	R–B1
37	P–B8=Q	*Resigns*

Since Q×Q is answered by Q×P *mate.*

CHAPTER VIII

Nimzo-Indian and Queen's Indian Defences

To obtain a view of contemporary chess which is as objective as the view one can gain of a past period is never wholly possible; it is like taking a ride on a bus the destination of which is obscured. All that is possible is to pick out a landmark here and there and hope to deduce at least the general direction. That is what has in effect been done in the second half of this book. A number of typical games have been selected to illustrate the Russian school, and for the sake of convenience these have been arranged in groups according to openings.

First, in the Nimzo-Indian Defence the Russian demand for dynamic energy led to a general abandonment of the old orthodox line of 4 Q–B2 for White, as in Game 36, and to a return to Sämisch's idea of an early P–QR3, as in Game 24. Since the doubling of White's QB pawn was therefore accepted, there was no need either to forestall it or hasten it, and a developing move which came into regular use was Rubinstein's old move of 4 P–K3, frequently followed later by P–QR3, which as often as not transposed back directly into a Sämisch variation. The following game is a comparatively early example of this idea.

GAME 41

NIMZO-INDIAN DEFENCE

Botvinnik   *Capablanca*

AVRO Tournament, Holland, 1938

1	P–Q4		Kt–KB3
2	P–QB4		P–K3
3	Kt–QB3		B–Kt5
4	P–K3		P–Q4
5	P–QR3		B×Kt*ch*
6	P×B		P–B4

7	P×QP		KP×P
8	B–Q3		O–O
9	Kt–K2		P–QKt3
10	O–O		B–R3

A variation superficially similar to the old Staunton Defence in the Queen's Gambit Declined, but the transfer of White's QKt pawn to the QB file makes his complex of pawns on the black squares virtually unbreakable.

Taking a leaf out of Nimzovitch's

99

book, who played the same manœuvre in Game 16. By the exchange of Bishops, White's grip on the white squares is weakened and his P–K4 delayed.

11 B×B   Kt×B
12 B–Kt2

Hoping to play P–QB4 and obtain scope for his Bishop that way, but the bad situation of this Bishop shows the essential soundness of Black's play so far. Later Botvinnik sharpened the line considerably by substituting 10 P–QR4 for O–O and at this point playing 12 B–R3.

12 ...   Q–Q2
13 P–QR4

Forestalling Q–R5 as an answer to his intended Q–Q3. It will be seen that White has a poorer development of his Q Bishop as compared with the line in the previous note, but as will appear, he obtains some compensation for this seven moves later.

13 ...   KR–K1
14 Q–Q3   P–B5
15 Q–B2   Kt–Kt1
16 QR–K1   Kt–B3
17 Kt–Kt3   Kt–QR4

Compare the Botvinnik–Alexander game in the 1946 match. White plays to force P–K4, the natural reaction against Black's P–B5, while Black plays to get the Knight to QKt6, thus cutting off the defences of White's QR pawn.

18 P–B3   Kt–Kt6
19 P–K4   Q×P
20 P–K5

By not having to defend a QB on QR3, White gains time in exchange for his worse placed Bishop.

20 ...   Kt–Q2
21 Q–B2   P–Kt3

To prevent Kt–B5, and played in the conviction that the white Bishop cannot readily make any capital out of the weak black squares.

22 P–B4   P–B4

White's P–B5, breaking open his King's position, can only temporarily be delayed.

23 P×P*e.p*   Kt×BP
24 P–B5   R×R
25 R×R   R–K1
26 R–K6   R×R

Saving his King's position at the cost of allowing White a strong passed pawn. But if K–Kt2; 27 R×Kt, K×R; 28 P×P*dis. ch*, K×P; 29 Q–B5*ch*, K–Kt2; 30 Kt–R5*ch*, K–R3; 31 P–Kt4, Q–B3; 32 B–R3, and White wins.

27 P×R   K–Kt2
28 Q–B4

Threatening Q–Kt5 followed by Kt–B5*ch*, or even the same moves in the reverse order.

28 ...   Q–K1
29 Q–K5   Q–K2

(See Diagram 30)

Now there comes another of Botvinnik's brilliant combinative finishes.

| 30 | B–R3 | Q×B |

If Q–Kt2; 31 B–B8*ch*, K×B; 32 Q×Kt*ch*.

31	Kt–R5*ch*	P×Kt
32	Q–Kt5*ch*	K–B1
33	Q×Kt*ch*	K–Kt1
34	P–K7	Q–B8*ch*
35	K–B2	Q–B7*ch*
36	K–Kt3	Q–Q6*ch*

The best chance of perpetual check. After Q×BP*ch* White escapes by 37 K–R4, Q–K8*ch*; 38 K–R3, Q–K6*ch*; 39 P–Kt3.

37	K–R4	Q–K5*ch*
38	K×P	Q–K7*ch*
39	K–R4	Q–K5*ch*
40	P–Kt4	Q–K8*ch*
41	K–R5	*Resigns*

Diagram 30

Since the previous game is really only a Sämisch Variation with a few moves transposed, it is not uncommon for the Russian school to play the moves in the same order chosen by Sämisch and illustrated in Game 24.

GAME 42
NIMZO-INDIAN DEFENCE

Bronstein   Najdorf

Budapest Candidates Tournament, 1950

1	P–Q4	Kt–KB3
2	P–QB4	P–K3
3	Kt–QB3	B–Kt5
4	P–QR3	B×Kt*ch*
5	P×B	P–B4

With the idea of fixing the doubled pawns in order to carry out the same attack on them as was employed in Game 24, namely bringing the QB to QR3 and the QKt to QR4. But the results of this strategy have been almost consistently unfavourable.

6	P–K3	Kt–B3
7	B–Q3	O–O
8	Kt–K2	P–Q3
9	P–K4	Kt–K1

To avoid the pin after 10 B–Kt5. The Knight has more scope from K1 than from Q2.

| 10 | O–O | P–QKt3 |
| 11 | P–B4 | B–R3 |

Reluctant to abandon his attack on the doubled pawns, but the dynamic energy of White's game in this variation is now so apparent that it must be neutralized by 11 ..., P–B4; 12 P–Q5, Kt–K2 (this piece too

101

must abandon intentions on the doubled pawns); after which Black's game is still tenable.

12 P–B5   P–K4

Intending to continue with P–B3, blocking White's attack quite effectively. Of course if 12 ..., P × P; 13 R × P, followed by P–K5, gives the white Bishops the freedom of the K side.

Diagram 31

13 P–B6

A tactical pawn sacrifice which undermines Black's strategy completely. Now 13 ..., Kt × P would allow the pin 14 B–Kt5 after all, and then might follow 14 ..., Kt–QR4; 15 Kt–Kt3, B × P; 16 B × B, Kt × B; 17 Kt–R5, with a crushing attack. Even worse would be 13 ..., P × P allowing 14 B–R6, Kt–Kt2; 15 Kt–Kt3 threatening Q–Kt4 and Kt–B5. But even declining the offer

cannot restore his game.

13 ...   K–R1
14 P–Q5

A neat finesse while his other pawn is still on KB6. The black Knight is forced away from the vital sector, and ironically to the place Black originally intended for it.

14 ...   Kt–R4
15 Kt–Kt3   P × P

P–Kt3 was preferable, though it left him very stifled. But gasping for air this way merely lets in the draught.

16 Kt–B5   B–B1

If 16 ..., Kt–KKt2; 17 Kt × Kt, K × Kt; 18 Q–R5, with a conclusion similar to that which now follows.

17 Q–R5   B × Kt
18 P × B   R–KKt1
19 R–B3   R–Kt2

The threat was 20 Q × P*ch*, K × Q; 21 R–R3*ch*, K–Kt2; 22 B–R6*ch*, K–R2; 23 B–B8*dis. ch mate*, and even 19 ..., Kt–Kt2 will not prevent it.

20 B–R6   R–KKt1
21 R–R3   *Resigns*

For if 21 ..., Kt–Kt2 (against 22 B–B8); 22 Q–R4, threatening 23 B–Kt5, P–R4; 24 Q × P*ch*, with the same mate as before.

Unless White plays the Sämisch move of P–QR3 on the fourth move, as in the preceding game, it is more logical to defer it as long as possible in the hope that Black will exchange Bishop for Knight anyway, and so gain White a tempo. Actually Black is not likely to give away a tempo so readily, but the long deferment of P–QR3 leads to variations quite different from the Sämisch variation; they are, in fact, variations of the Rubinstein line.

GAME 43
NIMZO-INDIAN
DEFENCE

Kotov   Matanovic

Saltsjöbaden Tournament,
1952

1	P–Q4	Kt–KB3
2	P–QB4	P–K3
3	Kt–QB3	B–Kt5
4	P–K3	P–B4
5	B–Q3	P–Q4
6	Kt–B3	Kt–B3
7	O–O	O–O

It is the old Staunton Defence to the Queen's Gambit Declined again, except that Black's KB is developed outside instead of inside his QBP.

8 P–QR3   B×Kt

Black can, with slight loss of time, avoid giving White the Sämisch pawn skeleton by playing 8 ..., BP × P; 9 KP × P, P × P; 10 B × P, B–K2. But in that case it hardly seems worth playing the KB to QKt5 in the first place.

9	P×B	QP×P
10	B×P	Q–B2
11	P–QR4	

Part of the strategical struggle for the black central squares. Black has P–K4 available, so White plays to pin the black QBP on the Rook by B–R3.

11 ...   R–Q1

The alternative is to play 11 ..., P–K4; 12 B–R3, P–QKt3.

12	B–R3	P×P
13	BP×P	Kt×P

The point of Black's play. He wins a pawn, reduces White's central advantage, and removes one of the two Bishops. But in spite of that the exchanges leave him with an exposed King and a majority of undeveloped pieces, whose helplessness reveals the fine tactical quality of White's pawn sacrifice.

14	Kt×Kt	Q×B
15	B–K7	R–Q4
16	B×Kt	P×B
17	Q–B3	B–Q2

He can hardly try and hold the extra pawn. If 17 ..., P–B4; 18 KR–B1, Q–Q6 (Q–R3; 19 Kt× BP); 19 Q–Kt3ch, K–R1 (K–B1; 20 Q–R4, K–Kt1; 21 Q–K7); 20 Q–B7, R–Q2; 21 Q–K5ch with advantage. While if 17 ..., K–Kt2; 18 Q–Kt4ch, K–R1 (K–B1; 19

Kt × P*ch* wins the Queen); 19 Q–B4, K–Kt2; 20 Kt–B5*ch*.

| 18 | Q × P | Q–B2 |

The threat now was 19 KR–B1, Q–R3; 20 R–B7, P–Kt3; 21 Q–K7, B–K1; 22 Kt × P.

| 19 | QR–Kt1 | P–Kt3 |

Of course not 19 ..., B × P; 20 Kt × P, P × Kt; 21 Q × P*ch*, Q–B2; 22 Q–Kt4*ch*, K–R1; 23 Q × B.

| 20 | Kt–B3 | Q–Q1 |

Against Kt–Kt5.

| 21 | Q–B4 | R–B1 |
| 22 | P–K4 | |

A tactical and not a strategical move in the centre. The idea is to force the Rook to desert the Bishop, after which the black King's position can be more easily breached.

| 22 | ... | R–QR4 |
| 23 | Kt–K5 | P–B3 |

He is almost forced to give up a pawn, for if B–K1; 24 QR–Q1, Q–B2; 25 R–Q3, K–B1; 26 Q–B6.

24	Kt × B	Q × Kt
25	Q × P	R–B1
26	Q–R6	R × RP

The material is still level, but the weakness of the black King's position now decides the issue.

27	R–Kt3	Q–K2
28	R–Kt3*ch*	K–R1
29	P–K5	R–R5
30	Q–B1	R(5)–KB5
31	R–QB3	

A sudden switch, threatening R–B7 with the win of the QRP.

31	...	P–QR4
32	R–B7	Q–Kt5
33	Q–K3	

Something must now fall, for he threatens Q–KR3 attacking the King and the KP, as well as R–B6 attacking two pawns.

33	...	P–R5
34	P–Kt3	R(5)–B2
35	R–B6	R–QKt2
36	R × KP	P–R6
37	R–KB6	R–R1
38	P–K6	Q–Kt7

Preventing R–R1 as an answer to P–R7, and at the same time attacking the other Rook, but White has seen further.

| 39 | Q–KB3 | R–KKt1 |

Naturally if P–R7; 40 R–B8*ch*, K–Kt2; 41 R × R wins.

40	R–B8	R–R2
41	R × R*ch*	K × R
42	Q–Q5	*Resigns*

For if 42 ..., P–R7; 43 P–K7 *dis. ch*, K–Kt2; 44 P–K8=Q, P–R8=Q; 45 Q(8)–Kt8*ch* followed by Q(5)–Kt5*mate*, and if 42 ..., K–Kt2; 43 Q–Kt5*ch*, K–B1; 44 Q–Q8*ch*, K–Kt2; 45 P–K7, P–R7; 46 P–K8=Q, P–R8=Q; 47 Q–B8 *ch*, K–Kt3; 48 Q–Q3*ch* followed by Q(3)–B5*mate*.

An attempt to avoid these lines and introduce a somewhat different emphasis was made by Black playing his QKt to Q2 instead of to B3, but the following game indicates that the problem is not so easily solved.

GAME 44
NIMZO-INDIAN
DEFENCE

Tal   Tolush

Russian Championship, 1958

1 P–Q4	Kt–KB3
2 P–QB4	P–K3
3 Kt–QB3	B–Kt5
4 P–K3	P–B4
5 Kt–B3	P–Q4
6 B–Q3	O–O
7 O–O	QKt–Q2

This more restricted variation alters the emphasis entirely since this knight is now aiming at quite a different group of squares. A later technical improvement was to make the subsequent pawn exchange before this move.

8 P–QR3	P×QP

Safer was 8 ..., B×Kt; 9 P×B, P×BP; 10 B×P, Q–B2; 11 Q–K2, P–K4; 12 P–K4, BP×P; 13 P×P, P×P; 14 B–Kt2, Kt–K4. If Black hoped with the text move to preserve the two bishops, he is quickly and devastatingly disillusioned.

9 QKt×P	P×Kt
10 P×B	P×BP
11 B×P	Kt–Kt3

12 B–Kt3	P×P
13 B×P	Kt(Kt)–Q4

Black has difficulty in finding a satisfactory move here. The text prepares the fianchetto of the bishop. In an earlier game (Korchnoi–Darga, Hastings, 1956) Black endeavoured to retain the balance by giving up a pawn in the hope that White's extra doubled pawn would not count, but was disillusioned as follows: 13 ..., B–K3; 14 B×B, P×B; 15 Q×Q, KR×Q; 16 R×P, R×R; 17 B×Kt, KR–R1; 18 B×R, R×B; 19 Kt–K5, K–B1; 20 R–B1, K–K2; 21 P–B4, Kt–Q4; 22 Kt–Q3, R–R3; 23 K–B2, R–Kt3; 24 R–B4, R–R3; 25 R–K4, K–B3; 26 Kt–B5, R–R7; 27 R×P ch, K–B2; 28 R–K2, Kt×BP; 29 R–Q2, P–QKt3; 30 Kt–Q7, P–QKt4; 31 K–K3, Kt–K3; 32 Kt–B5, R–R2; 33 R–Q6, Kt–B1; 34 R–Kt6, R–R7; 35 Kt–Q3, Kt–Q2; 36 R×P, K–K3; 37 K–Q4, K–Q3; 38 R–QR5, Resigns.

14 B–B5	R–K1
15 R–K1	R×R ch
16 Q×R	P–QKt3
17 B–Q4	B–Kt2

Completing his plan which White shows to be faulty by developing pressure on the KBP now that the bishop can no longer defend it by B–B4–Kt3.

18	R–Q1	Q–K1
19	B–K5	Q–Kt4

Not Kt×P; 20 Q×Kt, B×Kt; 21 R–K1, B–Kt2; 22 B×Kt, Q–B3; 23 B×Pch, K–R1; 24 B×Pch, K×B; 25 B–Q5, Q×B; 26 R–K7ch, a most delightful winning variation.

20	QB×Kt	P×B

Somewhat better was Kt×B; 21 Q–K7, B–Q4; 22 B×B, Kt×B; 23 Q–Kt7, R–Q1; 24 P–R4, still with advantage to White. Now Tal produces a pulverizing finish.

21	Q–K4	Q×P

If R–K1; 22 R×Kt wins.

22	Kt–Q4	P–B4
23	Q–K5	Kt–K2
24	Q–B6	B–Q4

Slightly better was R–KB1, but then 25 P–R3, B–Q4; 26 R–Q3, B×B; 27 R–Kt3ch, Kt–Kt3; 28 Kt×P wins.

Diagram 32

25	Kt–B6	Q×B
26	Kt×Ktch	K–B1
27	R–K1	

Threatening Q–R8*mate*, a finish which Black can only temporarily prevent.

27	...	B–K3
28	Kt×P	*Resigns*

The masters consequently looked to less committing variations in the hope that, as in the early days of the Hypermoderns, these restricted lines would allow more complicated tensions to develop. The following game shows that even this was not entirely satisfactory.

GAME 45		1	P–Q4	Kt–KB3
NIMZO-INDIAN		2	P–QB4	P–K3
DEFENCE		3	Kt–QB3	B–Kt5
Bronstein	*Keres*	4	P–K3	P–B4
Göteborg Tournament, 1955		5	B–Q3	P–QKt3

The opening thus becomes a hybrid between the Nimzo-Indian and Queen's Indian Defences.

6	Kt–K2	B–Kt2
7	O–O	P×P
8	P×P	O–O
9	P–Q5	

Asserting an advantage in space in a manner which Black hoped his pawn exchange might have prevented. Nor could Black have forestalled the text by 8 ..., P–Q4; since he would then have lost a piece after 9 Q–R4*ch*, Kt–B3; 10 P×P, Kt×P (not B×Kt; 11 P×Kt); 11 B–QKt5, Q–Q3; 12 Kt×Kt, P×Kt; 13 B–KB4.

9 ...		P–KR3

He had nothing better than B–K2. White soon exploits this weakening of the King's position.

10	B–B2	Kt–R3
11	Kt–Kt5	

Threatening to win the bishop by P–QR3, P–QKt4 and P–Q6. More subtly he is offering a pawn for the attack.

11	...	P×P
12	P–QR3	B–K2
13	Kt–Kt3	P×P

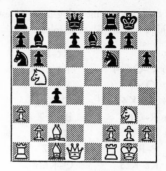

Diagram 33

14	B×P	P×B
15	Q–Q2	Kt–R2
16	Q×P	P–B4

Planning to break the attack by returning material, but events prove that his position is already too damaged.

17	Kt×BP	R×Kt
18	B×R	Kt–B1
19	QR–Q1	B–Kt4

He must act at once to forestall R–Q4–Kt4*ch*.

20	Q–R5	Q–B3
21	Kt–Q6	B–B3
22	Q–Kt4	K–R1

Hoping to trap White into the simplification 23 Q×B, Q×Q; 24 Kt–B7*ch*, K–Kt2; 25 Kt×Q, K–B3.

23	B–K4	B–R3
24	B×B	P×B
25	Q×P	

Starting a mopping-up process which renders Black helpless.

25 ...	Kt–B4	
26 P–QKt4	Kt(4)–K3	
27 Q×P	R–Kt1	
28 Kt–K4	Q–Kt3	
29 R–Q6	B–Kt2	
30 P–B4	Q–Kt5	
31 P–R3	Q–K7	
32 Kt–Kt3	Q–K6ch	

33 K–R2	Kt–Q5	
34 Q–Q5	R–B1	
35 Kt–R5	Kt–K7	
36 Kt×B	Q–Kt6ch	
37 K–R1	Kt×P	
38 Q–B3	Kt–K7	
39 R–R6ch	*Resigns*	

He is mated in two more moves. A brilliancy prize game.

More successful was a treatment in which Black moved closer to the Queen's Indian Defence, as in the following game.

GAME 46

NIMZO-INDIAN DEFENCE

Uhlmann   Botvinnik

Munich Team Tournament, 1958

1 P–Q4	P–K3
2 P–QB4	Kt–KB3
3 Kt–QB3	B–Kt5
4 P–K3	P–QKt3
5 B–Q3	B–Kt2
6 Kt–B3	Kt–K5

With P–B4 Black could have adopted a process nearer to that seen in the last game. The present position could equally have arisen from the Queen's Indian Defence by 1 P–Q4, Kt–KB3; 2 P–QB4, P–K3; 3 Kt–KB3, P–QKt3; 4 Kt–B3, B–Kt5; 5 P–K3, B–Kt2; 6 B–Q3, Kt–K5.

7 O–O	P–KB4

Following the true Nimzovitch pattern.

8 Q–B2	B×Kt
9 P×B	O–O
10 R–Kt1	P–B4

He has to deal with the threat of P–B5. At the same time he attacks the black centre squares.

11 P–QR4	Q–B2
12 P–R5	P–Q3
13 Kt–Q2	Kt×Kt
14 B×Kt	Kt–Q2
15 R–Kt2	

Still pursuing the will-o'-wisp of pressure on the QKt file. Black quite simply counters by making the QR file an issue with two passed pawns.

15 ...	P×RP
16 R–R1	Kt–Kt3
17 R×P	

Forestalling P–R5, but Black's threats really lie elsewhere. White suddenly finds that threats to his QBP may involve loss of the exchange.

17 ...	B–K5
18 B×B	P×B
19 Q–Kt3	

Similar positions are reached after 19 Q×P, Kt×P; 20 Q×KP*ch*, K–R1; 21 Q×Kt, Q×R; while the attempt to save the exchange by 19 R–R1, Kt×P; 20 R(2)–R2, P–Q4;

leaves his bishop quite useless.

19 ...	Kt×P
20 Q×Kt	Q×R
21 Q×P*ch*	K–R1
22 R–R2	Q–B2
23 Q×KP	

Allowing a fatal fork, but the game is past redemption.

23 ...	Q–B2
Resigns	

There were some players who preferred to throw Black more on his own resources, even at the cost of some personal insecurity, and the following game is a good example of this.

GAME 47

NIMZO-INDIAN DEFENCE

Spassky   *Smyslov*

Bucharest Tournament, 1953

1 P–Q4	Kt–KB3
2 P–QB4	P–K3
3 Kt–QB3	B–Kt5
4 B–Kt5	

An attempt to exploit Black's last move by imposing a pin which Black will be reluctant to try and break by a bishop retreat.

4 ...	P–KR3
5 B–R4	P–B4
6 P–Q5	P–Q3

The modern dynamic player accepts a backward QP as part of his springboard for counter-attack, but

a possibility here was 6 ..., P–QKt4; and if 7 QP×P, BP×P.

7 P–K3	P×P

After P–K4 his position might be less vulnerable but would certainly offer less scope for action; Smyslov naturally makes the dynamic choice.

8 P×P	QKt–Q2
9 B–QKt5	O–O
10 Kt–K2	Kt–K4
11 O–O	Kt–Kt3
12 B–Kt3	Kt–R4

A promising alternative to the elimination of White's bishop would be the development of his own by P–R3; 13 B–Q3, P–Kt4.

13 B–Q3	Kt×B
14 Kt×Kt	Kt–K4
15 B–K2	B×Kt

Fearing 16 P–B4, Kt–Kt3; 17 P–B5, Kt–K4; 18 P–B6, he plans Q–R5 so as to play the knight to KKt5 when it is attacked; but first he prevents a counter-attack on his QP by White's Kt–Kt5.

16	P×B	Q–R5
17	P–KB4	Kt–Kt5
18	B×Kt	B×B

A development of the bishop at last, but one that proves illusory against White's next threat of P–B5.

19	Q–R4	B–B1
20	P–K4	Q–Kt5

Threatening B–Q2 and P–QKt4, but White's thrust is in the centre and therefore proves superior.

21	Q–B2	P–KR4
22	R–B2	P–QKt4
23	P–K5	P–R5
24	Kt–B1	B–B4
25	Q–Q2	P×P

Allowing White too much scope. Better was simply QR–Q1; 26 Kt–K3, Q–Kt3; 27 Kt×B, Q×Kt; 28 R–K1, KR–K1. White now builds up an attack with great speed.

26	P×P	B–Kt3

His pawn exchange has meant that White's Kt–K3 now threatens to win a piece.

27	R–K1	P–R6
28	P–Q6	B–K5
29	Kt–K3	Q–K3
30	R–B4	B×P

If he expected 31 Kt×B, simplifying, he is disappointed.

31	Kt–B5	KR–K1

The threat was 32 Kt–K7*ch* and R–R4*mate*.

32	R–K3	QR–Q1

Diagram 34

33	Kt×P	R×P

Despair. If 33 ..., K×Kt; 34 R–Kt3*ch*, K–B1; 35 R×P*ch*, Q×R (K×R; 36 Q–B4*ch*); 36 Q–R6*ch*.

34	Kt×Q	*Resigns*

Unlike the Nimzo-Indian Defence, the Queen's Indian Defence, which had been equally or more favoured by the Hypermoderns, had now gone right out of favour because it led to simplifying manœuvres which left the position almost devoid of dynamic stresses. After 1 P-Q4, Kt-KB3; 2 P-QB4, P-K3; 3 Kt-KB3, P-QKt3; 4 P-KKt3, B-Kt2; 5 B-Kt2, B-K2; 6 O-O, O-O; 7 Kt-B3, Kt-K5 the resulting positions did not appeal to the Russians, whether they had White or Black, since in either case the game was comparatively dead. Consequently there arose a tendency, on the few occasions when the Queen's Indian Defence was played, for White to adopt older lines which in theory were less satisfactory since Black more easily obtained a grip on the white squares, but which by avoiding simplification left White some chances of developing dynamic possibilities. The following game is typical of this new approach by White and of the hazards involved in so doing.

GAME 48
QUEEN'S INDIAN DEFENCE

Geller	Boleslavsky

Neuhausen–Zürich Candidates Tournament, 1953

1	P-Q4	P-K3
2	Kt-KB3	Kt-KB3
3	P-B4	P-QKt3
4	Kt-B3	B-Kt2
5	B-Kt5	P-KR3
6	B×Kt	

To reduce Black's grip on the white squares, but it would be more in keeping with the dynamic views of the Russian school to play 6 B-R4 and allow Black's P-KKt4 on the grounds that Black's K side weakness would offset the loss of control of the white squares.

6	...	Q×B

7	P-K4	B-Kt5
8	B-Q3	P-B4

Since White has successfully won the battle for the white squares, Black switches his attentions to the black squares.

9	O-O	P×P
10	Kt-QKt5	Q-Q1
11	Kt(5)×QP	O-O
12	Q-K2	Kt-B3
13	QR-Q1	Kt×Kt
14	Kt×Kt	B-B4
15	B-B2	

The results of the opening are now clarified. White has managed to occupy the centre, though still under some pressure, but Black has the two Bishops.

15	...	R-B1
16	P-K5	

Giving up much of his white

square control for a rather nebulous pressure on the Q file and against the Q pawn.

| 16 ... | Q–Kt4 |
| 17 P–B4 | |

Against the threat of mate, but he now weakens his black squares as well as his white. 17 B–K4 would have retained the balance of forces, since then 17 ..., Q × P loses a piece after 18 B × B.

| 17 ... | Q–K2 |
| 18 K–R1 | P–B4 |

Finally controlling the white squares and preventing White's B–K4. If now 19 P × P*e.p.*, P × P; and Black can effectively deploy a further attack along the KKt file.

| 19 Kt–Kt5 | P–R3 |
| 20 Kt–Q6 | B × Kt |

Fine play. He gives up the advantage of the two Bishops, realizing that his resources for attack are now adequate and that White's pressure on the Q file can be held.

21 R × B	R–QB3
22 R(1)–Q1	R × R
23 R × R	B–B3
24 P–QKt4	

Hoping to dislodge the black Bishop by P–Kt5, but as Black now shows, the last chance of doing so was 24 Q–B2 followed by B–Q1–B3.

| 24 ... | Q–R5 |
| 25 R–Q4 | |

Not 25 P–Kt5, P × P; 26 P × P, B × P; 27 Q × B, Q–K8*ch*.

| 25 ... | P–KKt4 |

The loose positions of the white pieces are excellently exploited in a logical build-up of the long prepared attack.

| 26 K–Kt1 | P × P |
| 27 Q–B2 | Q–K2 |

After Q × Q*ch*; 28 K × Q, the advanced KB pawn would fall.

| 28 P–QR3 | Q–Kt2 |
| 29 R × BP | |

P–B6 was threatened.

29 ...	Q × P
30 R–Q4	R–B2
31 B–Q3	P–B5
32 B–B1	Q–B3
33 R–Q2	P–Kt4

Stabilizing this flank before proceeding to the final assault.

| 34 P–B5 | Q–R8 |

An idle excursion. P–K4 at once would do.

35 Q–R4	Q–B3
36 Q × Q	R × Q
37 K–B2	P–K4
38 P–Kt3	P × P*dbl. ch*
39 K–K1	R–B6
40 P × P	R × KtP
41 R–Q6	K–Kt2
42 B–Q3	P–K5
43 B–K2	R × P
44 B–Kt4	R–Q6
Resigns	

CHAPTER IX

King's Indian and Old Indian Defences

IT was a sign of the times that as the Queen's Indian Defence went out of favour, the King's Indian Defence came in. It was a defence that had not been greatly favoured by the Hypermoderns because it led to such cramped and difficult positions for Black. It was recognized that in spite of all new analysis White could still gain an early advantage in the centre, but what was now seen was that Black's game, properly handled, contained great dynamic force, and expansion at the right time could produce adequate chances in a game of intense tension. The following is a typical example.

GAME 49

KING'S INDIAN DEFENCE

Botvinnik	*Smyslov*

14th Match Game, Moscow, 1954

1	P–Q4	Kt–KB3
2	P–QB4	P–KKt3
3	P–KKt3	

The Rubinstein procedure, seeking to hold both the black and the white centre squares.

3	...	B–Kt2
4	B–Kt2	O–O
5	Kt–QB3	P–Q3
6	Kt–B3	QKt–Q2
7	O–O	P–K4
8	P–K4	P–B3

Better than the old Hypermodern idea of playing P–Kt3, as in Game

26. Note that if now 9 P × P, P × P; Black's pawn structure in the centre is even better than White's, for White could post no outpost piece on Q5, whereas Black's Q5 is available for a black outpost.

9	B–K3

The old plan was to play P–KR3 first so as to be able to make this move without fear of Kt–Kt5 in reply. Here, however, White actually invites the move in the expectation that he will thereby increase his dynamic chances.

9	...	Kt–Kt5
10	B–Kt5	Q–Kt3

White has expected the usual 10 ..., P–B3; 11 B–B1, P–KB4; when he has drawn Black into an advance of his KB-pawn which may prove weakening as White has not previously played P–Q5. However, Smyslov has found a new way of keeping Black's game dynamic. If now 11 B–K7, R–K1; 12 B×P, P×P; 13 Kt–QR4, Q–R3 threatening P–QKt4 with advantage owing to veiled threats against two of White's minor pieces.

| 11 P–KR3 | P×P |

A temporary sacrifice of the Knight which quite overturns the refutation planned by White's last move.

| 12 Kt–QR4 | Q–R3 |
| 13 P×Kt | P–Kt4 |

Recovering his piece at the cost of a weak long diagonal, which White at once exploits.

| 14 Kt×P | P×Kt |
| 15 Kt×P | |

The Knight can only be captured at the cost of the exchange, but after 15 ..., B–Kt2; 16 Kt–K7ch (not 15 ..., B×P; 16 R–Kt1, B–KKt2; 17 P–K5, B–Kt2; 18 Kt–K7ch), the disintegrated black pawns would prove an insuperable handicap. Accordingly Black prefers to get rid of the pawn weaknesses and lose the exchange, a truly dynamic choice, to which he was in fact committed when he played his 10th move.

15 ...	Q×Kt
16 P–K5	Q×P
17 B×R	Kt×P

After P × P Black would have such difficulty in developing his Q-Bishop that his dynamism would be much reduced. Now Black threatens to get two pieces for his Rook by 18 ..., B×P. White's best line is simply to play 18 B–Kt2, or else to remove his Queen from the threat by Q×QP, instead of which he aims for an ultimate Q×RP, which is brilliantly refuted.

| 18 R–B1 | Q–Kt5 |
| 19 P–R3 | |

Still pursuing his faulty plan, while Black is preparing to seize the long diagonal against the white King with a development of his Q-Bishop on Kt2.

19 ...	Q×QKtP
20 Q×RP	B–Kt2
21 R–Kt1	

Falling into a dastardly trap by playing for the win of a piece after 21 ..., Q moves; 22 B×B. He has to consider that otherwise Black threatens to get the second piece for the Rook either by B×B or by Kt–B6ch and Kt×B; while if 21 B×B, Q×B; 22 R–Kt1, Q–R1; there is no adequate answer to Kt–B6ch followed by the discovered check. All the same, 21 B×B, Q×B was his best line, followed by 22 R–B3, Kt–B6ch; 23 R×Kt, though even then Black not only recovers his material but keeps a strong initiative.

Diagram 35

21 ...   Kt–B6*ch*

Although the white Bishop is still on the board, the diagonal has passed out of its control.

22 K–R1   B × B

The climax of Black's play, giving up the Queen for three minor pieces, and much better than Kt–Q7*dis. ch*; 23 B × B, Kt × QR; 24 B–QB6, with approximately equal chances.

23 R × Q   Kt × B*dis. ch*
24 K–R2   Kt–B6*ch*

| 25 | K–R3 | B × R |
| 26 | Q × P | B–K5 |

Preventing White's R–QKt1, and threatening R–R1, winning the white QR-pawn, which pawn now becomes White's best chance, though in fact he is unable to advance it far enough for it to affect the issue.

27	P–R4	K–Kt2
28	R–Q1	B–K4
29	Q–K7	R–B1

Threatening mate in three by R–B7, R × P and R–R7, while if White tries 30 R × P, offering the exchange to break the power of the two Bishops, then 30 ..., R–B8 forces mate.

30	P–R5	R–B7
31	K–Kt2	Kt–Q5*dis. ch*
32	K–B1	B–B6
33	R–Kt1	Kt–B3
	Resigns	

For the threat of B–Q5 means that he must submit to further loss.

The next example is once again the same variation, but on this occasion the position is reached by a transposition from the Old Indian Defence, a device which gives Black the opportunity of keeping out of the King's Indian Defence if it suits his purpose.

GAME 50

KING'S INDIAN DEFENCE

Zita   *Bronstein*

Prague–Moscow Match, 1946

1 P–QB4   P–K4

It begins as an English Opening.

2	Kt–QB3	Kt–KB3
3	Kt–B3	P–Q3
4	P–Q4	

Becomes an Old Indian Defence.

| 4 | ... | QKt–Q2 |
| 5 | P–KKt3 | P–KKt3 |

And is now the King's Indian Defence with White playing the accepted Rubinstein line.

6	B–Kt2	B–Kt2
7	O–O	O–O
8	P–Kt3	

Instead of direct occupation of the centre by P–K4, as in the previous games, White adopts a more truly Hypermodern method of countering Black's attempt to play on the black squares.

8	...	R–K1
9	B–Kt2	P–B3
10	P–K4	P×P

The same manœuvre as in the preceding game to give life to the K-Bishop.

11	Kt×P	Q–Kt3

The usual line is Kt–B4; 12 Q–B2, P–QR4; 13 QR–Q1, and only then Q–Kt3. Finding his Q–B2 now not possible, White is lured into a weak alternative. The best reply was Kt(4)–K2 attacking the black Q-pawn.

12	Q–Q2	Kt–B4
13	KR–K1	P–QR4
14	QR–Kt1	

Against P–R5, which is a strong move anyway.

14	...	P–R5
15	B–R1	P×P
16	P×P	Kt–Kt5
17	P–R3	

Diagram 36

17	...	R×B

An astonishing climax to the fight for the long diagonal.

18	R×R	Kt×BP

Now White is faced with cross-fire on two black diagonals, KR8–QR1 and QR7–KKt1. If now 19 K×Kt, Kt×KtP and the pin of the Knight on Q5 comes on the new diagonal, while if 19 Q×Kt, Kt–Q6; in either case forking Queen and Rook.

19	R–K3	Kt×P*ch*
20	K–R2	Kt–B7

This time if 21 Q×Kt, B×Kt.

21	R–B3	Kt(4)×KP
22	Q–B4	Kt–Kt5*ch*
23	K–R1	P–KB4

Note that this move, once regarded as the themic freeing move for Black (see Game 26) is now relegated to a much later stage, if indeed it is played at all. Here it indicates the final collapse of White's game.

24	Kt×Kt	R×Kt
25	Q×QP	R×Kt
26	Q–Kt8	R–Q1

27 R–R8	B–K4	He is threatened with Q–B8*ch*
28 Q–R7	Q–Kt5	and with R–Q7. The zigzag move-
29 Q–R2	Q–B1	ment of the black Queen from QKt3
30 B–R3	Q–R3	to KR3 for the winning manœuvre
Resigns		is highly original.

While the Rubinstein line with its fianchetto of the K Bishop seemed logical enough for White in the early days of the King's Indian Defence, when the new conceptions of the centre were still in an over-simplified form, it came to be regarded as less adequate when the later views on central play, as exemplified in the preceding games, came into vogue.

One of the lines tried instead was the so-called Lasker Variation, seen in Game 27. But the Russians, with their search for dynamic situations, tended to look askance at P–Q5 for White. Tarrasch's day of winning by space alone was long since past. The locking of the centre pawns led to positions where Black could bring about a stronger reaction than White. P–KB4 by Black was both natural and good, whereas P–KB4 by White only led, after Black's P × P, to a backward White K-pawn and a strong outpost square for Black on his K4. Nor were the Russians very enthusiastic about a pawn-storming attack on a very narrow front, as tried by Nimzovitch in Game 27.

However, the avoidance of the move P–Q5 by White still led to problems for White, as shown in the following game.

GAME 51

KING'S INDIAN DEFENCE

Alatortsev   *Smyslov*

Moscow Championship, 1943

1 P–Q4	Kt–KB3
2 P–QB4	P–KKt3
3 Kt–QB3	B–Kt2
4 P–K4	P–Q3
5 KKt–K2	P–K4
6 P–B3	O–O
7 B–K3	

It was now or never if he wanted to play P–Q5. However, White here has only played P–KB3 to bolster up his K-pawn which, as seen in Games 49 and 50, comes under severe fire from Black.

7 ...	P × P
8 Kt × P	P–B3
9 Kt–B2	R–K1
10 Q–Q2	P–Q4

Black at once sets about weakening White on the K file, even at the cost of allowing him a passed pawn. In the process he induces White to place his King on the more hazardous Q flank.

11	O–O–O	Q–R4
12	BP×P	P×P
13	P×P	QKt–Q2
14	B–Q4	P–QR3
15	B–B4	P–QKt4
16	B–Kt3	P–Kt5
17	Kt–K4	

This does not give back a pawn by exchanges on K4, since in return he can win a pawn on QKt4, but it does seriously weaken the defences of his King and for this reason Kt–R4 was better.

17	...	Kt×Kt
18	P×Kt	Kt–K4

Avoiding the exchange of his K-Bishop which in this game has the additional merit of pointing at the hostile King, whereas after 18 ..., R×P; 19 B×B, he would have sacrificed all attacking chances to recover his pawn.

19 Q×P

Over-greedy. The win of this second pawn opens lines for Black's attack.

19 ...   Q–Q1

A retreat to permit a later advance. Black's tactical play is first class.

20	B–R4	B–Q2
21	B×B	Q×B
22	B–B3	QR–B1
23	Kt–R3	Q–Kt5

White has been building up the defences of his King, but the black

Queen's return to action comes on the other flank.

24	K–Kt1	Q×P
25	Q–Q4	R×B

Another example of a sacrifice of the exchange as a means of clearing the vital long diagonal.

26 Q×R

If 26 P×R, then R–Kt1*ch* followed by Q–Kt7*mate*.

26 ...   Kt–B5

Triumph on the diagonal again. Naturally if now 27 Q×Kt, Q× KtP*mate*.

27	Q–Kt4	P–QR4
28	Q–Kt3	Kt×Kt*ch*

Much better than merely winning the QKtP. White's last move betokened an intention of replying to the text move with 29 Q×Kt, but then would come 29 ..., R–Kt1; 30 P–Kt3, Q×KP*ch*; 31 K–B1, R–B1*ch*; 32 K–Q2, R–B7*mate*. So White has to expose his King still more.

29	P×Kt	Q×KP*ch*
30	Q–Q3	R–Kt1*ch*
31	K–B1	R–B1*ch*
32	K–Kt1	

Not 32 K–Q2, B–R3*ch*.

32 ... *Resigns*

For if 33 Q–Q2, then Q–R8*mate*.

A still more logical and direct method of meeting the King's Indian Defence was, however, available, and with the doubts thrown on other lines this line came increasingly into favour. It dispensed with all indirect pawn moves in the opening and only involved the advance of the centre pawns, without however being as over-optimistic as the Four Pawns Advance seen in Game 25.

GAME 52
KING'S INDIAN DEFENCE
Filip   *Tolush*
Bucharest Tournament, 1953

1 P–Q4	Kt–KB3
2 P–QB4	P–Q3
3 Kt–QB3	P–K4
4 Kt–B3	

His idea is to play P–K4 early, but he waits until Black has played QKt–Q2, for if 4 P–K4 Black gets a powerful game, as shown by the score of the game Alatortsev–Boleslavsky from the 1950 Russian Championship, which continued 4 ..., P×P; 5 Q×P, Kt–B3; 6 Q–Q2, P–KKt3; 7 P–QKt3, B–Kt2; 8 B–Kt2, O–O; 9 B–Q3, Kt–KKt5; 10 Kt–B3, Kt(5)–K4; 11 B–K2, Kt×Kt*ch*; 12 B×Kt, Kt–Q5; 13 B–Q1. P–KB4; 14 P×P, B×P; 15 Kt–K2, Kt×Kt; 16 B×Kt, B×B; 17 Q×B, Q–Kt4; 18 P–Kt3, QR–K1; 19 O–O, B–R6; 20 P–B4, B×R; 21 P×Q, R×B; 22 Q–B3, B–Kt7; 23 Q–Q3, B–B6; 24 R–KB1, R–Kt7*ch*; 25 K–R1, B–B3; 26 R×R*ch*, K×R; 27 Q–B1*ch*, R–B7*dis. ch*; *Resigns.*

4 ...	QKt–Q2
5 P–K4	P–KKt3
6 B–K2	B–Kt2
7 O–O	O–O
8 R–K1	

Reaching the orthodox position in this line. Against the alternative 8 P–Q5 Black is at once able to post a Knight on his QB4 and then continue with the old themic move of P–KB4, which has been shown to be a successful type of reaction to a pawn lock ever since the days of Steinitz.

8 ...	P–B3
9 B–B1	R–K1
10 R–Kt1	

Now 10 P–Q5 is met by P–B4 and White will have chances neither in the centre nor on the Q side after Black's P–KB4, so that although Black may not be able to win he is at least in virtually no danger of losing. The text move which is more dynamic and therefore in the spirit of the times, prepares for action on the Q side in order to force Black's hand.

10 ...	P×P
11 Kt×P	Kt–B4

12 P–B3	P–QR4
13 B–K3	KKt–Q2

An increase in energy created by a temporary retreat is frequently found in Russian games. Now pressure on the long diagonal is emphasized and the Knight will be posted more aggressively on K4.

14 Q–Q2	Kt–K4
15 R(K)–Q1	Q–K2
16 Kt–Kt3	

Giving Black a chance to expand on the Q side without loss of time. Kt–B2 was more promising. It is notable that Black does not continue with the obvious Kt × Kt.

16 ...	P–R5
17 Kt × Kt	P × Kt
18 QR–B1	

He finds after all that he cannot win the doubled pawn, for if 18 Q–Q6, Q × Q; 19 R × Q, B–K3; 20 B × P, then B–KB1 wins the exchange.

18 ...	B–K3
19 Q–QB2	

This lets Black in on the Q side. P–QKt3 was a little better.

19 ...	B × P
20 Kt × P	P–QKt4
21 Kt–Kt6	

If 21 Kt–B3, B × P.

21 ...	R × P
22 Kt × B	P × Kt
23 KB × P	

Diagram 37

23 ...	R × P

Yet one more astonishing climax to the play on the vital diagonal.

24 Q–R4

Of course if 24 Q × R, Kt × P*ch* wins the Queen.

24 ...	Q–Kt2
25 B × P	

This allows the Queen to be trapped, but Black leads into a won ending after 25 R–Q2, R × R; 26 B × R, R–R1; 27 Q–B2, Kt × B; 28 Q × Kt, B–Q5*ch*; 29 K–R1, Q–Kt4.

25 ...	R–R1
26 Q–R3	R × Q
27 R–Q8*ch*	B–B1
28 R × B*ch*	

If 28 B × B, Q–Kt3*ch*; 29 B–B5 *dis. ch*, Q × R; 30 B × R, Q–Q5*ch*.

28 ...	K–Kt2
Resigns	

For after 29 B × R, Q–R2*ch*; 30 K–B1, Q × B White has no chance.

For players who wished to keep off the analysed lines there was always the Old Indian Defence, but Black's position then tended to be more cramped than in the King's Indian owing to the less dynamic position of the KB.

GAME 53

OLD INDIAN DEFENCE

Botvinnik   *Tartakover*

Nottingham Tournament, 1936

1 Kt–KB3	Kt–KB3
2 P–B4	P–Q3
3 P–Q4	QKt–Q2
4 P–KKt3	P–K4
5 B–Kt2	B–K2

Going definitely into an Old Indian style of game.

6 O–O	O–O
7 Kt–B3	P–B3
8 P–K4	Q–B2

The game now bears some resemblance to close variations of the Philidor Defence, except that White has fianchettoed his KB and advanced his QBP.

9 P–KR3

Preventing Kt–Kt5 before playing B–K3.

9 ...	R–K1
10 B–K3	Kt–B1

Black cannot clear the decks for action with P × P as in the previous games, because he has no strong

pressure on the long diagonal to compensate for his weak QP.

11 R–B1

A mysterious Rook move in the Nimzovitch style. He wants to gain space in the centre by P–Q5 without meeting the reply P × P.

11 ...	P–KR3
12 P–Q5	B–Q2
13 Kt–Q2	P–KKt4

Hoping in vain to prevent White's next advance of P–B4. The resulting exposure of both Kings reacts more unfavourably on Black than on White because Black's cramped game prevents him from easily defending weak points.

14 P–B4	KtP × P
15 KtP × P	K–Kt2
16 BP × P	QP × P
17 P–B5	

Philidor would have played thus to force a passed pawn. Modern strategy recognizes that such a pawn would be weak, and plays the move to create an outpost square on Q6 together with a clearance of QB4 so that the outpost Knight can reach his destination.

17 ...	P×P
18 Kt×P	Q–B3
19 Kt–QB4	

Everything works with machine-like precision. Of course 19 ...,
B×BP would be answered by 20
R×Kt.

19 ...	Kt–Kt3
20 Kt–Q6	

The outpost is wonderfully invulnerable owing to the counter-threat on KB6. Black is already reduced to time-losing defensive manœuvres in an attempt to get rid of the Knight on Q5 instead.

20 ...	B–K3
21 Kt×B	

Steinitz once said that once he had an outpost Knight established on the sixth rank, he could virtually let the game play itself. Botvinnik similarly will not squander his invaluable outpost by 21 Kt×R*ch* merely to win the exchange. By weakening Black on the black squares instead and at the same time keeping his outpost, he creates a situation where the game will similarly play itself.

21 ...	Kt×Kt

Even worse would be 21 ...,
R×Kt; 22 Kt–B5*ch*, K–R1 (or
B×Kt; 23 P×B, winning a piece);

23 Kt×R, Kt×Kt; 24 R×Kt, and
White is a piece ahead.

22 R×Kt	

At once exploiting the weak black squares in neat style.

22 ...	K×R
23 Q–R5	Kt–Kt3
24 Kt–B5	

Decisive. Black cannot capture the Knight because it will cost him a piece, and meanwhile his King is put in a mating net. He is faced not only with Q×P–Kt7*mate* but also with Q×P and B–Kt5*mate* or even B×P and Q–Kt5*mate*. Thus he must move his Bishop to create a flight square, which does not leave him sufficient time to contest the Q file on which White will then threaten R–Q6*ch*. A perfect example of a player overwhelmed by a multiplicity of threats.

24 ...	R–KKt1
25 Q×P	B×P
26 R–Q1	QR–Q1
27 Q–Kt5*ch*	K–K3
28 R×R	P–B3
29 R×R	Kt–B5

Quite fatal would be P×Q; 30
R×Kt*ch*, K–Q2; 31 R×Q, K×R;
and White is two pieces ahead.

30 Q–Kt7	*Resigns*

More original methods of keeping off the analyzed lines were then developed, as in the next game.

GAME 54

OLD INDIAN DEFENCE

Pachman   *Petrosyan*

Portorož Tournament, 1958

1	P–QB4	Kt–KB3	
2	Kt–KB3	P–Q3	
3	P–Q4	B–Kt5	
4	Kt–B3	P–KKt3	
5	P–K4	B×Kt	
6	Q×B	KKt–Q2	

Typical of Petrosyan's subtle positional appreciation. He contests his K4 against a possible P–K5 by White with both knights and his KB.

7	P–K5	Kt–QB3
8	P×P	Kt×P

A sharp dynamic line in preference to the more positional BP×P with approximate equality.

9	Q–K4	P–K4
10	P×P	Q×P
11	Kt–Q5	

Hoping ultimately to exploit the weak black squares on the King's wing.

11	...	Q–Q3
12	B–B4	

To answer Kt–QB4 with Q×P*ch*, and at the same time threatening 13 B×P, Q×B; 14 Q×Q*ch*, Kt×Q; 15 Kt–B7*ch*.

12	...	Kt–K3
13	B–K3	B–Kt2
14	O–O–O	

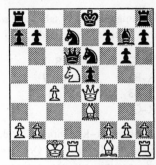

Diagram 38

With this move White seems to have turned Black's sharp opening against him, for the threats of Kt–B6*ch* and Kt–Kt6 appear to force a defensive move by the black queen. But Black has more startling ideas.

14	...	O–O
15	Kt–Kt6	Q×R*ch*
16	K×Q	P×Kt
17	P–QR3	Kt(2)–B4
18	Q–B2	P–K5
19	P–B3	

Somewhat better was B–K2.

19	...	QR–Q1*ch*
20	K–K1	

The alternative was 20 K–B1, Kt–Q6*ch*; 21 B×Kt, P×B; 22 Q–Q2, Kt–B4; and White has to deal with the threat of Kt–Kt6*ch*.

20 ...	Kt–Q5
21 B×Kt	B×B
22 P×P	Kt×P

The knight is clearly taboo and so another centre file is opened.

23 B–K2	KR–K1
24 R–B1	R–K2
25 R–B3	R(1)–K1
26 R–Q3	

To answer Kt–Kt4 with 27 R×B, R×B*ch*; 28 Q×R, R×Q*ch*; 29 K×R, coming out the exchange ahead.

26 ...	B–Kt8
27 P–R3	B–R7

Kt–Kt4 at once would be met by 28 R–Q2, but now the threat is on again since Black can follow with B–B5. So White must save his bishop.

28 B–B3	B–Kt6*ch*
29 K–Q1	Kt–B7*ch*
30 K–Q2	B–B5*ch*
31 K–B3	Kt×R
32 K×Kt	R–K6*ch*
33 K–Q4	B–R3

The long diagonal at last! He threatens 34 ..., B–Kt2*ch*; 35 K–Q5, R–Q1*mate*.

34 P–B5	P–QKt4
35 B×P	B–Kt2*ch*
36 K–Q5	R(1)–K3

Overcome by his difficulties, White lost on time, but after 37 P–B6, R(6)–K4*ch*; 38 K–Q4, R–K7*dis. ch*, it is all over.

CHAPTER X

Grünfeld and Bastard Grünfeld Defences

As might be expected, the Grünfeld Defence with its theme of producing a more dynamic form of King's Indian Defence received considerable attention from a school of chessmasters so skilled in the exploitation of positions of dynamic energy. Since its early introduction, when the old Exchange Variation (see Game 28 and the introductory note to it) seemed to permit Black too much pressure on the long diagonal to White's QR1 and too dangerous a Q side pawn majority, White had adopted more restrained methods of development, designed to create difficulties for Black by cramping his game. In the following example, however, Black once again succeeds in establishing a good and free position.

GAME 55

GRÜNFELD DEFENCE

Lilienthal   *Boleslavsky*

Russian Championship, 1944

1 P–Q4	Kt–KB3
2 P–QB4	P–KKt3
3 Kt–QB3	P–Q4
4 B–B4	B–Kt2
5 P–K3	O–O
6 Kt–B3	P–B4

Offering a temporary sacrifice of his QBP in order to open the important long diagonal, an offer which White unwisely accepts, thereby undermining the whole purpose of the quiet opening he has adopted. He should play B–K2 followed by O–O, maintaining his theme of play.

In the game Petrosyan–Benko in the Curaçao Candidates' Tournament, 1962, White had the interesting idea of playing his KP forward more vigorously, so he substituted R–B1 for P–K3 on move 5 and the game went on 5 ..., O–O; 6 Kt–B3, P–B4; 7 QP×P, P×P; 8 P–K4, Q–R4; 9 P–K5, R–Q1; 10 B–Q2, Kt–Kt5; 11 B×P, Q×BP; 12 Kt–K4, Q–Kt3; 13 B×Pch, K×B; 14 R×B, R×R; 15 Kt(3)–Kt5ch, K–Kt1; 16 Q×Kt, Q–QB3; 17 Kt–Q6, Q–Q2; but then missed the win by 18 Q–KR4, and played 18 Q×Q, Kt×Q; 19 Kt×R, R×Kt; 20 P–B4, R–B7; 21 K–K2, B–R3; 22 Kt–B3, R×P; 23 P–Kt3, P–KKt4. *Drawn.*

7 QP×P   Q–R4
8 Kt–Q2

Black threatens Kt–K5 with fearful pressure on QB3. Already White is repenting of his 7th move.

8 ...   P×P
9 Kt×P

Snatching at the chance of reducing the pressure, but it was still better to play B×P and O–O.

9 ...   Q×BP
10 B–K2   Kt–B3
11 O–O   R–Q1
12 Q–Kt3   B–K3
13 Q–Kt5

Against Kt–QR4. Black already has an easy initiative.

13 ...   Q×Q
14 Kt×Q   Kt–Q4
15 B–Kt3

If 15 Kt–B7, Kt×B; 16 P×Kt, B×Kt; 17 B×B (Kt×R, B×B; 18 KR–K1, R×Kt), QR–B1 with advantage to Black.

15 ...   QR–B1
16 P–QR4

Black threatened to gain ground by P–QR3 and P–QKt4, ending up with the win of White's QKtP. Nor can White try to gain the initiative by 16 P–K4 because then Kt(4)–Kt5; 17 P–QR3, Kt–B7; 18 QR–B1, Kt(7)–Q5; 19 Kt×Kt, Kt×Kt; 20 B–Q3, Kt–Kt6 and Black wins material.

16 ...   Kt(4)–Kt5
17 Kt(5)–R3

Defending the square QB4 which Black was able to exploit in the variation in the preceding note.

17 ...   Kt–Q6
18 QR–Kt1   B–B4
19 P–B3

White cannot save his QKtP, for if 19 P–Kt3, then Kt–B4.

19 ...   Kt×P
20 P–K4   B–K3
21 Kt×Kt   R–Q7

Recovering the piece.

22 B–QB4   R×Kt
23 B×B   P×B
24 R×R   B×R
25 Kt–Kt5

Safer was Kt–B4. From Kt5 the Knight can only go forward into still greater hazards. In any event, Black's extra pawn, though slightly offset by his doubled pawn, is technically sufficient for the win.

25 ...   P–QR3
26 Kt–B7   B–Q5ch
27 K–R1   K–B2
28 R–QKt1   Kt–Q1
29 R–Q1   P–K4

Adequately putting an end to White's brief initiative, though a more effective tactical opportunity occurred after 29 ..., B–Kt3; 30 R–Q7 in the pawn sacrifice 30 ..., P–K4; 31 B×P, Kt–K3 winning a piece.

30 Kt–Q5	R–B5
31 P–R5	Kt–B3
32 B–K1	R–R5
33 Kt–Kt6	

White must give up the position of one pawn holding two, for otherwise he loses the pawn altogether.

33 ...	B × Kt
34 P × B	K–K3
35 K–Kt1	R–R7
36 K–B1	P–QR4
37 R–Q3	P–R5
38 B–Q2	R–Kt7
39 B–K3	Kt–Q5
40 B × Kt	P × B
41 R–R3	

Not 41 R × P, P–R6; 42 R–R4, P–R7 and Queens after R–Kt8*ch*.

41 ...	K–K4

More direct than R–Kt5; 42 K–K2, K–K4; 43 P–Kt3, and Black is little further forward.

42 R × P	P–Q6
43 K–K1	

Against 43 ..., R–Kt8*ch*; 44 K–B2, P–Q7 winning.

43 ...	R × KKtP
Resigns	

For Black threatens K–B5–K6 with mate in the air.

To give White a stronger initiative by playing the KP forward two squares instead of one on its first move, the Russian school developed a different variation, while yet avoiding the hazards of the old Exchange Variation.

GAME 56
GRÜNFELD DEFENCE

Euwe   *Smyslov*

The Hague–Moscow World Championship Tournament, 1948

1 P–Q4	Kt–KB3
2 P–QB4	P–KKt3
3 Kt–QB3	P–Q4
4 Kt–B3	B–Kt2
5 Q–Kt3	P × P

After P–B3; 6 P–K3, O–O; the Schlechter Variation is reached. Schlechter as Black actually used this line as his version of the Slav Defence, thus: 1 P–Q4, P–Q4; 2 P–QB4, P–QB3; 3 Kt–KB3, Kt–B3; 4 Kt–B3, P–KKt3; 5 P–K3, B–Kt2; 6 Q–Kt3, O–O. Modern players regard Black's position as too lacking in dynamic energy.

6 Q × BP	O–O
7 P–K4	

Thus White has achieved his aim without loss of time. His centre is strong and Black is hard put to it to find an adequate continuation.

7 ...	B–Kt5
8 B–K3	KKt–Q2

Diagram 39

Black's last two moves initiate the Smyslov line. The unexpected text move is contrary to all theory except that of dynamics. Smyslov's idea is that the combined operation of Knights and pawns on the Q side plus the range of the KB along the diagonal will give adequate counter-play to meet White's centre.

9 Q–Kt3	Kt–Kt3
10 P–QR4	

An alternative line is 10 R–Q1, Kt–B3; 11 P–Q5, Kt–K4; 12 B–K2, Kt×Kt*ch*; 13 P×Kt, B–R6. Euwe aims to prevent Black getting so far with his QKt.

10 ...	P–QR4
11 P–Q5	B×Kt
12 P×B	Q–Q3

After this Black never ceases to exert at least a little pressure on the black squares.

13 Kt–Kt5	Q–Kt5*ch*
14 Q×Q	P×Q

15 Kt×P	R×P
16 R–QKt1	

Allowing Black more scope than he need. Better was 16 R×R, Kt×R; 17 P–Kt3, when the black Bishop is left biting on thin air.

16 ...	Kt(3)–Q2
17 Kt–Kt5	R–B1
18 B–K2	P–Kt6

Fixing a target on QKt7 which will not now run away.

19 Kt–R3

Offering his own KtP in the expectation that he will win the advanced black pawn. It says much for the fine judgment of the Russian master that he takes the offer without losing his own pawn.

19 ...	B×P
20 R×B	R×Kt
21 K–Q2	

Not yet 21 B–Q1 because of Kt–K4, threatening Kt–Q6*ch*, and if then 22 K–Q2, Kt–B5*ch*.

21 ...	Kt–R3
22 R(1)–QKt1	Kt(3)–B4
23 B–Q4	

Now if 23 B–Q1, R–R7 and the pawn still cannot be captured.

23 ...	P–K4
24 P×P*e.p.*	Kt×P
25 B–K3	Kt(2)–B4
26 B×Kt	Kt×B
27 K–B3	R–R4

Of course not Kt–R5ch; 28 K–Kt4, winning.

28 K–Q2	K–Kt2
29 K–K3	

Here if 29 B–Q1, R–Q1ch; 30 K–K3 (K–B3 or K–B1 would lose the exchange, while K–K2 is still met by R–R7), R–R7; 31 B×P, R×R; 32 R×R, R–Q6ch and wins.

29 ...	R–Q1
30 R–QB1	P–Kt3
31 B–B4	R(1)–QR1
32 B–Q5	

Now B×P would allow some horrible pins by 32 ..., R–Kt4; 33 R–B3, R–R6.

32 ...	R–R7
33 R(1)–QKt1	R(1)–R5
34 K–Q2	R–Q5ch
35 K–K2	

No better is 35 K–B3, R–Q6ch; 36 K–Kt4, R×P.

35 ...	Kt–R5
36 R×R	P×R
37 R–QR1	

A final disappointment. 37 B×RP fails against Kt–B6ch; 38 K–K3, R–R5; 39 B–Kt3, R–R6; 40 R–Kt2, Kt–Q8ch.

37 ...	Kt–B6ch
38 K–K3	R–Q8
Resigns	

So vigorous were these new forms of Grünfeld Defence that once more the wheel turned full circle, and the Russian school began to look to the oldest of all Grünfeld variations, the Exchange Variation, to give White the dynamic play they always sought.

GAME 57

GRÜNFELD DEFENCE

Geller   Smyslov

5th Match Game, 1965

1 P–Q4	Kt–KB3
2 P–QB4	P–KKt3
3 Kt–QB3	P–Q4
4 P×P	

It is typical of the alert Russian attitude to opening theory that a line long since discarded may be revived if it can be infused with new life. This, the Exchange Variation, was out of fashion from the late 1920's until after the Second World War because Black's counter-chances on the long diagonal plus his majority of Q side pawns proved too formidable.

4 ...	Kt×P
5 P–K4	Kt×Kt
6 P×Kt	B–Kt2
7 B–QB4	P–QB4
8 Kt–K2	

The first of the new improvements in White's play. The old move was Kt–B3, but this way the pin by B–Kt5 can be answered with P–B3.

8	...	O–O
9	O–O	Kt–B3
10	B–K3	Q–B2
11	R–B1	R–Q1
12	P–B4	P–K3

B–Kt5 was a good alternative, even though it would not win the white QP after 13 P–KR3, B × Kt; 14 Q × B, P × P; 15 P × P, B × P; because of 16 B × P*ch*. Probably Black preferred the text as finally preventing this last move, and he may have had in mind a game Spassky–Shishkin, Tallinn, 1959, which went 12 ..., B–Kt5; 13 P–B5, KtP × P; 14 B × P*ch*, K × B; 15 Q–Kt3*ch*, P–K3; 16 Kt–B4, though Black was not obliged to play such a weak 13th move.

13 K–R1

Already envisaging a K side attack and not wanting to give Black the chance of a tempo-gaining check later.

13	...	P–Kt3
14	P–B5	Kt–R4.

Better and more logical was KP × P; 15 Kt–Kt3 (KP × P, B × P is not much use), Kt–R4 (not P × P; 16 R × P); 16 B–Q3, P × P. But not 14 ..., KtP × P; 15 KP × P, KP × P; 16 B–KKt5, R–B1; 17 Kt–B4, with adequate compensation for the pawn. As played Black drives White's bishop where it is wanted for

the reinforcement of the attack, while his own knight is left out on a limb.

15	B–Q3	KP × P
16	KP × P	B–Kt2
17	Q–Q2	R–K1

White at once forestalls the threat of B–K5. Note how well White's defensive moves (Q–Q2 defending the KtP and Kt–Kt3 defending K4) combine with the attack.

18 Kt–Kt3

Not 18 P–B6, Q–B3.

18	...	Q–B3

Threatening 19 ..., R × B.

19	R–KB2	QR–Q1

It is too late to try and win the QP now. A last desperate chance was 19 ..., R × B; 20 Q × R, P × QP; 21 P × QP, B × P; 22 Q–B4, Q × R*ch*; 23 Q × Q, B × R; with some slight hopes.

20	B–KR6	B–KR1

The threat was 21 B × B, K × B; 22 P–B6*ch* and 23 Q–R6.

21	Q–B4	R–Q2
22	Kt–K4	P–B5

Not 22 ..., R × Kt; 23 B × R, Q × B; 24 Q–Kt8*ch*, *mating*.

23	B–B2	R(2)–K2
24	R(1)–B1	

Repeating the invitation to capture the knight but now planning a devastating attack as Black's acceptance of the offer shows. However, Black had little option, being threatened with 25 P×P, RP×P (BP×P; 26 Q–B8*ch*); 26 Kt–Q6, R–Q1; 27 Kt× KBP.

24 ...   R×Kt

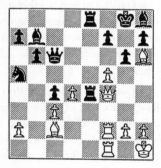

Diagram 40

25 P×P

A grim surprise. Clearly if 25 ..., R×Q; 26 P×RP*mate*. Nor can Black play 25 ..., Q×P; 26 Q×P*ch*, Q×Q; 27 R×Q, and if R–K8 against 28 R–B8*ch*, then 28 B×P*mate*.

25 ...   P–B3
26 Q–Kt5

Another elegant Q offer, threatening P–Kt7. Now 26 ..., R(5)–K2; would let the white KB in.

26 ...   Q–Q2
27 K–Kt1

Threatening 28 R×P, B×R; 29 Q×B, P×P (against Q–B8*ch*); 30 Q×P*ch*, K–R1; 31 B–Kt5, R(5)–K3; 32 B–B6*ch*, R×B; 33 R×R, winning because the text move has avoided the answer 33 ..., R–K8 *mate*.

27 ...   B–Kt2

R–Kt5 would fail against 28 P×P*dbl. ch*, K–B2; 29 R×P*ch*, B×R; 30 Q×B*mate*.

28 R×P	R–Kt5
29 P×P*ch*	K–R1
30 B×B*ch*	Q×B
31 Q×R	*Resigns*

If 31 ..., Q×Q; 32 R–B8*ch*, leads to *mate*.

A somewhat less satisfactory defence is the Bastard Grünfeld, in which Black plays P–Q4 without waiting for the parent move of Kt–QB3 by White. The disadvantage of this line is that after White's P–K4 Black must lose a move saving his Knight instead of being able to exchange it for White's QKt. The idea, however, is that the additional pressure exerted by this Knight on the Q side will prevent White from being able to exploit his gain in time, a tactical view which has hardly been borne out in practice.

GAME 58
BASTARD GRÜNFELD DEFENCE

Botvinnik   *Novotelnov*

Moscow Tournament, 1947

1 P–Q4	Kt–KB3
2 P–QB4	P–KKt3
3 Kt–KB3	B–Kt2
4 P–KKt3	O–O
5 B–Kt2	P–Q4

This Bastard Grünfeld is now the only form of Grünfeld open to him, and he would be better advised to content himself with P–Q3, leading to an orthodox King's Indian. In the Neuhausen–Zürich Candidates' tournament of 1953 Smyslov tried a Bastard Grünfeld against Euwe, as follows: 1 P–Q4, Kt–KB3; 2 P–QB4, P–KKt3; 3 P–KKt3, B–Kt2; 4 B–Kt2, P–Q4; and Euwe as White obtained the better game by 5 P × P, Kt × P; 6 P–K4, Kt–Kt3; 7 Kt–K2, P–QB4; 8 P–Q5, P–K3; 9 O–O, O–O; 10 P–QR4, Kt–R3; 11 Kt–R3, P × P; 12 P × P, B–B4; 13 Kt–B3, Kt–Kt5; 14 B–K3, R–B1; 15 P–Q6, B–Q6. Now, however, the game turned in Black's favour by 16 B × KtP, R–Kt1; 17 B–Kt2, B × R; 18 K × B, Kt–Q2; 19 Kt–B4, Kt–K4, whereas after 16 P–R5, Kt–R1; 17 B × KtP, R–Kt1; 18 P–R6 White retained good chances. The close balance of these positions shows that the Bastard Grünfeld, if a doubtful defence for

Black, is by no means a walkover for White.

6 P × P	Kt × P
7 O–O	P–QB4
8 P–K4	Kt–Kt3
9 P–Q5	P–K3

So far Black's loss of time with his Knight seems to have justified itself, for he now threatens to win a pawn on his Q4. To defend it adequately Botvinnik evolves a splendid tactical manœuvre which involves leaving his QKtP under-defended as well.

10 B–Kt5	P–B3

Not Q–Q2; 11 B–R3, B × P; 12 QKt–Q2, B × R; 13 Q × B threatening B–R6, an exchange sacrifice to win the long diagonal QR1–KR8, which was seen in the King's Indian Defence in Games 50, 51, and 52.

11 B–K3	Kt–R3
12 Kt–B3	Kt–B5
13 B–B1	

Giving back the gain of time, but retaining not only two Bishops but also the outpost pawn on Q5.

13 ...	P–K4
14 Kt–QKt5	

Threatening the manœuvre P–Q6 allowing access for his pieces to Q5 as in the preceding game. He has to play dynamically since Black has allowed the passed pawn with the obvious intention of following up with P–B4 undermining it.

14 ...	B–Q2

15 P–QR4	Q–Kt3
16 P–Kt3	Kt–R4

The correct strategical play was Kt–Q3 blockading the passed pawn after the Nimzovitch formula. The text move continues the play for win of a pawn on QKt4, the expected continuation being 17 Q–Q3, QR–B1 threatening P–B5.

17 R–K1

Another fine tactical-cum-strategical manœuvre. The move exerts pressure on the centre as a deterrent to Black's P–B4, and tactically it gains the advantage if Black wins the pawn because of the increased scope of the KB, as follows: 17 ..., B×Kt; 18 P×B, Q×P; 19 B–B1, Q–Kt3; 20 B×Kt, Q×B; 21 B–Q2, P–Kt3; 22 B×Kt, P×B; 23 Kt–Q2, threatening Kt–B4 with advantage.

17 ...	Kt–Kt5
18 Kt–R3	P–QR3
19 B–K3	Q–Q3
20 Kt–Q2	P–QKt4
21 B–B1	P–B4

Black has so far attained his strategical aims. His Q side majority is on the move, and his undermining of the white KP—and thereby of the passed QP—has started. With his next move, however, he forgoes the latter plan, and White's advantage in the passed pawn becomes permanent.

22 P–B3	P–KB5
23 B–B2	P×KtP

24 P×KKtP	B–R3

This shift to a new diagonal is very short-lived.

25 B–K3	B×B
26 R×B	Q–Kt3
27 K–B2	Kt–Kt2

Unable to advance further on the Q side, and having forgone his chances on the other flank, Black's tide starts to ebb.

28 Kt–B2	Kt×Kt
29 Q×Kt	P–Kt4
30 Q–B3	

A sudden resurgence of the long diagonal, but now with **White** exerting the pressure.

30 ...	Q–KB3
31 P×P	P×P
32 R×R	R×R
33 R–K1	P–R4
34 R–R1	R–K1
35 R–R7	Q–QKt3

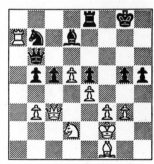

Diagram 41

So far Black has just managed to find time to rush from place to place defending everything. But **now**

Botvinnik ensures by an elegant sacrifice of the exchange that Black cannot return to the K side in time to prevent an entry there.

36	R×Kt	Q×R
37	Q–K3	P–KKt5
38	Q–Kt5*ch*	K–B1
39	Q–B6*ch*	K–Kt1
40	Q–Kt6*ch*	K–B1
41	Q×RP	R–R1
42	Q–R8*ch*	K–B2
43	Q–R7*ch*	K–B1
44	B×P	

The final stroke, recovering his material.

| 44 | ... | Q×B |

45	Q–R8*ch*	K–B2
46	Q×R	Q–Q6
47	Q–R5	B–Kt4
48	Q–B7*ch*	K–K1

If K–B3, White is able by a series of checks to bring his Queen to K3, when his material superiority is at last decisive.

49	Q×KP*ch*	K–Q2
50	Q–B5*ch*	K–K1
51	Q–R5*ch*	*Resigns*

For the white Queen can no longer be kept out of K3. (A few repetitive moves have been omitted in this score.)

CHAPTER XI

Sicilian Defence

It was hardly surprising that the Russians should be attracted by the fighting Sicilian Defence as an answer to 1 P–K4. After being almost entirely out of favour for the sixty years since Morphy's day—Capablanca, for example, practically never played it because, as he put it, "Black's game is full of holes"—the Sicilian Defence began to come into vogue under the influence of the Hypermoderns. Not surprisingly, the version then in vogue had some similarity to the Indian defences, for Black fianchettoed his K-Bishop and then played to combine pressure on the long diagonal with action on the open Q-Bishop file. This, the Dragon Variation, successfully rehabilitated the Sicilian Defence as a playable line.

A great deal of analysis was done on the Dragon Variation, until eventually all the dynamic possibilities, or at least most of them, seemed to have been whittled away, and in this respect the variation suffered in much the same way as the Queen's Indian Defence and similarly fell out of favour.

The Russians generally came to prefer other less exhausted lines of the Sicilian Defence, even though these might be very much more difficult to play, because they thereby retained dynamic opportunities. The following game, however, shows Black trying in vain to infuse some dynamic life into the old Dragon Variation.

GAME 59

SICILIAN DEFENCE
Ragosin   Taimanov
Leningrad Championship,
1945

1 P–K4   P–QB4
2 Kt–KB3   P–Q3

Played in preference to Kt–QB3

because, although only a transposition of moves, it avoids the dangerous Richter Attack, exemplified in Game 63.

3 P–Q4   P×P
4 Kt×P   Kt–KB3

In order to force White's QKt out in front of his QB-pawn. To allow the pawn to advance first would be to permit the so-called "Maróczy bind." This bind became less feared later because Black developed his game with Kt–KR3 and P–KB4, but there were still hazards as shown in the game Fischer–Reshevsky in the United States Championship, 1958, which went 1 P–K4, P–QB4; 2 Kt–KB3, Kt–QB3; 3 P–Q4; P×P; 4 Kt×P, P–KKt3; 5 Kt–QB3 (not using the bind move P–QB4), B–Kt2; 6 B–K3, Kt–B3; 7 B–QB4, O–O; 8 B–Kt3, Kt–QR4; 9 P–K5, Kt–K1; 10 B×P*ch*, K×B; 11 Kt–K6, and wins.

5 Kt–QB3	P–KKt3
6 B–K2	B–Kt2
7 B–K3	O–O
8 O–O	

That White cannot very well sharpen his attack by delaying castling was seen in the game Alekhin–Botvinnik at Nottingham in 1936, which went 8 Kt–Kt3, B–K3; 9 P–B4, Kt–B3; 10 P–Kt4, P–Q4; 11 P–B5, B–B1; 12 P×QP, Kt–Kt5; 13 P–Q6, Q×P; 14 B–B5, Q–B5; 15 R–KB1, Q×RP; 16 B×Kt, Kt×P; 17 B×Kt, Q–Kt6 *ch*; 18 R–B2, Q–Kt8*ch*. Drawn by perpetual check.

| 8 ... | Kt–B3 |
| 9 Kt–Kt3 | |

Preventing P–Q4.

9 ...	B–K3
10 P–B4	Kt–QR4
11 P–B5	B–B5

Diagram 42

A standard position in this variation, leading usually to simplifying exchanges, as in the Lasker line 12 Kt×Kt, B×B; 13 Kt×P, B×Q; 14 Kt×Q, B×P; or the Delayed Stockholm line 12 Kt×Kt, B×B; 13 Q×B, Q×Kt; 14 P–KKt4, or the immediate Stockholm line 12 P–Kt4, R–B1; 13 Kt×Kt, Q×Kt; 14 P–Kt5, Kt–Q2; 15 B×B, R×B.

12 B–Q3

The Johner line, usually met by 12 ..., B×B; 13 P×B, Kt×Kt; 14 RP×Kt, P–Q4. On this occasion Black tries to energize his game by a quicker central advance, but the result proves the unwisdom of this.

| 12 ... | P–Q4 |
| 13 P–K5 | Kt–K1 |

Exchanges will no longer serve. If Kt×Kt, White intended 14 B×B, Kt×R; 15 P×Kt, B×P; 16 Kt×P, B×P; 17 B–KR6, with a strong attack.

| 14 P–B6 | P×P |
| 15 B–QB5 | P×P |

16 B×R	KB×B
17 Kt×Kt	Q×Kt
18 B×B	P×B
19 Q–B3	

Materially there is still little in it, two pawns for the exchange being a fair balance, but White is now poised for a K side attack.

19 ...	Kt–Q3
20 QR–Q1	Q–Kt3*ch*
21 K–R1	Q×P

A clever trap which does not succeed, but if instead 21 ..., Q–B3; 22 Q×Q, P×Q; 23 KR–K1, P–B3; 24 Kt–K4, Kt×Kt; 25 R×Kt, the ending is in White's favour.

22 R×Kt	B×R
23 Kt–K4	

Avoiding the trap. 23 Q×P*ch*, K–R1; 24 Q–B6*ch*, K–Kt1; 25 Q–K6*ch*, K–R1; 26 Q×B, Q×Kt 27 R–B8*ch*, K–Kt2 leads only to a draw.

23 ...	B–B1
24 Q×P*ch*	K–R1
25 Kt–B6	B–Kt2
26 Kt–K8	*Resigns*

For if P–K5; 27 Q–B8*ch*, B×Q; 28 R×B*mate*.

In an attempt to obtain a more dynamic position with the Sicilian Defence the Russians took out of cold storage the old Scheveningen Variation, in which the black K-Bishop is developed on K2 instead of on KKt2. This variation had been a favourite with Euwe in the 1920s, but it gave Black a very cramped game and, like the King's Indian Defence at that time, was discarded as inferior. The cramped King's Indian Defence had now been shown to have powerful dynamic opportunities, and it was felt that the Scheveningen Variation might prove similar. Actually Black was not only cramped but suffered from a weak Q-pawn, and the variation remained very difficult for Black; the slightest error could lead to disaster, and often did even at the master level, let alone among less skilful players. The following is a case in point.

GAME 60

SICILIAN DEFENCE

Boleslavsky   *L. Steiner*

Saltsjöbaden Tournament, 1948

1 P–K4	P–QB4
2 Kt–KB3	Kt–QB3
3 P–Q4	P×P
4 Kt×P	Kt–B3
5 Kt–QB3	P–Q3
6 B–K2	P–K3

In the Scheveningen Variation Black makes no attempt to control any particular central squares, but he reserves options in the matter. He will, however, as in so many lines in the Sicilian Defence, make strong play on the Q-Bishop file in order to prevent White having a free run of the board. A somewhat sharper line for White was 6 B–QB4, P–K3; and the game Fischer–Olafsson, Stockholm, 1962, continued: 7 B–Kt3, B–K2; 8 P–B4, O–O; 9 B–K3, Kt×Kt; 10 B×Kt, P–QKt4; 11 P–K5, P×P; 12 P×P, Kt–Q2; 13 O–O, P–Kt5; 14 Kt–K4, B–Kt2; 15 Kt–Q6, B×Kt; 16 P×B, Q–Kt4; 17 Q–K2, B–Q4; 18 QR–Q1, B×B; 19 RP×B, P–K4; 20 Q–Kt5, P–QR3; 21 Q×Kt, P×B; 22 Q–B5, Q×Q; 23 R×Q, KR–Q1; 24 R×QP, QR–B1; 25 R–B2, P–QR4; 26 R(B)–Q2, P–B3; 27 R–QB4, K–B2; 28 R–B7*ch*, K–Kt3; 29 R–K7, P–R4; 30 P–Q7, R–B2; 31 P–B4, K–R2; 32 P–R4, K–Kt3; 33 R–Q5, *Resigns.*

7 O–O   P–QR3

A move which goes right back to Paulsen, Morphy's old opponent, who prepared similarly for the development of his Queen on QB2. In the true Paulsen system, however, the Q-pawn was not advanced.

8 B–K3   Q–B2
9 P–B4

So far all according to long established theory. Black can now continue non-committally with B–K2 or

continue to build up his Q side pressure with B–Q2 and R–QB1. In this particular game Black plays in a still more forthright style to put on the Q side pressure, but in spite of following a line strongly recommended at the time he finds that it leads to trouble.

9 ...   Kt–QR4
10 K–R1   B–K2
11 Q–K1

Preparing to play P–QKt3, which would foil Black's plan for the occupation of his QB5, and also threatening Q–Kt3 with a direct K side attack.

11 ...   Kt–B5
12 B–B1   P–QKt4
13 P–QKt3   Kt–Kt3
14 B–B3   B–Kt2

Better was P–Kt5, ensuring some counter-play on the Q-Bishop file, which White now prevents, leaving himself free to operate elsewhere.

15 P–QR3   Kt(Kt)–Q2
16 B–Kt2   Kt–B4
17 P–QKt4

Already he is confident enough to create a theoretical weakness, offering Black a strong outpost on QB4. He sees Black will not be able to complete the manœuvre Kt(4)–Q2–Kt3–B5.

17 ...   Kt(4)–Q2
18 P–K5   P×P

If Kt–Q4; 19 Kt × Kt, B × Kt;
20 B × B, P × B; 21 P × P, Q × QP;
22 Kt–B5, and White wins. And if
B × B, White gains a piece by 20
P × Kt.

19 P×P	Kt–KKt1

Now if Kt–Q4; 20 Kt × Kt,
B × Kt; 21 B × B, P × B; 22 P–K6.

20 Q–Kt3	B–KB1

What a comi-tragedy of a position!
If P–Kt3; 21 B × B, Q × B; 22
Q–B4 with a fearsome attack, and if
K–B1; 21 Kt × P*ch*, P × Kt; 22
B × B*dis. ch.*

21	QR–K1	Kt–R3
22	B×B	Q×B
23	B–B1	P–Kt3
24	B×Kt	B×B
25	Q–R3	B–Kt4
26	Kt–K4	B–K2

Diagram 43

27 R×P	

An elegant finish. Black cannot
reply K × R because of 28 Q × KP*ch.*

27 ...	Q–Q4
28 R×B*ch*	K×R
29 Q–R4*ch*	K–B2
30 Kt–Q6*ch*	K–Kt2
31 Q–K7*ch*	K–R3
32 R–K3	*Resigns*

For after K–R4; 33 ⌐R–R3*ch*,
K–Kt5; 34 Q–R4*mate.*

A more successful treatment by Black is seen in the following
game. The ending, with its Bishops of opposite colours, is a fine
example of Smyslov's excellent endgame technique.

GAME 61
SICILIAN DEFENCE
Petrosyan   *Smyslov*
Russian Championship, 1949

1	P–K4	P–QB4
2	Kt–KB3	P–Q3
3	P–Q4	P×P
4	Kt×P	Kt–KB3
5	Kt–QB3	P–QR3
6	B–K2	P–K3
7	O–O	B–K2
8	B–K3	O–O
9	P–B4	Q–B2
10	P–B5	

White's position looks good enough
for this early advance, but now the

dynamic force latent in the Scheveningen layout reveals itself. Better was the orthodox 10 Q–K1, Kt–B3.

| 10 ... | P–K4 |

Cheerfully leaving his QP backward and an outpost square for White on his Q4 in a manner which would have horrified the Classical school.

| 11 Kt–Kt3 | P–QKt4 |
| 12 P–QR3 | |

Occupation of the outpost square would lead to exchanges leaving his KBP weak. He wants to continue his attack with P–Kt4, but must first limit Black's Q side activities.

12 ...	B–Kt2
13 B–B3	R–Q1
14 Kt–Q2	

Now if 14 P–Kt4, Black plays P–Q4; 15 P×P, P–K5; 16 Kt×KP, Kt×QP; 17 Q–K2, Kt–Q2 and White's chances have all evaporated.

14 ...	QKt–Q2
15 K–R1	QR–B1
16 Q–K2	Kt–Kt3
17 Q–B2	Kt–B5
18 Kt×Kt	Q×Kt
19 B–Kt5	P–R3
20 B×Kt	B×B
21 QR–Q1	Q–B4
22 B–K2	Q×Q
23 R×Q	P–Q4

Black has judged the dynamics of his position very accurately, and with this surprising advance not only rids himself of a weakness but emerges with the better game. Should White hope to win a pawn by 24 P×P, then P–K5; 25 Kt×KP, B×KtP; 26 B–B3, B×RP and the two Bishops will give Black a slight but definite pull. As played, White secures Bishops of opposite colours and therefore decided drawing chances.

24 Kt×QP	B×Kt
25 P×B	R×BP
26 P–QKt3	P–K5
27 P–KKt4	P–K6
28 R–Kt2	R–Q7

Winning White's QP, but the technique of winning the resulting position is still very difficult.

29 R×R	P×R
30 B–Q1	R×P
31 K–Kt1	K–B1
32 K–B1	B–Kt4
33 P–QR4	P–KR4
34 P–R3	

If 34 P×RP, R×Pch and Black would have a second passed pawn.

34 ...	P–R5
35 P×P	P×P
36 R–B2	K–K2
37 R–B3	R–K4
38 B–K2	R–Q4

Not B–K6; 39 P–B6ch, P×P; 40 R–B5, forcing a drawn position.

39 B–Q1	K–B3
40 R–B3	B–B5
41 K–K2	K–Kt4

42 R–B3   P–Kt5
43 K–B1

He is now forced to give ground,
for if 43 R–Q3, then R–K4*ch*; 44
K–B2, R–K8; 45 B–B3, P–B3;
46 B–K2, R–KR8 and White is in
Zugzwang.

43 ...   R–K4

44 B–K2   B–K6
45 B–Q1   K–B3
46 B–K2   R–K5
   Resigns

For nothing can now stop the
black King from marching across the
board to QB8 to assist the queening.
A most masterly performance.

White thereupon developed sharper attacking lines by replacing the
quiet move 6 B–K2 with the more aggressive 6 B–Kt5 as in the next
game.

GAME 62
SICILIAN DEFENCE
Keres   Tolush
Russian Championship, 1957

1 P–K4   P–QB4
2 Kt–KB3   P–Q3
3 P–Q4   P×P
4 Kt×P   Kt–KB3
5 Kt–QB3   P–QR3
6 B–Kt5   P–K3
7 P–B4   Q–Kt3

Chosen on the assumption that
White has already overplayed his
hand with his 7th move, but safer is
B–K2 as played in the game Keres–
Fischer, Yugoslavia Candidates'
Tournament, 1959, which con-
tinued: 8 Q–B3, Q–B2; 9 O–O–O,
QKt–Q2; 10 B–K2, P–Kt4; 11
B×Kt, Kt×B; 12 P–K5, B–Kt2;
13 P×Kt, B×Q; 14 B×B, B×P;

15 B×R, P–Q4; 16 B×P, B×Kt;
17 R×B, P×B; 18 Kt×QP, Q–
B4; 19 R–K1*ch*, K–B1; 20 P–B3,
P–KR4; 21 P–B5, R–R3; 22 P–B6,
P×P; 23 Kt–B4, P–R5; 24 R–
Q8*ch*, K–Kt2; 25 R(1)–K8, Q–
Kt8*ch*; 26 K–Q2, Q–B7*ch*; 27 Kt–
K2, R–Kt3; 28 P–KKt3, P–B4; 29
R–Kt8*ch*, K–B3; 30 R×R*ch*, P×R;
31 P×P, Q×P(7); 32 R–Q4, Q–
R8; 33 K–B2, K–K4; 34 P–R4, Q–
B8; 35 Kt–B1, Q–Kt7*ch*; 36 K–Kt3,
P×P*ch*; 37 K–R3, Q–QB7; 38 Kt–
Q3*ch*, K–B3; 39 Kt–B5, Q–B8; 40
R×P, Q–K6; 41 Kt×P, P–B5; 42
R–Q4, K–B4; 43 Kt–Kt4, Q–K2;
44 K–Kt3, Q×P; 45 Kt–Q3, P–
Kt4; 46 P–B4, Q–Kt6; 47 P–B5,
P–B6; 48 K–B4, P–B7; 49 Kt×P,
Q×Kt; 50 P–B6, Q×P; 51 K–B5,
Q–B6*ch*; 52 K–Q5, P–Kt5; 53 R–
B4, Q–K4*mate*.

8 Q–Q2   Q×P

Preventing White's Q side castling with a pawn-grab that is notoriously dangerous.

| 9 R–QKt1 | Q–R6 |
| 10 P–K5 | P×P |

More disastrous was KKt–Q2 as in the game Keres–Fuderer, Göteborg, 1955, which continued 11 P–B5, Kt×P; 12 P×P, P×P; 13 B–K2, QKt–B3; 14 Kt×Kt, P×Kt; 15 Kt–K4, P–Q4; 16 O–O, Q–R5; 17 B–R5*ch*, K–Q2; 18 R×B, *Resigns*.

| 11 P×P | KKt–Q2 |
| 12 B–QB4 | B–K2 |

Not Kt×P; 13 Kt×P, with a savage attack.

13 R–Kt3	B×B
14 Q×B	Q–K2
15 Q×P	Q–B1
16 Q–Kt5	R–Kt1
17 Q–B4	Kt–B4
18 O–O	

He has reduced Black to such a sorry state that he can offer the exchange by 18 ..., Kt×R; 19 B×Kt, and the threat of Kt–K4 is quite overwhelming.

| 18 ... | Q–Kt2 |
| 19 R–B2 | Kt(1)–Q2 |

Diagram 44

| 20 Kt–Q5 | Kt×R |

Now he is forced to make this capture for if P×Kt; 21 R–Kt3, Q–B1; 22 B×QP, and the end is in sight.

21 Kt–B7*ch*	K–K2
22 B×Kt	Q×P
23 Q×P*ch*	K–Q3
24 Kt(4)×P	Kt–B3
25 R×Kt	Q–K8*ch*
26 R–B1	Q–K6*ch*
27 K–R1	B×Kt
28 Kt×B	QR–QB1

Against Q–B7*mate*.

| 29 Q×KtP | *Resigns* |

For a time P–Q3 quite supplanted Kt–QB3 as Black's 2nd move in the Sicilian Defence, since in that way Black could avoid the Richter Attack. At a time when the Dragon Variation was still in favour and the Scheveningen Variation considered inferior, Black was prepared to find every possible means of ensuring that he could develop his K-Bishop on KKt2 and would not be forced into the weakening development on K2. The Richter Attack virtually forced the K2 development and was accordingly much feared by players of the Sicilian Defence.

Then the Russians went a long way towards rehabilitating the Scheveningen Variation and the K2 development of the black K-Bishop was no longer looked on as disadvantageous. At once the Richter Attack lost much of its terror, and in the following game, for example, is quite cheerfully invited by Black.

GAME 63

SICILIAN DEFENCE

Smyslov   Botvinnik

The Hague–Moscow World Championship Tournament, 1948

1 P–K4	P–QB4
2 Kt–KB3	Kt–QB3
3 P–Q4	P×P
4 Kt×P	Kt–B3
5 Kt–QB3	P–Q3
6 B–KKt5	P–K3
7 B–K2	

Alternatively White can play Q–Q2 with O–O–O to follow, as in Tal–Nievergelt, Zürich, 1959, which went 7 Q–Q2, P–KR3; 8 B×Kt, P×B; 9 O–O–O, P–R3; 10 P–B4, B–Q2; 11 B–K2, P–KR4; 12 K–Kt1, Q–Kt3; 13 Kt–Kt3, O–O–O; 14 KR–B1, B–K2; 15 R–B3, QR–Kt1; 16 B–B1, K–Kt1; 17 R–Q3, B–QB1; 18 P–QR3, P–R5; 19 Q–K1, R–Kt5; 20 Kt–Q5, P×Kt; 21 P×P, Kt–K4; 22 P×Kt, BP×P; 23 Kt–R5, B–Q1; 24 Kt–B6ch, K–R1; 25 R–QKt3, Q–B2;

26 R–QB3 (here Tal admits he gambled on the ensuing complications), P×Kt; 27 R×P, Q–Kt2; 28 R×P, R–R5; 29 R–Q3, B–B2; 30 R–KB6, B–Q1; 31 R–B6, P–K5; 32 R–QKt3, B–R4; 33 Q–K3, Q–R2; 34 Q–R6 (allied to genius the gamble succeeds), R–Q1; 35 B×P, B–Q7; 36 Q–B6, Q–Q2; 37 B×B, *Resigns.*

7 ...	B–K2
8 O–O	O–O

This permits White to force the doubling of pawns on the K side, because Black's K-Bishop has to defend the Q-pawn. For this reason P–QR3 has generally been preferred here, but Botvinnik judges that his position with the positional weakness of the doubled pawn will have more dynamic strength than a position with a more solid K side.

9 Kt(4)–Kt5	P–QR3
10 B×Kt	P×B
11 Kt–Q4	K–R1
12 K–R1	R–KKt1
13 P–B4	B–Q2
14 B–B3	R–QB1
15 Kt×Kt	

This only strengthens Black's centre. Q–Q2, with a more gradual build-up of forces, would be better.

15 ...   P×Kt
16 Kt–K2

Preparing to get a strong grip on the centre with P–B4, an idea which Black immediately forestalls.

16 ...   P–Q4
17 P–B5

Hoping to fix the weakness of the doubled pawns so that they become a really permanent feature which can later be attacked. Nevertheless, the move gives up all hold upon the black central squares, a vacuum into which Black immediately moves.

17 ...   Q–B2
18 P–B4   P×QBP
19 Q–Q4   P–B4
20 Q×P(4)   B–Q3

Now the two Bishops make themselves felt.

21 P–KKt3   B–Kt4
22 Q–B2

There is nothing in 22 Q–B3, B–K4. The weakness of the black pawns is no weakness, because to the very end White cannot attack them. In fact, Black now shows that he has no expectation that White will kindly play P×P and undouble the pawns, so makes the one move that condemns them for ever to their doubled state, his object being to open the K file.

22 ...   P×P
23 P×P   R(B)–K1
24 R–B2   R–K6

Proving that an outpost does not necessarily have to be defended.

25 B–Kt2

If 25 Kt–B3, threatening Kt–Q5, Black calmly plays B–B3; 26 Kt–Q5, R×B; 27 Kt×Q, R×KtP*dis. ch* and wins. Or if White tries 26 B–Kt2, then B×P; 27 P×B, R(6)×P and wins.

25 ...   Q–K2
26 Kt–Kt1

Forced by the threat of R–K8*ch.*

26 ...   B–Q6

A devasting example of the power of the two Bishops in a fairly open position.

27 Q–Q2   P–B5
28 R–B3   R–K1
29 R–Q1

He cannot even simplify out of his troubles, for if 29 R×R, Q×R; 30 Q×Q, R×Q; 31 P–KKt4, B–K4.

29 ...   B–B4
30 P–Kt3   R–K8

Threatening B×Kt.

31 P×P   B×QBP
32 B–B1   R×R
33 Q×R   R–Q1
34 Q–B2   B–Q4

Now the harvest begins to come in.

35	Q–B3	B–Q5

Elegantly meeting White's last effort against the doubled pawns. If now 36 Q × B, B × R*ch*; 37 Kt × B, R × Q.

36	Q–Q3	Q–K6
37	Q × Q	B × Q
38	B–Kt2	B × R
39	B × B	R–Q7
40	Kt–K2	R × P

Resigns

The advance of Black's K-pawn to the fourth rank, leaving the Q-pawn backward, was a primitive manœuvre, long since recognized as leaving Black with serious weaknesses. It is amusing to observe how this very manœuvre has returned to favour among the leading masters.

In the Scheveningen Variation Black has already accepted the idea of a weak Q-pawn, so that in playing his K-pawn to K4 instead of to K3 he is not weakening the pawn any further but only his Q4 square. This additional weakness is offset, in the dynamic view, by Black having a less cramped position and one with more opportunities for a counter-stroke.

There was a glimpse of the idea in Game 61, where it occurred primarily as a device to block a dangerous attack, but the modern players of the Sicilian Defence, with their deeper understanding of the dynamics of the situation, frequently play it at an early stage of the game. White's attack is thus to some extent blocked even before it starts.

The next two games illustrate the move P–K4 by Black, although in the former game it is again partly motivated by White's play.

GAME 64

SICILIAN DEFENCE

Gereben   *Geller*

Budapest Tournament, 1952

1	P–K4	P–QB4
2	Kt–KB3	P–Q3
3	P–Q4	P × P
4	Kt × P	Kt–KB3

5	Kt–QB3	P–QR3
6	P–KR3	

Black is preparing to play a Scheveningen Variation, as evidenced by his fifth move, against which White has good chances so long as he acts with vigour. This can hardly be said of the text move.

6 …		Kt–B3

| 7 P–KKt4 | Kt × Kt |
| 8 Q × Kt | P–K4 |

In spite of leaving the Q-pawn backward and giving White a strong outpost on his Q5, this is less cramping than P–K3, and further it seizes an outpost square for Black on KB5 without loss of time. Black judges that the resulting position will give him chances sufficient to compensate for his weaknesses on the Q file.

9 Q–Q3	B–K2
10 B–Kt2	B–K3
11 P–Kt3	

It would have been better to take some of the force out of Black's 8th move by playing 11 P–B4, R–QB1; 12 P–B5, B–B5; 13 Q–B3.

11 ...	O–O
12 B–Kt2	P–QKt4
13 O–O–O	

His King is not particularly secure on either flank, but the K side offers Black fewer opportunities.

| 13 ... | P–Kt5 |
| 14 Kt–K2 | |

Note how Black's judgment on his 8th move begins to be justified. If 14 Kt–Q5, B × Kt; 15 P × B, and the centre is blocked and no frontal attack on the Q-pawn is possible, while Black has plenty of time to proceed with his attack by Kt–Q2–B4 followed by P–QR4–R5.

14 ...	P–QR4
15 P–KB4	Kt–Q2
16 P–B5	Kt–B4
17 Q–KB3	P–R5

The energy in his position threatens to burst out if White accepts the offer and plays 18 P × B, for then follows BP × P; 19 Q–Kt3, B–R5; 20 Q–R2, P × P; 21 RP × P, B–Kt4ch; 22 K–Kt1, R–B7; 23 Kt–B1, Q–R4 and wins.

18 P–R4	P × P
19 RP × P	R–R7
20 P × B	P × P
21 Q–K3	Q–R4

Threatening 22 ..., R × B; 23 K × R, Q–R6ch; 24 K–Kt1, R–R1.

22 P–B4

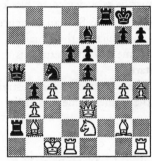

Diagram 45

22 ...	R × B
23 K × R	Q–R6ch
24 K–Kt1	

Not 24 K–B2, Q–R7ch; 25 K–B1, Kt × Pch.

146

24 ...   R–R1

Now Q–R7*ch* followed by Kt×P
ch is definitely threatened.

25 Kt–B1   Q–R8*ch*
26 K–B2   R–R7*ch*

A beautiful final stroke, which
won for Black the tournament prize
for brilliancy.

27 Kt×R   Q×Kt*ch*
28 K–B1   Kt×P*ch*
29 Q×Kt   Q×Q
30 R–Q2   Q–B6*ch*

31 R–B2   Q–K6*ch*
32 K–Kt2   Q–R6*ch*
33 K–Kt1   P–Kt6
34 R–Kt2   Q–Kt5

Threatening 35 ..., B×P; 36
R×B, Q–K8*mate.*

35 P–Kt5   B–Q1
36 R–QB1   B–Kt3
37 B–R3   K–B2
38 P–R5   B–Q5
39 P–Kt6*ch*   P×P
40 P×P*ch*   K–K2
     Resigns

The move P–K4 can, however, be played by Black in the Sicilian
Defence not in order to exploit some irregular action on White's part
in the opening, but as part of the ordinary defensive structure, the
theory being that the black QP is no weaker than if the KP had
advanced one square only, that its inability to advance to Q4 does not
matter as this advance is not themic to the Scheveningen Variation
anyway, and that the increase in dynamic possibilities for Black
offsets the weakness of his Q4. The following game illustrates these
views in practice.

GAME 65
SICILIAN DEFENCE
Stoltz   Boleslavsky
Groningen Tournament, 1946

1 P–K4   P–QB4
2 Kt–KB3   Kt–QB3
3 P–Q4   P×P
4 Kt×P   Kt–B3
5 Kt–QB3   P–Q3
6 B–K2   P–K4

Known as the Opocensky Variation, after the Czech master who

first played it in master chess, this
move would have been viewed with
horror by the Classical school and
would hardly have met with the
approval of the Hypermoderns, although Nimzovitch conducted a
certain number of games with central
holes and backward central pawns.

7 Kt–B3   P–KR3

Not a mere idle move on the flank,
but part of his fight for the white
centre squares by preventing B–
KKt5 with a pin on his Knight.

8	B–QB4	B–K2	
9	Q–K2	O–O	
10	P–KR3	B–K3	
11	O–O	R–B1	

Starting the standard Sicilian counter-action on the QB file.

12	B–Kt3	Kt–QR4
13	R–Q1	Q–B2
14	P–Kt4	

He cannot occupy the outpost square with 14 Kt–Q5 because of Kt × Kt; 15 B × Kt, B × B; 16 R × B, Q × P, yet if he captures on Q5 with his KP the whole of Black's plan is justified. While if 14 B–K3, preparing for QR–B1, with occupation of Q5 to follow, Black simply plays Kt × B.

14	...	Kt × B
15	RP × Kt	P–R3
16	K–R1	P–QKt4

Threatening P–Kt5 followed by Q × P.

17	P–Kt4	Q–B5
18	Q × Q	R × Q
19	R–K1	

Already White is short of a good plan, but a better chance was 19 Kt–Q2, R × KtP; 20 R × P. Now the two Bishops and the win of the QKt-pawn will be ample compensation to Black for his weak Q-pawn.

19	...	B–B1
20	P–Kt5	P × P

21	B × P	B–Kt2
22	K–R2	R × KtP
23	P–Kt3	R–B1

For White has a weak backward pawn as well now.

24	R–K3	R–Q5

Once more revealing how full of energy his position is. If 25 Kt × R, P × Kt; 26 R–K2, P × Kt with two pieces for the Rook.

25	R–KKt1	K–B1
26	B × Kt	B × B
27	R–Kt4	P–Kt5
28	Kt–QR4	

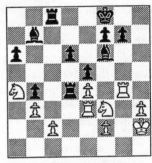

Diagram 46

28	...	R × BP

Elegantly winning the backward pawn, not to mention some other pawns as well, at the cost of the exchange.

29	Kt × R	P × Kt
30	R–K1	R × P*ch*
31	R–Kt2	R–B6
32	R–QB2	P–Q6

33 R–B7	B–K4ch
34 K–Kt1	P–Q7
35 R–Q1	B–Q5ch
36 K–R2	R–B7ch
37 K–Kt3	B × P

The game is now completely in Black's hands.

38 R–B4	R–B6ch
39 K–R2	B–K4ch
40 K–Kt1	P–Q4

At last this pawn advances, and to good effect.

41 R–B8ch	K–K2
42 R × P	B–B5
43 R–QKt2	B–K6ch
44 K–R2	R–B8
45 K–Kt3	R–Kt8ch
46 K–R2	

Not 46 K–R4, B–Kt4ch; 47 K–R5, B–Kt3mate.

46 ...	R–Kt3
Resigns	

There is no adequate defence to B–B5ch.

Versions of the defence where Black omitted the move P–Q3 altogether and reverted to the old P–K3 line, usually in a modified form of the old Paulsen Variation, were also resurrected and met with considerable favour.

GAME 66
SICILIAN DEFENCE
Unzicker   *Tal*
Zürich Tournament, 1959

1 P–K4	P–QB4
2 Kt–KB3	P–K3
3 P–Q4	P × P
4 Kt × P	P–QR3
5 P–QB4	

Suspecting Black of wishing to play P–Q4 in one move, he adopts a Maróczy-type bind.

5 ...	Kt–KB3
6 Kt–QB3	B–Kt5
7 B–Q2	

More usual is 7 B–Q3, Kt–B3; 8 Kt–B2, B × Ktch; 9 P × B, P–Q4.

7 ...	O–O
8 P–K5	B × Kt

The dynamic Tal prefers his KKt to advance rather than retreat.

9 B × B	Kt–K5
10 Q–B2	P–Q4
11 P × Pe.p.	Kt × B

Again avoiding a retreat by Kt × QP; 12 O–O–O, when White would have an attack.

12 Q × Kt	Q × P
13 R–Q1	

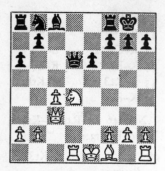

Diagram 47

White's position is apparently the better developed and looks quite threatening, yet by a sharp Morphy-like pawn sacrifice Black reveals its shortcomings and proves that 13 B–K2 would have been wiser.

13 ...	P–K4
14 Kt–B3	Q–KKt3
15 B–Q3	

He tries to correct his error, for if 15 Q×P, B–Kt5; 16 B–K2, Kt–B3; 17 Q–B3, KR–K1; with a powerful attack, while 15 Kt×P is even worse since a piece is lost after 15 ..., R–K1; 16 B–K2, Q×P; 17 K–Q2, Q–Kt4ch.

| 15 ... | P–K5 |

But in spite of his development, White is given no chance to recover.

16 B–Kt1	P–B4
17 Kt–R4	Q–K3
18 P–KKt3	Kt–B3

When he finally develops a minor piece as well as his queen, the win of a pawn is already certain.

19 R–Q5	Q–B2
20 O–O	B–K3
21 R–Q6	B×P
22 R(1)–Q1	B–K3
23 B–B2	QR–K1
24 Kt–Kt2	Q–B3
25 Q×Q	

A little more promising was 25 Q–B5, Q–K2; 26 B–R4, B×P; 27 P–Kt3, R–Q1; 28 Q–B4ch, K–R1; 29 R×R, R×R; 30 R×Rch, Kt×R; 31 Q–B2, P–QKt4; 32 Q×B, Q–Kt5; though Black still has a pull.

25 ...	R×Q
26 P–QR3	Kt–K4
27 Kt–B4	B–B2
28 R×R	P×R
29 R–Q6	Kt–B6ch
30 K–R1	R–QB1
31 B–Q1	R–B8
32 R–Q8ch	K–Kt2
33 K–Kt2	

B–Kt6 was threatened.

| 33 ... | Kt–K8ch |
| 34 K–R3 | Kt–Q6 |

Everything is suddenly attacked. 35 Kt×Kt, is no reply because of 35 ..., R×B; and the knight falls as well. White's only way out is to let more pawns go.

35 B–K2	Kt×Ktch
36 P×Kt	R–B7
Resigns	

CHAPTER XII

French and Caro-Kann Defences

THE French Defence yielded Black, as did the Sicilian, dynamic positions from which critical variations offering chances of victory might be developed. The French Defence did not perhaps present so wide a field of unexplored territory nor such a variety of critical variations as the Sicilian, but in some lines at least the chances it gave were more than enough to attract the attention of the Russian experts.

An excellent example is provided by the Chatard Attack, for in Game 29 Black's position was seen to be devoid of all energy, whereas in the following game, between two of the most prominent of Russian analysts, Black's energy breaks out continually.

GAME 67

FRENCH DEFENCE

Panov   Yudovitch

Russian Championship, 1937

1 P–K4	P–K3
2 P–Q4	P–Q4
3 Kt–QB3	Kt–KB3
4 B–Kt5	B–K2
5 P–K5	KKt–Q2
6 P–KR4	P–KB3

That the attempt to win a pawn by B×B is too rash was seen in Game 29. Of the alternative lines this is the most critical, Black obtaining some immediate activity at the cost of a weakness on the diagonal K1–KR4.

7 B–Q3

Probably the best move is also the simplest, namely 7 Q–R5*ch*, K–B1; 8 P×P, Kt×P; 9 Q–B3. But the text move with its reinforced threat of Q–R5*ch* is certainly vigorous.

7 ...   P–QB4

With this move the Russian master infuses new life into the defence. His game would be quite dead after the older move 7 ..., P×B; 8 Q–R5*ch*, K–B1 (not P–Kt3; 9 B×P*ch*); 9 R–R3, P×P; 10 R–B3*ch*, Kt–B3; 11 Kt–R3, Q–K1; 12 Q×P(4).

8 Q–R5*ch*   K–B1

(See Diagram 48)

9 Kt×P

Taking the bull by the horns and offering a piece, the alternative to which was giving up the centre by

9 KP × P, Kt × P; 10 B × Kt, B × B; 11 P × P.

Diagram 48

9 ...   P × B

Still playing for a dynamic position, which he would hardly have after 9 ..., P × Kt; 10 P–K6, Q–K1; 11 P × Kt, B × P; 12 Q × Q *ch.*

10 R–R3

He must go all out for attack or perish, for after 10 Kt × B, Q × Kt; 11 P × KtP it is very doubtful if he has adequate play for his material. Now if 10 ..., P × Kt; 11 R–B3*ch*, Kt–B3; 12 P × Kt, P × BP (B × P; 13 P × KtP recovering his material); 13 B–Kt6, K–Kt2 (against Q–R6*ch*); 14 P × KtP, P × P; 15 R–B7*ch*, K–Kt1; 16 B × P*ch* and wins.

10 ...   P–Kt5

11 Kt–B4

Not 11 Q × KtP, P × Kt; 12 R–B3*ch*, Kt–B3 and Black is a piece ahead.

11 ...   Kt × P

The only way to forestall the two threatened checks (on K3 and KKt3). The offer to return some material also assists in energizing his game.

12 P × Kt   P × R

It is at this point that White must find an adequate continuation or admit the failure of his sacrifice. 13 Kt–Kt6*ch* fails against P × Kt; 14 Q × R*ch*, K–B2; 15 Q–R7, Q × B; 16 P × Q, P–R7. The best line yet discovered seems to be 13 Kt(1) × P, K–Kt1; 14 R–Q1, Q–B1; 15 Kt–Kt5, P–KR3 (not Q × Kt; 16 B × P*ch*, K–B1; 17 R–Q3); 16 Kt(5) × P, B × Kt; 17 Kt × B, Q–B2; 18 Q–Kt4, P–KR4; 19 Q–R3, Kt–B3; 20 B–B4, Kt × P; 21 B–Q5.

13 B × P   R × B
14 Q × R   P–R7
15 K–K2   P–R8=Q

A triumphant progress by the KBP which Black made the key pawn in his defence only nine moves back. The scales are now weighted too heavily in Black's favour.

16 Kt–Kt6*ch*   K–B2
17 Kt–R8*ch*   Q × Kt

The most straightforward line is now to simplify. The alternative 17 ..., K–K1; 18 Q–Kt8*ch*, K–Q2; 19 R–Q1*ch* is less attractive.

18 Q × Q   Kt–B3
19 Q–R5*ch*   K–Kt1
20 Kt–R3

A last trap. If now 20 ..., Q × R;

21	Q–K8*ch*,	B–B1;	22	Kt–Kt5,

Kt × P; 23 Q–R5, B–Q3; 24
Q–K8*ch* and draws.

20	...	Q × P
21	Q–K8*ch*	B–B1
22	Kt–Kt5	Kt × P
23	P–B4	

Now Q–R5 would be answered by
Q–Kt5*ch*.

23	...	Q–Kt5*ch*
24	K–B1	Q × P*ch*
25	K–Kt1	Q–Kt5*ch*
26	K–B1	B–Q2
	Resigns	

The Winawer Variation, which had been reintroduced and developed by the Hypermoderns, especially fulfilled the dynamic requirements of the Russian school, and many critical games were played with this line.

GAME 68

FRENCH DEFENCE

Smyslov   Letelier

Venice Tournament, 1950

1	P–K4	P–K3
2	P–Q4	P–Q4
3	Kt–QB3	B–Kt5
4	P–K5	P–QB4
5	P–QR3	B × Kt*ch*

Games like the present, which restored White's position in this line, led Black to seek some other way of increasing his dynamic chances, and B–R4 was accordingly tried in this position. Black, however, came badly unstuck with this move in the following short game between Smyslov and Botvinnik in their 1954 match in Moscow: 5 ..., B–R4; 6 P–QKt4, P × QP; 7 Q–Kt4, Kt–K2; 8 P × B, P × Kt; 9 Q × KtP, R–Kt1; 10 Q × P, Kt–Q2; 11 Kt–B3, Kt–B1; 12 Q–Q3, Q × P; 13 P–KR4, B–Q2; 14

B–Kt5, R–B1; 15 Kt–Q4, Kt–B4; 16 R–QKt1, R–B5; 17 Kt × Kt, P × Kt; 18 R × P, R–K5*ch*, 19 Q × R, QP × Q; 20 R–Kt8*ch*, B–B1; 21 B–Kt5*ch*, Q × B; 22 R × Q, Kt–K3; 23 B–B6, R × P; 24 P–R5, B–R3; 25 P–R6, *Resigns*.

6	P × B	Kt–K2
7	P–QR4	Q–R4
8	Q–Q2	

Far better than B–Q2, as played on many occasions.

8	...	QKt–B3
9	Kt–B3	P × P

The alternative to this simplifying line is O–O; 10 B–B3, P–QKt3; 11 B–K2, B–R3.

10	P × P	Q × Q*ch*
11	B × Q	

Now he can afford to give up the idea of developing the Bishop on R3, since he can restrict Black's Q-Knight. Black accordingly plays to force White's P–B3, but gets a sharp surprise.

11 ...	Kt–B4
12 B–B3	B–Q2
13 B–Q3	R–QB1
14 K–Q2	O–O
15 P–R5	R–B2

The immediate threat was 16 KR–QKt1.

16 KR–K1

A Nimzovitch-like mysterious Rook move, which will achieve meaning only if Black plays P–B3, which very rashly he immediately does. Smyslov thought Black should strengthen his Q side by playing P–QR3, Kt–R2 and B–Kt4.

16 ...	P–B3

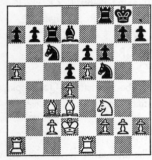

Diagram 49

17 B×Kt

Allowing Bishops of opposite colours in order to open the K file. So far from there being an increased danger of drawing, the presence of other pieces emphasizes the weakness of Black's Bishop in defence of the squares QB5 and K5.

17 ...	P×B
18 P×P	R×P
19 QR–Kt1	P–KR3
20 R–Kt5	B–K3
21 R(1)–QKt1	R(3)–B2

Not Kt–Q1; 22 Kt–K5.

22 Kt–K1	P–B5
23 P–B3	P–Kt4
24 Kt–Q3	K–R2
25 R–K1	R–B3
26 R–B5	

Now the threat of Kt–Kt4 is bound to loosen Black's game. As played, White finds a clever exchanging combination.

26 ...	R–QB1
27 Kt–Kt4	Kt×Kt
28 R×B	R(3)×R
29 R×R	Kt–B3

To answer 30 R–B7*ch* with R–K2, but White forces an advantage.

30 P–R6	P×P
31 R–B7*ch*	K–Kt3
32 R–Q7	Kt–K2
33 B–Kt4	Kt–B4
34 R×QP	Kt–K6
35 R–Q8	Kt×KtP
36 P–Q5	R–Kt3
37 B–B5	R–Kt2
38 R–QB8	

Forestalling R–QB2, and so ensuring the advance of his Q-pawn.

38 ...	Kt–R5
39 K–K2	Kt–B4
40 R–B6*ch*	K–R4

If K–B2; 41 R×QRP, R–B2;

42 R×QRP, and the two united passed pawns must win.

41 P–Q6   R–Q2
42 R–B7   *Resigns*

For after R–Q1 White wins by 43 P–Q7, P–Kt5; 44 P×P*ch*, K×P; 45 R×P, P–B6*ch*; 46 K–B2, Kt–R5; 47 B–Kt6.

One of the great exponents of the Winawer Variation was Botvinnik, and it was his prestige and success which did so much to establish its popularity. In later years, however, even he has not always found it an easy defence to handle and the older lines are beginning to attract attention once again. In the following game Botvinnik finds his favourite defence most roughly treated.

GAME 69

FRENCH DEFENCE

Tal   *Botvinnik*

1st Match Game, Moscow, 1960

1 P–K4   P–K3
2 P–Q4   P–Q4
3 Kt–QB3   B–Kt5
4 P–K5   P–QB4
5 P–QR3   B×Kt*ch*
6 P×B   Q–B2

This variation invites White to go for quick tactical play on the K side in the belief that it will not lead to any enduring advantage and then Black's positional pressure on the Q side and in the centre will assert itself. But Botvinnik finds he has caught a tactical Tartar.

7 Q–Kt4   P–B4
8 Q–Kt3   Kt–K2

Even P×P here has to be followed by Kt–K2 later and the same tactical opportunity is on. The positional players do not continue as Tal does but prefer 9 B–Q2, O–O.

9 Q×P   R–Kt1
10 Q×P   P×P
11 K–Q1

Not as bad as it looks, but the fact that he has to avoid checking captures of both his QBP and KP shows the positional validity of Black's plan.

11 ...   B–Q2
12 Q–R5*ch*   Kt–Kt3

A critical moment. It is still uncertain whether this move, which White will try and answer with Kt–K2–B4, is valid or whether he should content himself with K–Q1.

13 Kt–K2   P–Q6

This sacrifice of a further pawn is hardly justified by the ensuing attack and better was Kt–B3, or he could even have tried P×P; 14 Kt–B4, K–B2; 15 Q–R7*ch*, R–Kt2; 16 Q–R6, Q×P; 17 Kt–R5, Kt–B3; 18 Q×R*ch*, Q×Q; 19 Kt×Q, K×Kt; though after 20 P–B4, Black's centre pawns are not easy to mobilize.

| 14 | P×P | B–R5*ch* |
| 15 | K–K1 | Q×P |

Fearing that White's P–Q4 will leave him nothing to play for. Yet Kt–B3 and O–O–O, carrying on a pawn down, was his best chance.

16	B–Kt5	Kt–B3
17	P–Q4	Q–B2
18	P–R4	P–K4

It was still desirable to try and protect his king by Kt–K2 and O–O–O.

19 R–R3

The way Tal develops both his rooks in this game is most striking.

19	...	Q–B2
20	P×P	Kt(B)×P
21	R–K3	K–Q2

Not R–R1; 22 R×Kt*ch*.

22	R–Kt1	P–Kt3
23	Kt–B4	QR–K1
24	R–Kt4	B–B3

Diagram 50

25 Q–Q1

A magnificent conception. The attack has to be launched along the centre files.

25	...	Kt×Kt
26	R(4)×Kt	Kt–Kt3
27	R–Q4	R×R*ch*
28	P×R	

28 B×R, P–B5; would allow Black some small counter-possibilities.

| 28 | ... | K–B2 |
| 29 | P–B4 | |

Although Black has fought effectively to reduce the impact of the breakthrough, he cannot prevent it and now makes it worse by answering with a move that loses the exchange.

29	...	P×P
30	B×P	Q–Kt2
31	B×R	Q×B
32	P–R5	*Resigns*

Another version of the French Defence which led to critical situations was the Tarrasch Variation, illustrated in Game 28. In the following example Black avoids the inferior 3 ..., Kt–KB3 which was played there.

GAME 70

FRENCH DEFENCE

Botvinnik   Boleslavsky

Leningrad–Moscow Tournament, 1941

1	P–K4	P–K3
2	P–Q4	P–Q4
3	Kt–Q2	P–QB4

With a freer game than in most modern versions of the French Defence at the cost of a probable isolated Q-pawn. An unusual line is the Guimard Variation 3 ..., Kt–QB3; which leads to play akin to the Nimzovitch Defence, seen in Game 16. A game Keres–Botvinnik, Russian Championship, 1955, went 3 ..., Kt–QB3; 4 P–QB3, P–K4; 5 KP×P, Q×P; 6 KKt–B3, B–KKt5; 7 B–B4, B×Kt; 8 Q–Kt3, Kt–R4; 9 Q–R4*ch*, Q–Q2; 10 B×P*ch*, K–Q1; 11 Q×Q*ch*, K×Q; 12 Kt×B, P×P; 13 Kt×P, P–B4; 14 Kt–B3, K–K2; 15 B–Q5, Kt–KB3; 16 B–Kt5, P–KR3; 17 B×Kt*ch*, K×B; 18 O–O–O, B–Q3; 19 P–KKt3, KR–K1; 20 Kt–Q2, B–B1; 21 Kt–K4*ch*, K–B4; 22 P–B3, KR–Q1; 23 P–KR4, Kt–B3; 24 P–R5, B–K2; 25 KR–K1, Kt–K4; 26 Kt–B2, P–KKt4; 27 P×P *e.p.*, Resigns.

4	KP×P	KP×P
5	B–Kt5*ch*	Kt–B3
6	KKt–B3	B–Q3
7	O–O	Kt–K2
8	P×P	B×P
9	Kt–Kt3	B–Kt3
10	B–K3	

White has been playing to set up a blockade of the black Q-pawn by occupying his Q4. Black has resisted strongly, but with the fine text move, allowing the isolation of his own K-pawn, Botvinnik establishes his right to the square in question.

10	...	B×B
11	B×Kt*ch*	P×B

If Kt×B; 12 R–K1 and White even escapes the isolation of his K-pawn.

12	P×B	O–O
13	Q–Q2	Q–Kt3
14	Q–B3	

Another strong move, putting pressure on the two black squares Q4 and QB5.

14	...	R–Kt1
15	QR–Kt1	R–K1
16	KR–K1	Kt–Kt3
17	Kt–B5	

Now the occupation of the weak centre squares begins.

17	...	B–Kt5
18	Kt–Q4	Kt–K4
19	P–Kt4	QR–Q1
20	P–K4	

With control and occupation of the important squares completed, White now rids himself of his isolated pawn. Black would do best to let White exchange, for by doing so himself he not only accelerates White's doubling of Rooks on the K file, but exposes a weakness on his K4.

20	...	P×P
21	R×P	P–QR4
22	P–QR3	

With 22 Q–KKt3, threatening after P–B3 to play 23 R×Kt followed by Q×B, White could take advantage of Black's 20th move— a tactical opportunity missed.

22	...	P×P
23	P×P	P–B3
24	R(1)–K1	K–R1
25	K–R1	B–Q2

After this White is able to exchange the Bishop and add play on the white squares to his existing control of the black squares. For this reason it was better to play B–R4 to preserve the Bishop.

| 26 | Kt×B | R×Kt |
| 27 | Q×P | |

The beginning of a period of delightful combinative play. Of course if Kt×Q; 28 R×R*mate*.

| 27 | ... | Q–Q1 |
| 28 | Kt–B3 | R–QB2 |

Allowing White the opportunity for further liquidation; it was better to play R(2)–K2.

| 29 | Kt×Kt | P×Kt |

If R×Q; 30 Kt–B7*ch*, K–Kt1; 31 Kt×Q, R×Kt; 32 P–B4 with a great advantage. But White still has a devastating combination up his sleeve.

Diagram 51

30	Q×R*ch*	Q×Q
31	R×P	Q–KKt1
32	R–K8	R×P
33	R×Q*ch*	K×R
34	R–QKt1	

It is now a question of technique.

34	...	K–B2
35	P–Kt5	K–K3
36	P–Kt6	R–B1
37	P–R3	R–QKt1
38	K–R2	K–Q4
39	K–Kt3	K–B3
40	K–Kt4	K–Kt2

After R×P; 41 R×R*ch*, K×R; 42 K–B5, White wins easily.

| 41 | R–K1 | |

The pawn is still taboo, for if

158

41 ..., K × P; 42 R–Kt1*ch*. Meanwhile White threatens 42 R–K7*ch*.

41 ...	R–Kt1
42 R–K6	K–R3
43 K–Kt5	K–Kt2
44 P–R4	K–R3
45 P–R5	K–Kt2
46 P–Kt4	K–R3
47 K–R4	K–Kt2
48 P–R6	

White's method of making further
progress is elegantly worked out.

48 ...	P × P
49 R × P	R–Kt2
50 K–R5	K–R3
51 R–QB6	R–K2

Not K–Kt2; 52 R–B7*ch*, R × R;
53 P × R, K × P; 54 K–R6 and
wins.

52 R–B7	R–K4*ch*
53 P–Kt5	K × P
54 R × P	K–B3
55 K–R6	K–Q3
56 P–Kt6	R–K8
57 R–KB7	K–K3
58 R–B2	R–R8
59 P–Kt7	R–R8*ch*
60 K–Kt6	R–Kt8*ch*
61 K–R7	R–R8*ch*
62 K–Kt8	K–K2
63 R–K2*ch*	K–Q2
64 R–K4	R–R7
65 K–B7	*Resigns*

A defence which was less popular because it offered fewer opportunities of dynamic positions was the Caro-Kann Defence. Those
who still played it did so mainly with the idea of obtaining equality
and nothing more, and so most of the dynamic innovations were on
the White side in an attempt to avert these deadening intentions. The
chief innovation was the introduction of the Panov Variation, in
which it was only after many years of exhaustive practice and analysis
that Black found how to counter White's dynamic chances successfully.

GAME 71

CARO-KANN DEFENCE

Botvinnik   Kmoch

Leningrad Tournament, 1934

1 P–QB4	P–QB3
2 P–K4	P–Q4
3 KP × P	P × P
4 P–Q4	

Arriving by transposition at the
Panov Variation, usually reached by

1 P–K4, P–QB3; 2 P–Q4, P–Q4;
3 P × P, P × P; 4 P–QB4.

4 ...	Kt–KB3
5 Kt–QB3	Kt–B3
6 B–Kt5	

The Botvinnik line. The first idea
of defence against it was 6 ..., P × P
but White obtained a strong game
by 7 P–Q5, Kt–K4; 8 Q–Q4,
Kt–Q6*ch*; 9 B × Kt, P × B; 10

Kt–B3. An astonishing game occurred in the Moscow tournament
of 1935, when Spielmann in his game
against Botvinnik tried 6 ...,
Q–Kt3 and the continuation was
7 P×P, Q×KtP; 8 R–B1, Kt–
QKt5; 9 Kt–R4, Q×RP; 10
B–QB4, B–Kt5; 11 Kt–B3, *Resigns.*

6 ...	P–K3
7 P–B5	

The alternative line 7 Kt–B3
allows Black to transpose into a kind
of Queen's Gambit by 7 ..., P×P.
A game Hasenfuss–Flohr in the
Kemeri tournament of 1937 went
7 Kt–B3, P×P; 8 B×P, B–K2;
9 O–O, O–O; 10 R–B1, P–QR3;
11 P–QR3, P–Kt4; 12 B–R2,
B–Kt2; 13 Q–Q3, Kt–Q4; 14
Kt–K4 (better B–Kt1), Kt(3)–Kt5;
15 Q–Kt1 (not P×Kt, Kt×P; 16
Q–Kt1, Kt×B; 17 Q×Kt, B×Kt),
Kt×B; 16 Q×Kt, B×B; 17
Kt(4)×B, P–R3; 18 Kt–K4, Kt–
B5; 19 QR–K1, B–Q4; 20 P–
QKt3, P–B4; 21 Kt(4)–Q2, Q–B3;
22 K–R1, QR–B1; 23 Q–Kt1,
Kt×P; 24 K×Kt, Q–Kt4*ch;* 25
K–R1, Q×Kt; 26 R–K3, Q×QP,
Resigns.

7 ...	B–K2

The Black plan is to play Kt–K5
so as to prevent White's P–QKt4,
and then follow with P–QKt3, thus
breaking up White's pawn grip.

8 B–Kt5	O–O
9 Kt–B3	

A later improvement was 9 KKt–

K2, so as to retain the option of
P–QKt4. Then Black's Kt–K5 can
be answered with 10 B–KB4 and
not only is Black's P–QKt3 virtually
prevented but he will have great
difficulty in developing his forces.

9 ...	Kt–K5
10 B×B	Kt×B

Now he has the option of advancing his QKt-pawn, though he
does not elect to do so. The alternative line was Q×B, intending to
play Kt–Kt4 as a preparation for
P–K4.

11 R–QB1	Kt–Kt3
12 O–O	B–Q2
13 B–Q3	P–B4
14 P–QKt4	B–K1
15 P–Kt3	

Taking the sting out of Black's
threatened K side attack.

15 ...	R–B1
16 R–K1	Q–B3
17 P–QR3	Kt–K2
18 Kt–K5	Q–R3
19 P–B3	

Diagram 52

19 ...	Kt–B7
20 Q–K2	

Of course if 20 K × Kt, then Black draws by Q × P*ch*; 21 K–K3, P–B5*ch*; 22 P × P, Q × P*ch*.

20 ...	Kt–R6*ch*
21 K–Kt2	P–KKt4

22 Kt–Kt5	B × Kt
23 B × B	R–KB3
24 B–Q7	R–Q1
25 P–Kt5	Q–R4
26 P–B6	R–R3

Threatening Kt–B5*ch*.

27 K–R1	*Resigns*

With Black discovering how to take the sting out of the Panov Variation, the masters reverted to older lines, since it was found that after all they contained more dynamic chances.

GAME 72
CARO-KANN DEFENCE

Tal	Fuster

Portorož Tournament, 1958

1 P–K4	P–QB3
2 P–Q4	P–Q4
3 Kt–QB3	P × P
4 Kt × P	Kt–Q2

The old move was Kt–B3 allowing the doubling of a pawn, which this move is intended to forestall. It is not a line, however, which has proved entirely satisfactory in practice. Consequently B–B4, the other old move, has also been revived, as in the game Spassky–Foguelman at Amsterdam, 1964, which went 4 ..., B–B4; 5 Kt–Kt3, B–Kt3; 6 B–QB4, Kt–B3; 7 Kt(1)–K2, P–K3; 8 P–KR4, Kt–R4; 9 Kt × Kt, B × Kt; 10 P–KB3, P–KR3; 11 Kt–B4, B–Q3; 12 Q–K2 (if 12 Kt × B, Q–R4*ch*), B × Kt; 13 B × B, Kt–Q2; 14 P–KKt4, B–Kt3; 15 O–O–O, Q–B3; 16 B–Q6, O–O–O; 17 B–QKt3,

P–KR4; 18 Q–K3, KR–Kt1; 19 B–KB4, Q–K2; 20 P–Q5, Kt–B4; 21 P–Q6, *Resigns*.

5 Kt–KB3	KKt–B3
6 Kt × Kt*ch*	Kt × Kt
7 B–QB4	B–B4
8 Q–K2	P–K3
9 B–KKt5	B–K2
10 O–O–O	P–KR3

Kt–Q4 with simplification was better. White's chances are now exploited by the world's best tactician.

11 B–R4	Kt–K5
12 P–KKt4	

A sharp surprise for Black, who merely thought he was eliminating the white bishop. Now if 12 ..., B × B; 13 P × B, Kt × P; 14 P × P, and Black's king is suddenly in jeopardy.

12 ...	B–R2
13 B–KKt3	Kt × B
14 BP × Kt	

Still with his eye on the black king.

14 ...	Q–B2
15 Kt–K5	B–Q3
16 P–KR4	P–B3

Expecting 17 Kt–B3, O–O–O; 18 B×P*ch*, K–Kt1; and he will recover the KKtP.

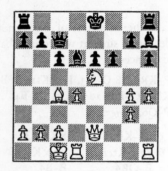

Diagram 53

17 B×P

Fixing the king in the centre and counting on the resulting tactical chances to provide the win.

17 ...	P×Kt
18 P×P	B–K2

He must keep at least one centre file closed, for if B×KP; 19 KR–K1, B×KtP; 20 B–Q7*dbl. ch*, K–B1; 21 Q–K7*ch*, K–Kt1; 22 B–K6 *mate*.

19 KR–B1	R–KB1

The threat now was 20 B–B7*ch*, K–B1; 21 B–Kt6*dis. ch*, B–B3 (not K–Kt1; 22 Q–B4*mate*); 22 B×B, R×B; 23 P×B, P×P; 24 R×P*ch*, winning.

20 R×R*ch*	B×R
21 Q–B3	

So that if 21 ..., R–Q1; 22 R×R*ch*, and mates next move. R–Q7 is also a threat.

21 ...	Q–K2
22 Q–Kt3	R–Kt1

Against 23 B–Q7*ch*, Q×B; 24 R×Q, K×R; 25 Q×P*ch*, winning; but White simply enters with his Q on the other side.

23 B–Q7*ch*	Q×B
24 R×Q	K×R
25 Q–B7*ch*	B–K2
26 P–K6*ch*	K–Q1

Of course not K–Q3; 27 Q–B4*ch*.

27 Q×P	*Resigns*

A piece is lost after B–K5; 28 Q–K5.

The younger generation went even further back to lines long since regarded as inferior, and infused them with new life as Tal does on the fourth move in the following game.

GAME 73

CARO-KANN DEFENCE

Tal   Golombek

Munich Team Tournament,

1958

1 P–K4	P–QB3
2 P–Q4	P–Q4
3 P–K5	B–B4
4 P–QB4	

Not entirely new, since it was recommended by Bogolyubov and tried by Alekhin, but still virtually an unknown line. Tal tried a less successful experiment in his second match with Botvinnik in 1961, when he played P–KR4 followed by P–KKt4 and came sadly to grief.

4 ...	P–K3
5 Kt–QB3	P×P

To avoid White's P–B5 and give himself a chance of using his Q4 for manœuvre. Also remotely in the air is the chance of attack on White's QP.

6 B×P	Kt–K2
7 KKt–K2	Kt–Q2
8 O–O	Kt–QKt3
9 B–Kt3	Q–Q2
10 P–QR4	

In case Black has any ideas on the QP by way of castling.

10 ...	P–QR4
11 Kt–Kt3	B–Kt3
12 B–B2	B×B
13 Q×B	Kt(2)–Q4

Q×P; 14 B–K3, would give White too much scope, and scope is all Tal ever asks.

14 Kt(B)–K4	Kt–Kt5
15 Q–K2	Kt(3)–Q4
16 P–B4	P–KKt3
17 R–R3	B–K2
18 B–Q2	Kt–B7
19 R–Q3	Kt(4)–Kt5
20 B×Kt	Kt×B
21 R(3)–Q1	

This rook has been developed from QR1 to Q1 by the most extraordinary rectangular manœuvre.

21 ...	R–Q1
22 K–R1	P–R4

After this White at once gets ideas about the weak black squares.

23 Kt–B6ch	B×Kt
24 P×B	K–B1

Not O–O; 25 Kt×P, with a winning break-through.

25 Kt–K4	P–R5

Bringing the knight back to the defence by Kt–Q4 was better.

26 Kt–B5	Q–B1

Diagram 54

27 P–B5

Initiating a wonderfully conceived

attack by which he penetrates to KKt7 at a cost of two pieces.

27 ...	KtP × P
28 Q–K3	P–Kt3
29 Q–Kt5	R–R2
30 R–B4	P × Kt
31 R × RP	R × R
32 Q–Kt7*ch*	K–K1
33 Q–Kt8*ch*	K–Q2
34 Q × P*ch*	K–Q3
35 Q–K7*ch*	*Resigns*

Because of K–Q4; 36 Q × BP*ch*, K–K5; 37 Q–K5*mate*.

CHAPTER XIII

Queen's Gambit Accepted and Declined

THE preceding chapters have indicated the predilection of the Russians for the asymmetrical defences on account of their dynamic possibilities, but this by no means eliminated all interest in the more direct replies to P–K4 and P–Q4.

Even the old Queen's Gambit Accepted, for example, produced its share of original thought.

GAME 74

*QUEEN'S GAMBIT
ACCEPTED*

Petrosyan   Bertok

Stockholm Tournament, 1962

1 P–Q4	P–Q4
2 P–QB4	P×P
3 Kt–KB3	Kt–KB3
4 Kt–B3	P–QR3
5 P–K3	P–K3
6 B×P	P–B4
7 O–O	P–QKt4
8 B–Kt3	B–Kt2
9 Q–K2	QKt–Q2
10 R–Q1	B–Q3

All book so far. Whatever line Black plays here, whether B–K2, Q–B2 or Q–Kt3, White still follows up with P–K4, trying for a central break.

11 P–K4	P×P
12 R×P	

But this is new, KKt×P having always been played before. The text avoids allowing Black to gain a move by 12 ..., Q–Kt1; 13 Kt–B3. And now if 12 ..., Q–Kt1; 13 R×B, Q×R; 14 P–K5.

12 ...	B–B4
13 R–Q3	Kt–Kt5

Safer was O–O.

14 B–Kt5	Q–Kt3

Diagram 55

15 Kt–Q5	Q–R4

White's startling move takes the sting out of Black's attack on the KBP, for now B×P*ch*; 16 K–R1, Q–R4; 17 R–KB1, and the open file merely benefits White. Nor can he play P×Kt because of 16 P× P*dis.ch*, K–B1; 17 P–Q6, B×P; 18 R(1)–Q1, R–K1; 19 Q–Q2, Q×P*ch*; 20 Q×Q, Kt×Q; 21 R×B, Kt×R; 22 R×Kt(7), B×Kt; 23 R×P*ch*, K–Kt1; 24 R×B*dis. ch*, and mates.

16 R–KB1	R–QB1

If now O–O; 17 Kt–K7*ch*, B×Kt; 18 R×Kt, B×B; 19 Kt×B, B–B3; 20 R×P, R×R; 21 Q×Kt, and wins.

17 Kt–B4	Kt(5)–K4

If P–KR3, there is the pretty line 18 Kt–Kt6, P×Kt; 19 B×KP, Kt(5)–B3; 20 P–K5. Such are the threats and pressures under which Black is now labouring.

18 Kt×Kt	Kt×Kt
19 R–R3	Kt–B5
20 R–Q1	Q–Kt3
21 Kt–R5	R–KKt1

22 R(R)–Q3	Kt–Q3
23 P–K5	Kt–K5
24 B–K3	

He could equally and more simply play 24 R–Q8*ch*, R×R; 25 R×R*ch*, Q×R; 26 B×Q, K×B; with material advantage.

24 ...	B×B
25 R×B	Q–B3
26 Q–Kt4	

Defending against the veiled mating threat and himself threatening 27 R×Kt, Q×R; 28 Kt–B6*ch*, P×Kt; 30 Q×R*ch*, winning easily.

26 ...	K–K2
27 R(1)–K1	P–B4
28 P×P*e.p.ch*	P×P
29 Q–R3	P–B4
30 P–B3	

Forcing the attack through at last.

30 ...	Kt–Kt4
31 Q×P	QR–B1
32 R×P*ch*	Kt×R
33 R×Kt*ch*	K–Q1
34 Q–Q3*ch*	*Resigns*

Besides the Pillsbury Attack, seen in Game 39, quieter forms of the Queen's Gambit Declined were often adopted, especially those leading to tensions in the centre arising from delayed forms of the Tarrasch Defence.

GAME 75
TARRASCH DEFENCE
Petrosyan   *Suetin*
Russian Championship, 1960

1 P–QB4	P–QB4
2 Kt–KB3	Kt–KB3
3 Kt–B3	Kt–B3
4 P–K3	P–K3
5 P–Q4	P–Q4

Staunton's old position in the Queen's Gambit Declined, which he developed further with a fianchetto of the QB.

6 BP×P	KP×P

The modern treatment is KKt×P with equality.

7 B–K2	P–QR3
8 O–O	P–B5

A development with no great reputation. But after his 6th move he has to reckon with an isolated QP.

9 Kt–K5	Q–B2
10 Kt×Kt	Q×Kt
11 P–QKt3	P–QKt4
12 P×P	KtP×P
13 P–K4	

The positional refutation of Black's whole plan of defence. It is all the more effective because Black has not yet started to get his king into safety. Nor does Black find the best answer, which is Kt×P.

13 ...	P×P
14 B–Kt5	B–KB4
15 P–Q5	Q–B2
16 B×Kt	P×B
17 B–Kt4	B×B

Not B–Kt3; 18 Kt×P, B×Kt; 19 R–K1, Q–K4; 20 Q–R4*ch*, and mates.

18 Q×B	Q–K4
19 Kt×P	P–B4
20 Q–R5	

The delightful key to White's last moves. Black dare not take the knight.

20 ...	O–O–O
21 Kt–Q2	P–B6
22 Kt–B4	Q–Q5
23 Q×P*ch*	R–Q2

If K–B2; 24 Q×P*ch*, R–Q2; 25 Q–K6, and Q×Kt is answered by 26 P–Q6*ch*.

24 Kt–K5	*Resigns*

For a time during the 1930s the Slav Defence appeared to offer all kinds of dynamic chances, and both Alekhin and Euwe adopted it with considerable frequency. But continuous analysis and practice seemed to show that with the best play Black was left with a game devoid of much chance and the Slav Defence suffered a loss of popularity in consequence. Smyslov alone of the Russians remained mildly faithful to the defence, but his experience was little more encouraging.

In the following game White adopts no very aggressive line, and yet Black still gets little or no play, which is symptomatic of the defence as a whole.

GAME 76
SLAV DEFENCE

Botvinnik	Smyslov

12th Match Game, Moscow, 1954

1	P–Q4	P–Q4
2	P–QB4	P–QB3
3	Kt–KB3	Kt–B3
4	Kt–B3	P×P
5	P–QR4	B–B4
6	P–K3	P–K3
7	B×P	B–QKt5
8	O–O	QKt–Q2

A line more generally preferred was 8 ..., O–O; 9 Q–K2, and then either 9 ..., Kt–K5 or 9 ..., B–Kt5. Smyslov himself had tried 8 ..., P–QR4; 9 Q–K2, Kt–K5; hoping to prevent the cramping of the Q side which follows White's P–QR5, but the efforts which Black has to make at this point in order to retain dynamic chances indicate that the defence does not easily yield such chances.

9 Kt–R4

A new and simplifying method of fighting for control of the white centre squares.

9 ...   O–O

Slightly more promising of dynamic play was the line 9 ..., B–Kt5; 10 P–B3, Kt–Q4.

10	P–B3	B–Kt3
11	P–K4	P–K4

The last chance of retaining any initiative at all, for if Kt×P; 12 Kt×B, Kt×Kt; 13 P×Kt, B×P; 14 Kt×R, B×R; 15 Kt×Kt, winning.

12	Kt×B	P×Kt
13	B–K3	

Having won control of the white centre squares, White turns his attention to the black squares, and for the next few moves Black is absorbed in fighting for these squares.

13	...	Q–K2
14	Q–K2	P×P
15	B×P	B–B4
16	B×B	Q×B*ch*
17	K–R1	P–KKt4

Thus far Black has at least held on to the black squares. The text move aims to prevent White's P–B4, but the subsequent play shows that KR–K1 was perhaps more promising.

18	P–KKt3	QR–Q1
19	B–R2	KR–K1

It would be worse than useless to play 19 ..., Kt–K4; 20 P–B4, Kt–Q6; 21 QR–Q1.

20	QR–Q1	Kt–B1
21	R×R	R×R
22	P–K5	

Now White moves on to the black squares after all. Black's reply is the only move to prevent 23 P–K6.

22	...	Kt–Q4
23	Kt×Kt	P×Kt
24	Q–Q2	Kt–K3
25	P–B4	P×P
26	P×P	Q–B3

Not to obtain a useless discovered check, which would only open a dangerous diagonal for White's Bishop, but to free his QB4 for the Knight in reply to the advance of the white KB-pawn. Saddled now with an isolated pawn, Black is devoid of winning chances, while his own King is by no means invulnerable, and taking vigorous advantage of the situation White now forces the issue with a most attractive attack.

27	P–B5	Kt–B4
28	Q–Kt5	R–Q2

After R–K1; 29 R–KKt1, Black would have no adequate defence for his KKt-pawn, but better was P–B3; 29 P×P, Q×BP; 30 Q–Kt2.

29	R–KKt1	P–B3
30	P×P	Kt–K5

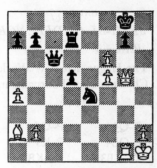

Diagram 56

31 P–B7*ch*

A delightful intermezzo, which by its renewed attack on the KKt-pawn forces an entry for the Queen on the eighth rank.

31	...	R×P
32	Q–Q8*ch*	K–R2

Of course not R–B1; 33 B × P*ch*, K–R2; 34 Q × R.

33	B×P	Kt–B7*ch*
34	K–Kt2	Q–B3
35	Q×Q	R×Q
36	K×Kt	R×P*ch*
37	B–B3	R–B5
38	R–Kt4	*Resigns*

Much more popular was the Semi-Slav Defence, a line which underwent great development. It is interesting that this was the form of defence which Breyer, the most dynamic of the Hypermoderns, especially favoured, and it provides therefore one more indication that the Russian school is working on the direct lines of the original Hypermodern idea.

GAME 77
SEMI-SLAV DEFENCE
Botvinnik   *Euwe*
The Hague–Moscow World Championship Tournament, 1948

1	P–Q4	P–Q4
2	P–QB4	P–K3
3	Kt–KB3	Kt–KB3
4	Kt–B3	P–B3
5	P–K3	

At any time since Pillsbury's day one might have expected B–Kt5 here, but the Russians generally, and Botvinnik in particular, prefer non-committal dynamic moves to more direct assaults which offer fewer possibilities of later subtlety and energy.

| 5 | ... | QKt–Q2 |
| 6 | B–Q3 | B–Kt5 |

Romi's line to avoid the hazards of the Meran Variation. Other lines are the less pointed B–Q3 and B–K2. The object of the text move is to relieve pressure on Black's QP so as to permit a later P–K4.

| 7 | P–QR3 | B–R4 |

Avoiding B × Kt which, after both sides had castled, Alekhin played against Euwe himself in their 1937 match, but without success.

8	Q–B2	Q–K2
9	B–Q2	P × P
10	B × BP	P–K4
11	O–O	O–O
12	QR–K1	B–B2
13	Kt–K4	

The strategical preliminaries having been successfully completed on both sides, there comes the first direct threat in the game in the form of B–Kt4.

| 13 | ... | Kt × Kt |
| 14 | Q × Kt | P–QR4 |

He weakens his Q side to prevent 15 B–Kt4, B–Q3; 16 B × B, Q × B; 17 P × P, but a more solid method was 14 ..., Kt–B3; 15 Q–R4, P–K5; 16 B–Kt4, B–Q3; 17 B × B, Q × B; 18 Kt–Q2.

15 B–R2

Envisaging the pawn sacrifice two moves later, or else he would have moved the other Bishop in order to make room for the Knight.

15 ...	Kt–B3
16 Q–R4	P–K5
17 Kt–K5	B × Kt
18 P × B	Q × KP
19 B–B3	Q–K2
20 P–B3	

The climax of the combination. If in reply 20 ..., P × P; 21 B–Kt1, P–R3; 22 R × P, Kt–Q4; 23 R–Kt3, Q × Q; 24 R × P*ch*, K–R1; 25 R–R7*dbl. ch*, K–Kt1; 26 R–R8 *mate*—a wonderful conception. The best chance for Black now is B–K3; 21 B–Kt1, Kt–Q4; 22 Q × Q, Kt × Q; 23 B × KP.

20 ...	Kt–Q4
21 Q × Q	Kt × Q
22 P × P	

As a result of his combination he can seize the open Q file at his pleasure. Black has one Rook tied to his QRP and the other to his KBP.

22 ...	P–QKt3

Trying to develop his Bishop by eliminating one weakness, for if B–Kt5; 23 R–B4, B–R4; 24 P–KKt4, B–Kt3; 25 R–Q1, KR–Q1; 26 R × R*ch*, R × R; 27 B × RP.

23 R–Q1	Kt–Kt3

The threat was 24 R × P, R × R; 25 R–Q8*mate*.

24 R–Q6	B–R3
25 R–B2	B–Kt4
26 P–K5	

Reserving R–Q7 until the subsequent threats of R–QKt7 or R × KBP are irresistible.

26 ...	Kt–K2

If QR–K1; 27 P–K6, P × P; 28 B × P*ch*, K–R1; 29 R–Q7, R × B; 30 R × P.

27 P–K4	

Preventing Kt–Q4.

27 ...	P–B4

The QKtP is doomed anyway by the threat of 28 R–Q7, QR–K1; 29 R–Kt7.

28 P–K6	

Much better than 28 R × KtP, B–B3; 29 P–K6, B × P; 30 P × P *ch*, K–R1. If Black now replies 28 ..., P × P White wins by 29 R × KP, R × R; 30 K × R, K–B1; 31 B × P*ch*, K × B; 32 R × Kt*ch*.

28 ...	P–B3
29 R × KtP	B–B3
30 R × B	

Resistance is finally broken.

30 ...	Kt × R
31 P–K7*dis. ch*	R–B2
32 B–Q5	*Resigns*

An elegant finish, and much stronger than B × R*ch*. Now if 32 ..., R–QB1; 33 P–K8 = Q*ch*, R × Q; 34 B × Kt, R(1)–K2; 35 B–Q5, R–R2; 36 B × R*ch* coming out a piece ahead.

If White on the other hand elected not to give Black the chance of playing the Meran Variation by playing 5 B–Kt5, then there was an extremely critical line worked out by the Russians for Black which quickly unbalanced the position and led to highly combinative possibilities. This, the Anti-Meran Gambit or Russian Variation, is beautifully illustrated in the following game.

GAME 78
SEMI-SLAV DEFENCE
Denker   *Botvinnik*

Russo-American Match, 1945

1 P–Q4	P–Q4
2 P–QB4	P–K3
3 Kt–QB3	P–QB3
4 Kt–B3	Kt–B3
5 B–Kt5	P×P
6 P–K4	

The critical lines which follow can be avoided by 6 P–QR4. Donner–Kotov, Venice, 1950, continued 6 P–QR4, B–Kt5; 7 P–K4, B×Kt*ch*; 8 P×B, Q–R4; 9 P–K5, Kt–K5; 10 B–Q2, Q–Q4; 11 Q–B2, P–QB4; 12 B–K3, Kt–QB3; 13 B–K2, P×P; 14 P×P, Kt–Kt5; 15 Q–B1, P–B6; 16 O–O, B–Q2; 17 Kt–K1, R–QB1; 18 P–B3, Kt–Q7; 19 B×Kt, Kt–R7; 20 R×Kt, Q×R; 21 B–KKt5, P–KR3; 22 B–Q3, P×B; 23 Q×KtP, Q–Q7; 24 P–B4, B–B3; 25 Q–Kt3, P–KKt3; *Resigns.*

6 ...	P–Kt4
7 P–K5	P–KR3

8 B–R4	P–Kt4
9 KKt×P	P×Kt

The critical nature of this line is well illustrated in the alternative move of 9 ..., Kt–Q4. A game Fridstein–Yudovitch, played in the Moscow Championship semi-finals of 1943, continued 9 ..., Kt–Q4; 10 Kt×BP, Q×B; 11 Kt×R, B–Kt5; 12 Q–Q2, P–B4; 13 P×P, Kt–Q2; 14 O–O–O, Kt×KP; 15 B–K2, B–Kt2; 16 P–KKt3, Q–B3; 17 P–B4, Q×Kt; 18 B–R5*ch*, Kt–B2; 19 Q–K2, K–B1; 20 B×Kt (correct was Q×KP), K×B; 21 Kt×Kt, B×Kt; 22 Q–R5*ch*, K–K2; 23 R×B, P×R; 24 Q×QP, R–Q1; 25 Q–Kt7*ch*, K–B1; 26 Q×KtP, B–Q7*ch*; 27 K–Kt1, Q–Q5; 28 Q–B6, Q–Q6*ch*; 29 K–R1, B–B6, *Resigns.*

10 B×KtP	QKt–Q2
11 P×Kt	B–QKt2
12 B–K2	Q–Kt3
13 O–O	O–O–O

Black's advantage in return for his pawn is now apparent. His Q side majority is already more advanced than White's K side majority, and moreover it can move on without exposing his King to the same extent as an advance by White would do.

14	P–QR4	P–Kt5
15	Kt–K4	P–B4
16	Q–Kt1	Q–B2
17	Kt–Kt3	

White's King is already under fire, but as the subsequent course of the game shows, a better defence was P–R3, going a little way towards blocking the activities of Black's KR on the file.

17	...	P×P
18	B×P	

Revealing the purpose of his 16th move. Black's majority is reduced to a passed QP. On the other hand, White's weakness on the diagonal QKt7–KKt2 now makes itself felt.

18	...	Q–B3
19	P–B3	P–Q6

A neat tactical move, opening up still further lines against the white King and threatening either 20 ..., Q×B followed by 21 R–B1, B–B4 *ch*; or 20 ..., Q–B4*ch* followed by Q×QB.

20	Q–B1	B–B4*ch*
21	K–R1	

Naturally if 21 B–K3, then P–Q7 wins.

21	...	Q–Q3
22	Q–B4	

Diagram 57

22	...	R×P*ch*

A fine combinative finish.

23	K×R	R–R1*ch*
24	Q–R4	

There is no defence, for if 24 Kt–R5, then follows R×Kt*ch*; 25 K–Kt3, R×B*ch*.

24	...	R×Q*ch*
25	B×R	Q–B5
	Resigns	

One of his Bishops must now be lost as well.

A more successful method of leaving Black's game without dynamic possibilities was found to lie in switching altogether from the normal close treatment given to the Semi-Slav Defence and employing an open treatment more reminiscent of the romantic days of gambit play.

GAME 79

SEMI-SLAV DEFENCE

Taimanov   *H. Steiner*

Saltsjöbaden Tournament,
1952

1 P–Q4	P–Q4
2 P–QB4	P–K3
3 Kt–QB3	P–QB3
4 P–K4	

The Open Variation, which entirely changes the character of the game.

4 ...	P×KP
5 Kt×P	B–Kt5*ch*
6 B–Q2	Q×P

Accepting the gambit, which can be safely declined by B×B*ch*; 7 Q×B, Kt–B3.

7 B×B	Q×Kt*ch*
8 B–K2	Kt–QR3

Q×KtP; 9 B–KB3 would merely help to give White a still greater lead in development.

9 B–Q6

An improvement on the older B–B3. A game Bronstein–Kotov in the Budapest Candidates' tournament of 1950 continued 9 B–B3, Kt–K2; 10 B×P, R–KKt1; 11 B–B3, Q×KtP; 12 Q–Q2, Q×R;

13 O–O–O, Kt–Q4; 14 Kt–B3, Q×R*ch*; 15 B×Q, Kt×B; 16 Q×Kt, K–K2; 17 Kt–K5, B–Q2; 18 Q–R3*ch*, P–B4; 19 Q–KB3, QR–Q1; 20 Q×P*ch*, K–Q3; 21 Q–B4, R(Q)–KB1; 22 Kt–B7*dbl. ch*, K–K2; 23 B–R5, B–B3; 24 Q–Q6*ch*, K–B3; 25 Kt–R6, R–Kt8 *ch*; 26 K–Q2, K–Kt2; 27 Kt–Kt4, R×Kt; 28 Q–K7*ch*, K–R3; 29 B×R, R×P*ch*; 30 K–K3, R–B8; 31 P–KR4, K–Kt3; 32 B–R5*ch*, *Resigns.*

9 ...	B–Q2
10 Kt–B3	P–QB4
11 Kt–K5	B–B3
12 Kt×B	P×Kt

Not Q×Kt; 13 B–B3, Q–Q2; 14 B–K5, and one of the Knight's pawns must fall.

13 O–O	Kt–K2

Diagram 58

14 Q–R4

The beginning of the end. If Black answers Q × B, then 15 Q × Kt, Q–K5; 16 KR–K1, and Black's pawn on QB6 can no longer be held.

If Q–R5; 17 B × Kt(4) wins a piece, and if Q × P; 17 B × Kt(7), K × B; 18 P–QR3 again wins a piece.

14 ...	Kt–Kt5	
15 B × P	P–QR4	

Now if Q × B; 16 Q × Kt, threatening Q–Kt7.

16 B–B3	Q–B7	

17	P–QKt3	R–QB1
18	Q × P	Kt–Q6
19	B–K4	Q–K7
20	KB × Kt	Q × B
21	QR–Q1	Q–B4
22	Q–R7	*Resigns*

CHAPTER XIV

Ruy Lopez

JUST as 1 P–Q4 was still often met with P–Q4, so, for all the new emphasis upon the Sicilian Defence, was 1 P–K4 met with P–K4, and especially where it led to the Ruy Lopez. Indeed, the Ruy Lopez remained as vigorous as ever and offered an apparently endless string of new refinements.

Of all the defences the Morphy Defence continued to be one of the most favoured, since the close and complicated nature of the opening led to positions which were capable of dynamic exploitation. A typically new outlook in an old line is seen in the following game at the 13th move.

GAME 80
RUY LOPEZ
Geller   *Keres*
Russian Championship, 1951

1	P–K4	P–K4
2	Kt–KB3	Kt–QB3
3	B–Kt5	P–QR3
4	B–R4	Kt–B3
5	O–O	B–K2
6	R–K1	P–QKt4
7	B–Kt3	O–O
8	P–B3	P–Q3
9	P–KR3	Kt–QR4
10	B–B2	P–B4
11	P–Q4	Q–B2
12	QKt–Q2	BP×P
13	P×P	B–Kt2

Keres' improvement on the old Kt–B3, after which White may have nothing better than to close the centre with P–Q5, a move which had been discarded as a response to Kt–B3. The move would be better here since now the black QKt would be left out on a limb; but the bishop would then simply return by B–B1 so as to play Kt–Kt2–B4, and White has gained nothing.

14 Kt–B1

Playing for a more dynamic game than would follow P–Q5.

14	...	QR–B1
15	B–Kt1	P–Q4

The dynamic idea behind Black's 13th move now becomes apparent. White gets nothing by replying 16 P×KP, Kt×P; 17 B–K3, Kt–B5;

18 Kt–Q4, P–B3; nor by 17 Kt–Kt3, P–B4; 18 P×P*e.p.*, B×P; 19 Kt×Kt, P×Kt; 20 B×P, B×B; 21 R×B, Q–B7.

| 16 P×QP | P×P |

The purpose of White's 15th move, in preference to B–Q3, now makes itself apparent, for if 15 B–Q3 had been played, Black could continue with 16 ..., P–K5; 17 B×KP, Kt×B; 18 R×Kt, B×P; 19 R–K1, Q–Kt2 with two Bishops and some pressure for his pawn. But with the Bishop on QKt1, Black's 16 ..., P–K5 would be answered by 17 Kt–Kt5. On such small refinements do the dynamics of modern chess depend.

17 B–Kt5	P–R3
18 B–R4	Kt×P
19 Q–Q3	P–Kt3
20 B–Kt3	B–Q3
21 B×B	Q×B
22 Q–Q2	

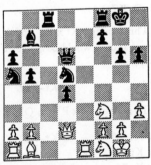

Diagram 59

Expecting the answer 22 ..., Kt–QB5; 23 Q×RP, threatening Kt–Kt5 winning. But play on the flanks in preference to the centre is notoriously dangerous, although in this position the proof of that fact calls for a display of high genius. Correct was Q×QP, while the last chance was B–K4 next move.

22 ...	Kt–KB5
23 Q×Kt(R)	B×Kt
24 P×B	Kt×P*ch*
25 K–Kt2	Kt–B5*ch*
26 K–Kt1	Q–Q4

The move on which Black has based his sacrifice. He threatens both Q×BP–Kt7*mate* and Q–R4–R6–Kt7*mate*. If 27 B–K4, Q–R4; 28 Q–Q2, Q–Kt4*ch*; 29 Kt–Kt3, Kt–R6*ch* winning the Queen.

27 Kt–Kt3

To answer Q × BP with 28 B–K4.

27 ...	P–Q6
28 Kt–K4	Q–KB4
29 Q–Kt4	

So that now if Q–R6, he can play 30 Kt–B6*ch*, K–R1; 31 Q×Kt.

29 ...   KR–K1
Resigns

For the threat is 30 ..., R×Kt; 31 Q×R, Q–Kt4*ch* and mates.

When, however, Black tried to improve this line by playing the move B–Kt2 at an earlier stage the position did not turn out to be as dynamic as was perhaps hoped. The following game is a striking example.

GAME 81

RUY LOPEZ

Keres   Gligoric

Zürich Tournament, 1959

1	P–K4	P–K4
2	Kt–KB3	Kt–QB3
3	B–Kt5	P–QR3
4	B–R4	Kt–B3
5	O–O	B–K2
6	R–K1	P–QKt4
7	B–Kt3	O–O
8	P–B3	P–Q3
9	P–KR3	B–Kt2
10	P–Q4	Kt–QR4
11	B–B2	Kt–B5

This proves loss of time. He has nothing better than P–B4, trying to get back into the book, and thus his novel 9th move already looks doubtful.

12	P–QKt3	Kt–Kt3
13	QKt–Q2	

Not 13 P×P, P×P; 14 Q×Q, QR×Q; 15 Kt×P, Kt×P; 16 B×Kt, B×B; 17 R×B, R–Q8*ch*; 18 K–R2, R×B.

13	...	QKt–Q2
14	B–Kt2	P–B4

He comes to it at last, but meanwhile White has made progress in his development.

15	Kt–B1	R–K1
16	P–QR4	B–KB1
17	Kt–Kt3	Q–B2
18	Q–Q3	P–B5
19	KtP×P	P×BP
20	Q–Q2	P–Kt3

Trying to get some play for his KB, but he would do better to defer this weakening move and try for play on the open file by QR–Kt1.

21	B–R3	QR–Q1
22	QR–Kt1	B–B1
23	Q–K3	B–KKt2
24	P×P	P×P
25	KR–Q1	B–B1

Forced to admit another loss of time in order to meet the threat of B–Q6.

26	B×B	R×B
27	Q–Kt5	Kt–K1
28	Q–K7	

Threatening Kt×P, which if played at once would be answered by P–B3.

28	...	Kt–Kt2

To answer Kt×P with QR–K1.

29	Kt–B1	Kt–K3
30	Kt–K3	Kt–B5
31	K–B1	P–B3
32	Kt–Kt4	

Threatening 33 R×Kt, R×R;
34 Kt×P*ch*.

32 ...   Kt–Q6

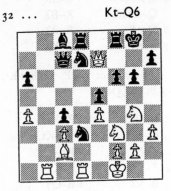

Diagram 60

33 R×Kt

A splendid forcing combination.

33 ...	P×R
34 B–Kt3*ch*	K–R1
35 Kt×BP	R×Kt
36 Kt–Kt5	R×P*ch*

A most subtle defence, intending to force the exchange of White's queen by 37 K×R, R–B1*ch*; 38 K–Kt1, Q–B4*ch*. But White's peculiar runaway defence triumphs.

37 K–Kt1	R–B8*ch*
38 K–R2	*Resigns*

Nor were more extravagant attempts to put new life into very old lines any more successful.

GAME 82

RUY LOPEZ

Spassky   *Taimanov*

Russian Championship, 1955

1	P–K4	P–K4
2	Kt–KB3	Kt–QB3
3	B–Kt5	P–QR3
4	B–R4	P–QKt4
5	B–Kt3	Kt–R4

A very old line, inviting 6 B×P*ch*, K×B; 7 Kt×P*ch*, which used to be considered a refutation. White has doubts and prefers a quieter process.

6	O–O	P–Q3
7	P–Q4	Kt×B
8	RP×Kt	P–KB3

Borrowing an old idea from the

Steinitz Defence Deferred in order to maintain his K4. But his position here is worse than in that defence since his QKtP is on QKt4 instead of QB3, which gives him less power of resistance in the centre, and in addition White has here an open QR file.

9	Kt–B3	B–Kt2
10	Kt–KR4	Kt–K2
11	P×P	QP×P
12	Q–B3	Q–Q2

A vain attempt to contest the white squares.

13	R–Q1	Q–K3
14	B–K3	P–Kt4

Inviting trouble. Safer was 14

..., P–Kt3; 15 B–B5, B–Kt2; 16
Kt–Q5.

15 Kt×P

A sharp shock for Black, who must
prevent White exploiting the open
QR file, for if 15 ..., R–B1; 16 Q–
R5ch, Q–B2; 17 R–Q8ch, R×R; 18
Kt×Pch.

15 ...   RP×Kt
16 Q–R5ch   Q–B2

Or Kt–Kt3; 17 R×Rch, B×R;
Kt×Kt, Q–B2; 19 Q–Kt4, Q×Kt;
20 Q–B8ch, K–B2; 21 R–Q7ch, B–
K2; 22 Q×P, R–K1; 23 B–B5.

17 R×Rch   B×R
18 R–Q8ch   K×R
19 Q×Q   P×Kt

Black's pieces have sufficient value
but insufficient co-ordination for successful resistance.

20 Q×BP   R–Kt1
21 P–KB3   P–R6

22 P–Kt3	K–K1
23 Q×P	R–Kt3
24 Q×Pch	B–B3
25 Q–Kt8ch	K–B2
26 Q×P	R–B3
27 B–Kt5	R–K3

Of course not R×P; 28 B×Kt,
B×B; 29 Q×QB.

28 P–QKt4	K–Kt1
29 Q–Kt8	Kt–Kt3
30 K–B2	Kt–K4
31 P–Kt5	B–K1
32 B–K3	B–Q3
33 Q–B8	K–B2
34 P–Kt6	R–B3
35 B–B4	B–Q2
36 P–Kt7	

The final blow.

36 ...	B–K3
37 B×Kt	B×B
38 P–Kt8=Q	QB×Q
39 Q×KB	Resigns

At a time when the new dynamic view was that small disadvantages
were acceptable if one thereby obtained an access of energy, it was
natural that there was a revival of interest in the active Tarrasch
Defence, which had only been jettisoned on account of Black's
backward QBP. Against this defence too the Russians evolved
certain critical variations.

GAME 83
RUY LOPEZ
Smyslov   Euwe
The Hague–Moscow World
Championship Tournament,
1948

1 P–K4	P–K4
2 Kt–KB3	Kt–QB3
3 B–Kt5	P–QR3
4 B–R4	Kt–B3
5 O–O	Kt×P
6 P–Q4	P–QKt4

7 B–Kt3   P–Q4
8 P×P   B–K3
9 Q–K2

The new Russian Variation, the idea of which is to pin Black's QP by R–Q1 and if possible to be the first to exert Q side pressure by following with P–B4. The older move, P–B3, is certainly less sharp though probably more permanent in its effects.

9 ...   Kt–B4

The main variation runs 9 ..., B–K2; 10 R–Q1, Kt–B4; 11 P–B4, P–Q5; 12 P×P, P–Q6; when Black has adequate counter-play.

10 R–Q1   Kt×B

He can either revert to the main line by B–K2, or play the Reshevsky move P–Kt5, which takes the sting out of the threatened P–B4.

11 RP×Kt   Q–B1

Diagram 61

12 P–B4

In spite of Black's attempt to forestall this move, White still makes it

as a pawn sacrifice, for the resulting open position will favour him as the better developed player.

12 ...   QP×P
13 P×P   B×P

Not P–Kt5; 14 Q–K4, Kt–Q1; 15 B–Kt5, with advantage.

14 Q–K4   Kt–K2

Now if Kt–Q1; 15 R×Kt*ch*, K×R (or Q×R; 16 Q–B6*ch*, K–K2; 17 B–Kt5*ch*); 16 B–Kt5*ch*, B–K2; 17 Kt–R3, P–QB3; 18 Kt×B, P×Kt; 19 R–Q1*ch*, K–K1; 20 B×B, K×B; 21 Q–R4*ch*, K–B1; 22 Q×BP, and wins.

15 Kt–R3   P–QB3

If B–K3; 16 Kt×P.

16 Kt×B   P×Kt
17 Q×BP

White has now recovered his pawn and still has by far the better position, with a threat of Kt–Kt5 giving an immediate attack on the King.

17 ...   Q–Kt2

Not Kt–Kt3; 18 Kt–Q4, Kt×P; 19 R–K1. While 17 ..., Q–K3 allows a lovely combination in 18 R×P, Q×Q; 19 R×R*ch*, Kt–B1; 20 R×Kt*ch*, K–K2; 21 R–B7*ch*, K–K3 (not K–K1; 22 B–Kt5 threatening both R–Q8*mate* and R–B8*mate*); 22 R×P*ch*, Q×R; 23 Kt–Q4*ch*, K–Q4; 24 Kt×Q, K×Kt; 25 R–Q8, and wins easily.

18 P–K6   P–B3

A virtual admission of defeat, but

if P × P; 19 Q × KP, Q–B1; 20 Q–B4, Kt–Q4; 21 Kt–K5.

19	R–Q7	Q–Kt4
20	Q × Q	BP × Q
21	Kt–Q4	

Restricting Black's Knight and threatening Kt × P.

21	...	R–B1
22	B–K3	Kt–Kt3

Not Kt–B3; 23 R–QB1, Kt–K2; 24 R × Kt*ch.*

23	R × RP	Kt–K4
24	R–Kt7	B–B4

At last he can develop his Bishop, since if 25 R × KKtP, then B × Kt and White cannot answer 26 B × B on account of R–B8*mate.*

25	Kt–B5	O–O
26	P–R3	*Resigns*

An alternative line in the Steinitz Defence Deferred was the critical Siesta Variation, in which the Russians introduced a highly novel line in order to strengthen White's hand.

GAME 84

RUY LOPEZ

Boleslavsky   *Ragosin*

Russian Championship, 1949

1	P–K4	P–K4
2	Kt–KB3	Kt–QB3
3	B–Kt5	P–QR3
4	B–R4	P–Q3
5	P–B3	P–B4

The Siesta Variation, a line which would have met with the approval of Philidor.

6 P × P

An attempt to force the issue by 6 P–Q4 was sharply rebutted in the game Réti–Capablanca at Berlin in 1928, which continued 6 P–Q4, P × KP; 7 Kt–Kt5, P × P; 8 Kt × KP, Kt–B3; 9 B–KKt5, B–K2; 10 Q × P, P–Kt4; 11 Kt × Kt *ch,* P × Kt; 12 Q–Q5, KtP × B; 13 B–R6, Q–Q2; 14 O–O, B–Kt2;

15 B–Kt7, O–O–O; 16 B × R, Kt–K4; 17 Q–Q1, B–B6; 18 P × B, Q–R6, *Resigns.*

6	...	B × P
7	O–O	

The Russian innovation, known as the Panov line, and played in preference to the older 7 P–Q4, P–K5 when White is in difficulties after 8 Kt–Kt5, P–Q4; 9 P–B3, P–R3.

7	...	B–Q6

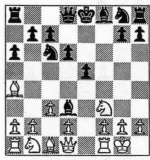

Diagram 62

In any former age this natural move would have been regarded almost as a winner, occupying a huge hole as it does and thoroughly tying White up. But the Russian view of dynamics is that Black has only a temporary grip, and once this is broken his efforts will in fact react against him.

8	R–K1	B–K2
9	R–K3	P–K5
10	Kt–K1	B×Kt

The end of the bind already.

11	R×B	Kt–B3
12	P–Q3	P–Q4
13	R–R3	Q–Q2
14	P–QKt4	

To deter Black from castling on the Queen's side.

14	...	P–QKt4
15	B–Kt3	Kt–K4
16	B–Kt5	R–Q1

His King would be better off on the threatened Q side than left in the centre like this. It was safer therefore to play 16 ..., O–O–O; 17 P–R4, KP×P; 18 Kt×P, Kt–B5 with good chances of resistance.

17	B×Kt	B×B
18	P×P	P×P
19	Q–B2	Q–B3
20	R–K3	K–Q2

Now that he is threatened by R×P, followed by Kt–B3, he has to admit his error.

21	R×P	K–B1

Better was KR–K1; 22 P–KB4,

Kt–Kt3. But not 22 ..., Kt–B5 on account of 23 R×Kt, P×R; 24 B–R4. Now, by a temporary win of material, White gains a decisive pawn advantage on the K side.

22	R×Kt	B×R
23	Q–B5ch	K–Kt1
24	Q×B	KR–K1
25	Q×P	Q–K5
26	Kt–B2	R–Q7
27	R–KB1	R×Kt
28	B×R	Q×B
29	P–KB4	

The climax of his combination. It is now only a question of technique, though great accuracy and a considerable amount of time are still required, for the ending is instructive and full of pitfalls.

29	...	Q×RP
30	Q×P	Q–Q7
31	Q–R3	R–K8
32	Q–B3	R–K6

After Q–B8; 33 P–B5, R×Rch; 34 Q×R, Q×P; 35 P–B6, Q×KtP; 36 P–B7, Q–B1; 37 P–R4, Black still cannot save the game, for if 37 ..., P–Kt5; 38 Q–B5, P–Kt6; 39 Q–K6, P–Kt7; 40 Q–K8ch, K–R2; 41 Q×Q, P–Kt8=Qch; 42 K–R2, Q–QB8; 43 Q–Kt7, Q–B5ch; 44 K–R3—a fascinating line.

33	Q–B2	Q×P
34	P–B5	R–K2
35	P–B6	R–B2
36	Q–B4	P–R4

37	P×P	P–Kt5	42 ...	Q×RP
38	P–R6	Q–B4*ch*	43 R–QKt1	Q–R6
39	K–R1	Q–Kt3	44 P–Kt6	R×P
40	P–Kt4	P–Kt6	45 P–Kt7	Q–QKt6
41	P–Kt5	P–Kt7	46 Q–K8*ch*	K–R2
42	Q–K4		47 P–Kt8=Q	R–B8*ch*

Threatening to force a quick win by Q–Kt7*ch*.

48	R×R	P–Kt8=Q
49	R×Q	*Resigns*

The more orthodox lines in the Steinitz Defence Deferred also supplied their quota to dynamic play.

GAME 85

RUY LOPEZ

Geller   Spassky

Russian Interzonal Tournament, 1964

1	P–K4	P–K4
2	Kt–KB3	Kt–QB3
3	B–Kt5	P–QR3
4	B–R4	P–Q3
5	O–O	

Black's reply to this move makes it more difficult for White to contest the centre than after the more usual moves of P–B3 or P–Q4 at once.

5	...	B–Kt5
6	P–KR3	B–R4

The aggressive line 6 ..., P–KR4; has not proved quite sufficient.

7	P–B3	Kt–B3
8	P–Q4	P–QKt4
9	B–Kt3	B–K2

Not Kt×KP; 10 B–Q5, nor need he play P×P; 10 P×P, B×Kt; 11 P×B to expose White's king, since White's king's position will open itself up anyway without the loss of central control involved in the above line.

10	B–K3	O–O
11	QKt–Q2	P–Q4

Spassky is as skilful as Tal at introducing a crisis and, being less spectacular, he is almost more dangerous.

12 P–Kt4

Virtually forced by the threat of 12 ..., P×KP or if 12 KP×P, of P–K5. Nor does 12 B×P, Kt×B, 13 P×Kt, Q×P solve White's problem.

12	...	B–Kt3
13	QP×P	

Safer was simplification by 13 Kt×KP, Kt×Kt; 14 P×Kt; Kt ×P.

| 13 ... | KKt×KP |
| 14 Kt–Kt1 | |

The sad corollary of avoiding the simplification on the previous move.

| 14 ... | Q–B1 |

Now threats like P–KR4 hang over White. He cannot answer 15 B×P because of R–Q1, nor 15 Q×P, Kt–R4; 16 P–K6 (not B–B2, R–Q1), P–KB4; 17 Kt–R2, R–Q1; 18 Q–K5, Kt×B; 19 P×Kt, B–Q3; 20 Q–Q5, B×Kt*ch*; winning the Q.

| 15 Kt–Q4 | Kt×KP |
| 16 P–KB4 | |

If 16 Kt–B3, Kt×KtP; 17 P×Kt, Q×P*ch*; 18 K–R1, B–R4.

| 16 ... | P–QB4 |
| 17 P×Kt | |

Now Kt–B3 would be worse because of 17 ..., Kt×KtP; 18 P×Kt, Q×P*ch*; 19 K–R1, Kt–Kt6*ch*.

17 ...	P×Kt
18 P×P	Q–Q2
19 Kt–Q2	P–B3

Opening lines for his bishops which will soon launch a strong K side attack.

20 R–B1	K–R1
21 B–KB4	P×P
22 B×KP	

Had he foreseen Black's lovely conception he would have chosen P×P here.

| 22 ... | B–Kt4 |
| 23 R–QB7 | |

Thinking he has successfully un-pinned his knight.

Diagram 63

23 ...	Q×R
24 B×Q	B–K6*ch*
25 K–Kt2	

25 K–R2 would lead to Kt×Kt; 26 R×R*ch*, R×R; 27 B×P, R–B7*ch*; 28 B–Kt2, B–K5. Though

down in material, Black has devastating bishops.

25	...	Kt×Kt
26	R×R*ch*	R×R
27	B×P	R–B7*ch*
28	K–Kt3	Kt–B8*ch*
29	K–R4	P–R3

30 B–Q8

Preventing B–Kt4*mate* only to be faced with the same threat on another diagonal.

30	...	R–B1
	Resigns	

CHAPTER XV

Assorted Irregulars

It was natural that, just as the Hypermoderns looked to a new range of openings for their dynamic opportunities, so the Russians should also enjoy fishing in comparatively unknown waters. Our selection of the play of the Russians is accordingly concluded with five examples in the less analyzed fields of opening theory, and it is no accident that this group includes two examples by their most violently aggressive tactician and three by their quietest and subtlest strategist.

The English Opening, though at least as old as Staunton whose adoption of it gave it its name, and though also much used in the days of the Hypermoderns since it was often allied to Réti–Catalan-style developments, nevertheless still provides ample opportunities for deserting the books and roaming in more or less uncharted areas.

GAME 86

ENGLISH OPENING

Petrosyan   *Korchnoi*

Curaçao Candidates' Tournament, 1962

1	P–QB4	P–QB4
2	Kt–KB3	Kt–KB3
3	P–Q4	P×P
4	Kt×P	P–KKt3

Many moves have been tried at this point in the past, the most usual being P–Q4, Kt–B3 and P–K3. The two fianchetto developments and P–K4 are less common. The line has by no means been fully worked out.

5	Kt–QB3	P–Q4

White threatens to play 6 P–K4, transposing to the Maróczy bind in the Sicilian Defence.

6 B–Kt5

Better than 6 P×P, as played in the Flohr–Euwe match, 1932, which went 6 ..., Kt×P; 7 Kt(4)–Kt5, Kt×Kt; 8 Q×Qch, K×Q; 9 Kt×Kt, B–Kt2; with equality.

6	...	P×P
7	P–K3	Q–R4

But this is decidedly premature, as Petrosyan beautifully shows. Best was simply B–Kt2. If Black hopes his two bishops will prove an advantage to him, he is in for a shock.

8 B×Kt	P×B
9 B×P	B–QKt5

That he has played for the fianchetto of the bishop and then develops it thus is an indication of why he is already behind in his development.

10 R–QB1	P–QR3

A further loss of time. O–O was indicated.

11 O–O	Kt–Q2
12 P–QR3	B–K2
13 P–QKt4	

Expanding his position very forcefully. If now Q×RP; 14 Kt–Q5, R–QKt1; 15 R–R1, Q–Kt7; 20 R–R2, trapping the queen. Black's best reply is the passive Q–Q1 and in trying to maintain some activity he runs into worse trouble.

13 ...	Q–K4

Diagram 64

14 P–B4

A terrible surprise for Black, since after 14 ..., Q×Pch; 15 K–R1, the black queen cannot get out again and must succumb to 16 R–B3.

14 ...	Q–Kt1
15 B×Pch	

The position is ripe for a combinative finish.

15 ...	K×B
16 Q–Kt3ch	K–K1

If K–Kt2; 17 Kt–K6ch, K–R3; 18 R–B3, P–KKt4; 19 P–B5, winning.

17 Kt–Q5	B–Q3

The threat of a fork on his QB2 is a recurring motif, which can no longer be satisfactorily resisted.

18 Kt–K6	P–QKt4
19 Kt(5)–B7ch	K–K2
20 Kt–Q4	K–B1

Of course not B×Kt; 21 Kt–B6ch.

21 Kt×R	*Resigns*

If Q×Kt; 22 Q–K6, B–K2; 23 R–B7, and Black's position collapses.

GAME 87
ENGLISH OPENING
Toran   *Tal*
Oberhausen Team Tournament, 1961

1 P–QB4	P–K4
2 Kt–QB3	P–Q3

The usual play is Kt–KB3 with the intention of disputing the centre quickly by P–Q4.

| 3 P–KKt3 | P–KB4 |
| 4 P–Q4 | |

At once contesting the black central squares, though a quieter positional line with B–Kt2 might have been better.

4 ...	P–K5
5 P–B3	Kt–KB3
6 B–Kt2	P × P
7 Kt × P	

His fight for the centre has been quite successful, but this is over-ambitious. His idea is to complete the campaign in the centre with P–K4, but this only rids Black of a KBP which is something of an obstruction to him. Better was P × P and KKt–K2.

7 ...	P–KKt3
8 O–O	B–Kt2
9 P–K4	

Logical, but his QP will be weak and under fire from Black's KB. It was therefore wiser to play B–Kt5 or B–B4 followed by P–K3.

9 ...	P × P
10 Kt–KKt5	O–O
11 Kt(5) × KP	Kt × Kt
12 R × R*ch*	

Already feeling the weakness of his QP, for if 12 Kt × Kt, R × R*ch*; he must play 13 B × R to preserve it.

| 12 ... | Q × R |
| 13 Kt × Kt | Kt–B3 |

Attacking the pawn before White has time for P–Kt3 and B–Kt2.

| 14 B–K3 | B–B4 |
| 15 Q–Q2 | |

This is no protection to his bishop against threats on the K file. Better was 15 Kt–B3, R–K1; 16 Kt–Q5.

15 ...	R–K1
16 Kt–Kt5	R × B
17 B–Q5*ch*	

Of course not 17 Q × R, B × P. But White still thinks he has a draw up his sleeve.

| 17 ... | K–R1 |
| 18 Kt–B7*ch* | |

Diagram 65

| 18 ... | Q × Kt |

A shock for White who had reckoned on a perpetual check.

19 B×Q   R–Q6

Starting a delightful series of rook manœuvres along the rank with the bishops in action behind.

20 Q–K2   B×Pch
21 K–Kt2   Kt–K4

All the black pieces join in the attack, but when White brings up a reserve next move, it serves no useful purpose, and there was more resistance in B–Q5, disputing the long diagonal.

22 R–Q1   R–K6
23 Q–B1   B–K5ch
24 K–R3   R–KB6
25 Q–K2   B–B4ch
      Resigns

After 26 K–Kt2 (not K–R4, R–B7), R–B7ch; 27 Q×R, B×Q; 28 K×B, Kt×B; Black has a winning material pull.

The Benoni Defence 1 P–Q4, P–QB4; had a slight revival under Alekhin but never proved very successful. It was left to Tal to revive it in a modified form and make a most dangerous attacking weapon out of it.

GAME 88

BENONI DEFENCE

Averbach   *Tal*

Russian Championship, 1958

1 P–Q4   Kt–KB3
2 P–QB4   P–K3
3 Kt–QB3   P–B4

This deferred Hromadka Variation of the Benoni is one which Tal has made especially his own. It gives ground in the centre in order to exploit the Q side, and though not found entirely satisfactory, it is far from harmless in the hands of a brilliant tactician. The usual order of moves is 1 P–Q4, Kt–KB3; 2 P–QB4, P–B4; 3 P–Q5, P–K3; 4 Kt–QB3.

4 P–Q5   P×P
5 P×P   P–Q3
6 P–K4   P–KKt3
7 B–K2   B–Kt2
8 Kt–B3

Probably better than the line in which White plays P–B4 first.

8 ...   O–O
9 O–O   R–K1

Tal's particular line, putting restraint on White's central intentions before undertaking any Q-side offensive.

10 Q–B2   Kt–R3
11 B–KB4

Better was P–QR3. Tal moves astonishingly quickly into the attack.

11 ...   Kt–QKt5
12 Q–Kt1

Diagram 66

12 ...   Kt × KP

Not necessarily a win yet, but sufficiently good and startling to stand a chance of throwing the opponent off balance.

13 Kt × Kt   B–B4
14 Kt(3)–Q2   Kt × QP
15 B × P

He could have retained good chances by 15 B–Kt3, Q–K2; 16 B–Kt5, B × Kt; 17 Kt × B, Q × Kt; 18 B × R, Q × B; 19 B × P, with the exchange for a pawn. Now Black recovers his piece with advantage.

15 ...   Kt–B3
16 B–B3

An attempt to save his QB by B × P fails against 16 ..., Kt × Kt; 17 Kt × Kt, B × Kt; 18 Q–Q1, Q–Kt4; still catching the bishop, while if 16 B–Kt3, the same series of exchanges is followed by 18 ..., B × QKtP with a won ending.

16 ...   Kt × Kt
17 Kt × Kt   B × Kt
18 B × B   Q × B
19 Q–B2

He cannot recover the pawn by B × QKtP because of 19 ..., QR–Kt1; 20 B–B3, B × P; and Black wins the exchange.

19 ...   R–K2
20 B–B3   QR–K1
21 QR–Q1   B–Q5
22 P–QR4   P–Kt3
23 P–QKt3   R–K4
24 R–Q2

Hoping to exchange some of the heavy material and come down to an ending with bishops of opposite colours.

24 ...   P–KR4
25 R–K2   R × R
26 B × R   P–R5
27 K–R1

Preparing to answer P–R6 with P–Kt3. If 27 P–R3, Black plays Q–B5 and B–K4.

27 ...   Q–B5
28 P–Kt3

Not 28 B–B4, B–K4; 29 Q × P*ch*, K–B1; and Black is home.

28 ...   Q–B3
29 Q–Q1

To answer Q–B3*ch* with B–B3.

29	...	R–Q1
30	B–Kt4	B×P
31	Q–K2	R–Q7

A fine idea. If 32 Q×R, Q–B3*ch*; is decisive.

32	Q–K8*ch*	K–Kt2
33	P×P	Q–Q5
34	B–R3	Q–Q6
35	B–Kt2	

He might have tried 35 Q–K5*ch*, K–R2; 36 Q–B4, hoping for Q×B;

37 Q×P*ch*, and draws by perpetual check but in fact Black would reply 36 ..., Q–Q4*ch*; 37 B–Kt2, Q×B*ch*; 38 K×Q, B–K6*dis.ch*; 39 K–R1, B×Q; 40 R×B, K–Kt2; with a won ending.

35	...	R–Q8
	Resigns	

Because of 36 Q–Kt5, R×R*ch*; 37 B×R, Q–K5*ch*; 38 B–Kt2, Q×KRP; winning easily.

Even the standard fianchetto defences were faced with irregular treatments and taken right out of the books as in the following example.

GAME 89

IRREGULAR QUEEN'S INDIAN

Petrosyan   *Nievergelt*

Belgrade Tournament, 1954

1	P–Q4	Kt–KB3
2	Kt–KB3	P–QKt3
3	B–Kt5	

Diverging in typical Russian style from the book which shows 3 P–B4, a move which has no part in Petrosyan's plans, though if Black had played 3 ..., Kt–K5 he would have had to think again.

3	...	B–Kt2
4	Kt–B3	P–Q4

This method of preventing P–K4 deadens his own game. The dynamic style as far back as Alekhin's day would have demanded P–B4.

5	P–K3	P–Kt3
6	B–Kt5*ch*	P–B3

He is forced to remove the support given by his bishop to his K5, so that 5 ..., P–QR3 is seen to have been better.

7	B–Q3	B–Kt2
8	P–K4	

As a result of Black's unfortunate 6th move White now assumes the initiative, though Black would have done better to reply P×P than to have allowed White his head.

8	...	O–O
9	P–K5	KKt–Q2
10	Kt–K2	P–B3
11	P × P	P × P
12	B–K3	Kt–R3

He would do better to hasten to the defence of his K side either by P–KB4, Kt–B3 and QKt–Q2 or by R–K1 and Kt–B1.

13	P–KR4	Kt–Kt5
14	P–R5	Kt × B*ch*
15	Q × Kt	Q–K1

He finds he is no better off for having eliminated the white KB, for now if 15 ..., P–KKt4; 16 Kt–Kt3 and 17 Kt–B5.

16	P × P	P × P
17	Kt–B4	Kt–K4

The ingenuity born of despair.

18	P × Kt	P × P
19	Q × P	

The riposte which Black has overlooked, expecting 19 Kt–R3, P–K5.

19	...	P × Kt
20	Q–R7*ch*	K–B2
21	R–R6	

Another unexpected surprise, If now 21 ..., P × B; 22 Kt–Kt5*ch*, K–K2; 23 R–K6*ch*, winning and if 21 ..., R–R1; 22 Kt–Kt5*ch*, K–B1; 23 Q–B5*ch*, K–Kt1; 24 R × R*ch*, B × R; 25 Q–R7*ch*, K–B1; 26 Q × B*ch*, winning.

21	...	Q–K2
22	Q–Kt6*ch*	K–Kt1
23	Kt–Kt5	*Resigns*

The immediate threat is Q–R7 *mate* and if 23 R–B3; 24 R–R8*ch*, K × R; 25 Q–R7*mate*.

Unusual fianchetto developments are apt to take the game completely out of all books on opening theory, and they therefore make an especial appeal to the player who likes a slow strategical game where there are no known charts to guide the play.

GAME 90
KING'S FIANCHETTO OPENING

Filip   *Petrosyan*

Amsterdam Candidates' Tournament, 1956

1	Kt–KB3	Kt–KB3

2	P–KKt3	P–Q3
3	B–Kt2	P–K4
4	P–Q3	P–KKt3
5	O–O	B–Kt2
6	P–K4	

He restores the symmetry as the best means of keeping Black's KB restricted.

6 ...	O–O
7 QKt–Q2	QKt–Q2
8 P–QR4	P–QR4
9 Kt–B4	Kt–B4
10 B–K3	Kt–K3
11 P–R3	

Apparently fearing Kt–Kt5, but in a close position where knights are as valuable as bishops this seems to have been a threat he could have ignored.

11 ...	P–Kt3
12 Q–Q2	B–QR3
13 P–Kt3	Kt–R4
14 P–B3	

An unnecessary move, whether intended to protect the black squares or, as the course of the game indicates, as part of a Q-side push. The main factor in the position is Black's threat of P–KB4, so a more promising line for White was Kt–Kt5.

14 ...	Q–K2
15 P–QKt4	P–KB4
16 KP × P·	

P–B5 was a serious threat.

16 ...	KtP × P
17 Kt–Kt5	P–B5

He still plays this move, since acceptance of the exchange by B × R would weaken White's K side irremediably.

18 Kt × Kt	Q × Kt

Not P × B; 19 Kt × P(3), Q × Kt; 20 B–Q5.

19 P–Kt5	

And again if 19 B × R, R × B; 20 P × BP, Q × P; the threat of B–Kt2 is decisive. But if now Black plays 19 ..., P × B; 20 Kt × P(3) and Black can only save his QB at the cost of his QR. Black, however, has a much more subtle answer, getting rid of the threat to his rook and weakening White's K side all in one.

19 ...	P–B6
20 P × B	P × B
21 K × P	P–Q4

It is now clear how completely and subtly White has been outplayed. Black controls the centre and White's pieces are driven to useless squares.

22 Kt–R3	R × P
23 Q–K2	Q–Kt3
24 K–R2	

24 P–Q4, R(3)–R1; 25 K–R2, R(R)–K1; leaves all the trumps in Black's hand.

24 ...	R(3)–R1
25 Kt–B2	R(R)–K1
26 R(R)–K1	P–B4
27 R–KKt1	Kt–B3
28 Q–Q2	

After this his bishop has to go to KKt5 where it is very vulnerable. Better was B–B1.

28 ...	P–Q5	35 Q–B1	R–Q8
29 P×P	BP×P	36 Q–Kt2	
30 B–Kt5	Kt–Q4		
31 R–Kt2	R–B6		

Decisive. White can only hold his QP for a move or so.

Or 36 Q–R3, B–B1; 37 Q–Kt2, R–QKt8; and the queen is still trapped, quite apart from the fact that his minor pieces are also *en prise*.

32 R–K4	Kt–B6
33 R–Kt4	P–R4
34 R–R4	R×QP

36 ...   R–QKt8

Resigns

Since the Russians so frequently go back to old lines and refurbish them, it is perhaps significant that Petrosyan's wonderful subtlety in the preceding game derives from an opening that has a closer affinity with those of the Hindus and Persians of a thousand years ago than with those of European masters of a mere century back. And with that provocative thought we bid our readers farewell.

A CATALOGUE OF SELECTED DOVER BOOKS
IN ALL FIELDS OF INTEREST

A CATALOGUE OF SELECTED DOVER BOOKS
IN ALL FIELDS OF INTEREST

AMERICA'S OLD MASTERS, James T. Flexner. Four men emerged unexpectedly from provincial 18th century America to leadership in European art: Benjamin West, J. S. Copley, C. R. Peale, Gilbert Stuart. Brilliant coverage of lives and contributions. Revised, 1967 edition. 69 plates. 365pp. of text.
21806-6 Paperbound $3.00

FIRST FLOWERS OF OUR WILDERNESS: AMERICAN PAINTING, THE COLONIAL PERIOD, James T. Flexner. Painters, and regional painting traditions from earliest Colonial times up to the emergence of Copley, West and Peale Sr., Foster, Gustavus Hesselius, Feke, John Smibert and many anonymous painters in the primitive manner. Engaging presentation, with 162 illustrations. xxii + 368pp.
22180-6 Paperbound $3.50

THE LIGHT OF DISTANT SKIES: AMERICAN PAINTING, 1760-1835, James T. Flexner. The great generation of early American painters goes to Europe to learn and to teach: West, Copley, Gilbert Stuart and others. Allston, Trumbull, Morse; also contemporary American painters—primitives, derivatives, academics—who remained in America. 102 illustrations. xiii + 306pp.
22179-2 Paperbound $3.00

A HISTORY OF THE RISE AND PROGRESS OF THE ARTS OF DESIGN IN THE UNITED STATES, William Dunlap. Much the richest mine of information on early American painters, sculptors, architects, engravers, miniaturists, etc. The only source of information for scores of artists, the major primary source for many others. Unabridged reprint of rare original 1834 edition, with new introduction by James T. Flexner, and 394 new illustrations. Edited by Rita Weiss. 6⅝ x 9⅝.
21695-0, 21696-9, 21697-7 Three volumes, Paperbound $13.50

EPOCHS OF CHINESE AND JAPANESE ART, Ernest F. Fenollosa. From primitive Chinese art to the 20th century, thorough history, explanation of every important art period and form, including Japanese woodcuts; main stress on China and Japan, but Tibet, Korea also included. Still unexcelled for its detailed, rich coverage of cultural background, aesthetic elements, diffusion studies, particularly of the historical period. 2nd, 1913 edition. 242 illustrations. lii + 439pp. of text.
20364-6, 20365-4 Two volumes, Paperbound $6.00

THE GENTLE ART OF MAKING ENEMIES, James A. M. Whistler. Greatest wit of his day deflates Oscar Wilde, Ruskin, Swinburne; strikes back at inane critics, exhibitions, art journalism; aesthetics of impressionist revolution in most striking form. Highly readable classic by great painter. Reproduction of edition designed by Whistler. Introduction by Alfred Werner. xxxvi + 334pp.
21875-9 Paperbound $2.50

EAST O' THE SUN AND WEST O' THE MOON, George W. Dasent. Considered the best of all translations of these Norwegian folk tales, this collection has been enjoyed by generations of children (and folklorists too). Includes True and Untrue, Why the Sea is Salt, East O' the Sun and West O' the Moon, Why the Bear is Stumpy-Tailed, Boots and the Troll, The Cock and the Hen, Rich Peter the Pedlar, and 52 more. The only edition with all 59 tales. 77 illustrations by Erik Werenskiold and Theodor Kittelsen. xv + 418pp. 22521-6 Paperbound $3.00

GOOPS AND HOW TO BE THEM, Gelett Burgess. Classic of tongue-in-cheek humor, masquerading as etiquette book. 87 verses, twice as many cartoons, show mischievous Goops as they demonstrate to children virtues of table manners, neatness, courtesy, etc. Favorite for generations. viii + 88pp. 6½ x 9¼. 22233-0 Paperbound $1.25

ALICE'S ADVENTURES UNDER GROUND, Lewis Carroll. The first version, quite different from the final Alice in Wonderland, printed out by Carroll himself with his own illustrations. Complete facsimile of the "million dollar" manuscript Carroll gave to Alice Liddell in 1864. Introduction by Martin Gardner. viii + 96pp. Title and dedication pages in color. 21482-6 Paperbound $1.25

THE BROWNIES, THEIR BOOK, Palmer Cox. Small as mice, cunning as foxes, exuberant and full of mischief, the Brownies go to the zoo, toy shop, seashore, circus, etc., in 24 verse adventures and 266 illustrations. Long a favorite, since their first appearance in St. Nicholas Magazine. xi + 144pp. 6⅝ x 9¼. 21265-3 Paperbound $1.75

SONGS OF CHILDHOOD, Walter De La Mare. Published (under the pseudonym Walter Ramal) when De La Mare was only 29, this charming collection has long been a favorite children's book. A facsimile of the first edition in paper, the 47 poems capture the simplicity of the nursery rhyme and the ballad, including such lyrics as I Met Eve, Tartary, The Silver Penny. vii + 106pp. 21972-0 Paperbound $1.25

THE COMPLETE NONSENSE OF EDWARD LEAR, Edward Lear. The finest 19th-century humorist-cartoonist in full: all nonsense limericks, zany alphabets, Owl and Pussycat, songs, nonsense botany, and more than 500 illustrations by Lear himself. Edited by Holbrook Jackson. xxix + 287pp. (USO) 20167-8 Paperbound $2.00

BILLY WHISKERS: THE AUTOBIOGRAPHY OF A GOAT, Frances Trego Montgomery. A favorite of children since the early 20th century, here are the escapades of that rambunctious, irresistible and mischievous goat—Billy Whiskers. Much in the spirit of Peck's Bad Boy, this is a book that children never tire of reading or hearing. All the original familiar illustrations by W. H. Fry are included: 6 color plates, 18 black and white drawings. 159pp. 22345-0 Paperbound $2.00

MOTHER GOOSE MELODIES. Faithful republication of the fabulously rare Munroe and Francis "copyright 1833" Boston edition—the most important Mother Goose collection, usually referred to as the "original." Familiar rhymes plus many rare ones, with wonderful old woodcut illustrations. Edited by E. F. Bleiler. 128pp. 4½ x 6⅜. 22577-1 Paperbound $1.25

PLANETS, STARS AND GALAXIES: DESCRIPTIVE ASTRONOMY FOR BEGINNERS, A. E. Fanning. Comprehensive introductory survey of astronomy: the sun, solar system, stars, galaxies, universe, cosmology; up-to-date, including quasars, radio stars, etc. Preface by Prof. Donald Menzel. 24pp. of photographs. 189pp. 5¼ x 8¼.
21680-2 Paperbound $1.50

TEACH YOURSELF CALCULUS, P. Abbott. With a good background in algebra and trig, you can teach yourself calculus with this book. Simple, straightforward introduction to functions of all kinds, integration, differentiation, series, etc. "Students who are beginning to study calculus method will derive great help from this book." Faraday House Journal. 308pp.
20683-1 Clothbound $2.00

TEACH YOURSELF TRIGONOMETRY, P. Abbott. Geometrical foundations, indices and logarithms, ratios, angles, circular measure, etc. are presented in this sound, easy-to-use text. Excellent for the beginner or as a brush up, this text carries the student through the solution of triangles. 204pp.
20682-3 Clothbound $2.00

TEACH YOURSELF ANATOMY, David LeVay. Accurate, inclusive, profusely illustrated account of structure, skeleton, abdomen, muscles, nervous system, glands, brain, reproductive organs, evolution. "Quite the best and most readable account,' *Medical Officer.* 12 color plates. 164 figures. 311pp. 4¾ x 7.
21651-9 Clothbound $2.50

TEACH YOURSELF PHYSIOLOGY, David LeVay. Anatomical, biochemical bases; digestive, nervous, endocrine systems; metabolism; respiration; muscle; excretion; temperature control; reproduction. "Good elementary exposition," *The Lancet.* 6 color plates. 44 illustrations. 208pp. 4¼ x 7. 21658-6 Clothbound $2.50

THE FRIENDLY STARS, Martha Evans Martin. Classic has taught naked-eye observation of stars, planets to hundreds of thousands, still not surpassed for charm, lucidity, adequacy. Completely updated by Professor Donald H. Menzel, Harvard Observatory. 25 illustrations. 16 x 30 chart. x + 147pp. 21099-5 Paperbound $1.25

MUSIC OF THE SPHERES: THE MATERIAL UNIVERSE FROM ATOM TO QUASAR, SIMPLY EXPLAINED, Guy Murchie. Extremely broad, brilliantly written popular account begins with the solar system and reaches to dividing line between matter and nonmatter; latest understandings presented with exceptional clarity. Volume One: Planets, stars, galaxies, cosmology, geology, celestial mechanics, latest astronomical discoveries; Volume Two: Matter, atoms, waves, radiation, relativity, chemical action, heat, nuclear energy, quantum theory, music, light, color, probability, antimatter, antigravity, and similar topics. 319 figures. 1967 (second) edition. Total of xx + 644pp. 21809-0, 21810-4 Two volumes, Paperbound $5.00

OLD-TIME SCHOOLS AND SCHOOL BOOKS, Clifton Johnson. Illustrations and rhymes from early primers, abundant quotations from early textbooks, many anecdotes of school life enliven this study of elementary schools from Puritans to middle 19th century. Introduction by Carl Withers. 234 illustrations. xxxiii + 381pp.
21031-6 Paperbound $2.50

AMERICAN FOOD AND GAME FISHES, David S. Jordan and Barton W. Evermann. Definitive source of information, detailed and accurate enough to enable the sportsman and nature lover to identify conclusively some 1,000 species and sub-species of North American fish, sought for food or sport. Coverage of range, physiology, habits, life history, food value. Best methods of capture, interest to the angler, advice on bait, fly-fishing, etc. 338 drawings and photographs. 1 + 574pp. 6⅝ x 9⅜.
22383-1 Paperbound $4.50

THE FROG BOOK, Mary C. Dickerson. Complete with extensive finding keys, over 300 photographs, and an introduction to the general biology of frogs and toads, this is the classic non-technical study of Northeastern and Central species. 58 species; 290 photographs and 16 color plates. xvii + 253pp.
21973-9 Paperbound $4.00

THE MOTH BOOK: A GUIDE TO THE MOTHS OF NORTH AMERICA, William J. Holland. Classical study, eagerly sought after and used for the past 60 years. Clear identification manual to more than 2,000 different moths, largest manual in existence. General information about moths, capturing, mounting, classifying, etc., followed by species by species descriptions. 263 illustrations plus 48 color plates show almost every species, full size. 1968 edition, preface, nomenclature changes by A. E. Brower. xxiv + 479pp. of text. 6½ x 9¼.
21948-8 Paperbound $5.00

THE SEA-BEACH AT EBB-TIDE, Augusta Foote Arnold. Interested amateur can identify hundreds of marine plants and animals on coasts of North America; marine algae; seaweeds; squids; hermit crabs; horse shoe crabs; shrimps; corals; sea anemones; etc. Species descriptions cover: structure; food; reproductive cycle; size; shape; color; habitat; etc. Over 600 drawings. 85 plates. xii + 490pp.
21949-6 Paperbound $3.50

COMMON BIRD SONGS, Donald J. Borror. 33⅓ 12-inch record presents songs of 60 important birds of the eastern United States. A thorough, serious record which provides several examples for each bird, showing different types of song, individual variations, etc. Inestimable identification aid for birdwatcher. 32-page booklet gives text about birds and songs, with illustration for each bird.
21829-5 Record, book, album. Monaural. $2.75

FADS AND FALLACIES IN THE NAME OF SCIENCE, Martin Gardner. Fair, witty appraisal of cranks and quacks of science: Atlantis, Lemuria, hollow earth, flat earth, Velikovsky, orgone energy, Dianetics, flying saucers, Bridey Murphy, food fads, medical fads, perpetual motion, etc. Formerly "In the Name of Science." x + 363pp.
20394-8 Paperbound $2.00

HOAXES, Curtis D. MacDougall. Exhaustive, unbelievably rich account of great hoaxes: Locke's moon hoax, Shakespearean forgeries, sea serpents, Loch Ness monster, Cardiff giant, John Wilkes Booth's mummy, Disumbrationist school of art, dozens more; also journalism, psychology of hoaxing. 54 illustrations. xi + 338pp.
20465-0 Paperbound $2.75

THE PRINCIPLES OF PSYCHOLOGY, William James. The famous long course, complete and unabridged. Stream of thought, time perception, memory, experimental methods—these are only some of the concerns of a work that was years ahead of its time and still valid, interesting, useful. 94 figures. Total of xviii + 1391pp.
20381-6, 20382-4 Two volumes, Paperbound $6.00

THE STRANGE STORY OF THE QUANTUM, Banesh Hoffmann. Non-mathematical but thorough explanation of work of Planck, Einstein, Bohr, Pauli, de Broglie, Schrödinger, Heisenberg, Dirac, Feynman, etc. No technical background needed. "Of books attempting such an account, this is the best," Henry Margenau, Yale. 40-page "Postscript 1959." xii + 285pp.
20518-5 Paperbound $2.00

THE RISE OF THE NEW PHYSICS, A. d'Abro. Most thorough explanation in print of central core of mathematical physics, both classical and modern; from Newton to Dirac and Heisenberg. Both history and exposition; philosophy of science, causality, explanations of higher mathematics, analytical mechanics, electromagnetism, thermodynamics, phase rule, special and general relativity, matrices. No higher mathematics needed to follow exposition, though treatment is elementary to intermediate in level. Recommended to serious student who wishes verbal understanding. 97 illustrations. xvii + 982pp.
20003-5, 20004-3 Two volumes, Paperbound $5.50

GREAT IDEAS OF OPERATIONS RESEARCH, Jagjit Singh. Easily followed non-technical explanation of mathematical tools, aims, results: statistics, linear programming, game theory, queueing theory, Monte Carlo simulation, etc. Uses only elementary mathematics. Many case studies, several analyzed in detail. Clarity, breadth make this excellent for specialist in another field who wishes background. 41 figures. x + 228pp.
21886-4 Paperbound $2.25

GREAT IDEAS OF MODERN MATHEMATICS: THEIR NATURE AND USE, Jagjit Singh. Internationally famous expositor, winner of Unesco's Kalinga Award for science popularization explains verbally such topics as differential equations, matrices, groups, sets, transformations, mathematical logic and other important modern mathematics, as well as use in physics, astrophysics, and similar fields. Superb exposition for layman, scientist in other areas. viii + 312pp.
20587-8 Paperbound $2.25

GREAT IDEAS IN INFORMATION THEORY, LANGUAGE AND CYBERNETICS, Jagjit Singh. The analog and digital computers, how they work, how they are like and unlike the human brain, the men who developed them, their future applications, computer terminology. An essential book for today, even for readers with little math. Some mathematical demonstrations included for more advanced readers. 118 figures. Tables. ix + 338pp.
21694-2 Paperbound $2.25

CHANCE, LUCK AND STATISTICS, Horace C. Levinson. Non-mathematical presentation of fundamentals of probability theory and science of statistics and their applications. Games of chance, betting odds, misuse of statistics, normal and skew distributions, birth rates, stock speculation, insurance. Enlarged edition. Formerly "The Science of Chance." xiii + 357pp.
21007-3 Paperbound $2.00

TWO LITTLE SAVAGES; BEING THE ADVENTURES OF TWO BOYS WHO LIVED AS INDIANS AND WHAT THEY LEARNED, Ernest Thompson Seton. Great classic of nature and boyhood provides a vast range of woodlore in most palatable form, a genuinely entertaining story. Two farm boys build a teepee in woods and live in it for a month, working out Indian solutions to living problems, star lore, birds and animals, plants, etc. 293 illustrations. vii + 286pp.

20985-7 Paperbound $2.50

PETER PIPER'S PRACTICAL PRINCIPLES OF PLAIN & PERFECT PRONUNCIATION. Alliterative jingles and tongue-twisters of surprising charm, that made their first appearance in America about 1830. Republished in full with the spirited woodcut illustrations from this earliest American edition. 32pp. 4½ x 6⅜.

22560-7 Paperbound $1.00

SCIENCE EXPERIMENTS AND AMUSEMENTS FOR CHILDREN, Charles Vivian. 73 easy experiments, requiring only materials found at home or easily available, such as candles, coins, steel wool, etc.; illustrate basic phenomena like vacuum, simple chemical reaction, etc. All safe. Modern, well-planned. Formerly *Science Games for Children*. 102 photos, numerous drawings. 96pp. 6⅛ x 9¼.

21856-2 Paperbound $1.25

AN INTRODUCTION TO CHESS MOVES AND TACTICS SIMPLY EXPLAINED, Leonard Barden. Informal intermediate introduction, quite strong in explaining reasons for moves. Covers basic material, tactics, important openings, traps, positional play in middle game, end game. Attempts to isolate patterns and recurrent configurations. Formerly *Chess*. 58 figures. 102pp. (USO) 21210-6 Paperbound $1.25

LASKER'S MANUAL OF CHESS, Dr. Emanuel Lasker. Lasker was not only one of the five great World Champions, he was also one of the ablest expositors, theorists, and analysts. In many ways, his Manual, permeated with his philosophy of battle, filled with keen insights, is one of the greatest works ever written on chess. Filled with analyzed games by the great players. A single-volume library that will profit almost any chess player, beginner or master. 308 diagrams. xli x 349pp.

20640-8 Paperbound $2.75

THE MASTER BOOK OF MATHEMATICAL RECREATIONS, Fred Schuh. In opinion of many the finest work ever prepared on mathematical puzzles, stunts, recreations; exhaustively thorough explanations of mathematics involved, analysis of effects, citation of puzzles and games. Mathematics involved is elementary. Translated by F. Göbel. 194 figures. xxiv + 430pp. 22134-2 Paperbound $3.00

MATHEMATICS, MAGIC AND MYSTERY, Martin Gardner. Puzzle editor for Scientific American explains mathematics behind various mystifying tricks: card tricks, stage "mind reading," coin and match tricks, counting out games, geometric dissections, etc. Probability sets, theory of numbers clearly explained. Also provides more than 400 tricks, guaranteed to work, that you can do. 135 illustrations. xii + 176pp.

20338-2 Paperbound $1.50

THE PHILOSOPHY OF THE UPANISHADS, Paul Deussen. Clear, detailed statement of upanishadic system of thought, generally considered among best available. History of these works, full exposition of system emergent from them, parallel concepts in the West. Translated by A. S. Geden. xiv + 429pp.

21616-0 Paperbound $3.00

LANGUAGE, TRUTH AND LOGIC, Alfred J. Ayer. Famous, remarkably clear introduction to the Vienna and Cambridge schools of Logical Positivism; function of philosophy, elimination of metaphysical thought, nature of analysis, similar topics. "Wish I had written it myself," Bertrand Russell. 2nd, 1946 edition. 160pp.

20010-8 Paperbound $1.35

THE GUIDE FOR THE PERPLEXED, Moses Maimonides. Great classic of medieval Judaism, major attempt to reconcile revealed religion (Pentateuch, commentaries) and Aristotelian philosophy. Enormously important in all Western thought. Unabridged Friedländer translation. 50-page introduction. lix + 414pp.

(USO) 20351-4 Paperbound $2.50

OCCULT AND SUPERNATURAL PHENOMENA, D. H. Rawcliffe. Full, serious study of the most persistent delusions of mankind: crystal gazing, mediumistic trance, stigmata, lycanthropy, fire walking, dowsing, telepathy, ghosts, ESP, etc., and their relation to common forms of abnormal psychology. Formerly *Illusions and Delusions of the Supernatural and the Occult.* iii + 551pp.   20503-7 Paperbound $3.50

THE EGYPTIAN BOOK OF THE DEAD: THE PAPYRUS OF ANI, E. A. Wallis Budge. Full hieroglyphic text, interlinear transliteration of sounds, word for word translation, then smooth, connected translation; Theban recension. Basic work in Ancient Egyptian civilization; now even more significant than ever for historical importance, dilation of consciousness, etc. clvi + 377pp. 6½ x 9¼.

21866-X Paperbound $3.95

PSYCHOLOGY OF MUSIC, Carl E. Seashore. Basic, thorough survey of everything known about psychology of music up to 1940's; essential reading for psychologists, musicologists. Physical acoustics; auditory apparatus; relationship of physical sound to perceived sound; role of the mind in sorting, altering, suppressing, creating sound sensations; musical learning, testing for ability, absolute pitch, other topics. Records of Caruso, Menuhin analyzed. 88 figures. xix + 408pp.

21851-1 Paperbound $2.75

THE I CHING (THE BOOK OF CHANGES), translated by James Legge. Complete translated text plus appendices by Confucius, of perhaps the most penetrating divination book ever compiled. Indispensable to all study of early Oriental civilizations. 3 plates. xxiii + 448pp.   21062-6 Paperbound $3.00

THE UPANISHADS, translated by Max Müller. Twelve classical upanishads: Chandogya, Kena, Aitareya, Kaushitaki, Isa, Katha, Mundaka, Taittiriyaka, Brhadaranyaka, Svetasvatara, Prasna, Maitriyana. 160-page introduction, analysis by Prof. Müller. Total of 826pp.   20398-0, 20399-9 Two volumes, Paperbound $5.00

JIM WHITEWOLF: THE LIFE OF A KIOWA APACHE INDIAN, Charles S. Brant, editor. Spans transition between native life and acculturation period, 1880 on. Kiowa culture, personal life pattern, religion and the supernatural, the Ghost Dance, breakdown in the White Man's world, similar material. 1 map. xii + 144pp.
22015-X Paperbound $1.75

THE NATIVE TRIBES OF CENTRAL AUSTRALIA, Baldwin Spencer and F. J. Gillen. Basic book in anthropology, devoted to full coverage of the Arunta and Warramunga tribes; the source for knowledge about kinship systems, material and social culture, religion, etc. Still unsurpassed. 121 photographs, 89 drawings. xviii + 669pp.
21775-2 Paperbound $5.00

MALAY MAGIC, Walter W. Skeat. Classic (1900); still the definitive work on the folklore and popular religion of the Malay peninsula. Describes marriage rites, birth spirits and ceremonies, medicine, dances, games, war and weapons, etc. Extensive quotes from original sources, many magic charms translated into English. 35 illustrations. Preface by Charles Otto Blagden. xxiv + 685pp.
21760-4 Paperbound $4.00

HEAVENS ON EARTH: UTOPIAN COMMUNITIES IN AMERICA, 1680-1880, Mark Holloway. The finest nontechnical account of American utopias, from the early Woman in the Wilderness, Ephrata, Rappites to the enormous mid 19th-century efflorescence; Shakers, New Harmony, Equity Stores, Fourier's Phalanxes, Oneida, Amana, Fruitlands, etc. "Entertaining and very instructive." *Times Literary Supplement.* 15 illustrations. 246pp.
21593-8 Paperbound $2.00

LONDON LABOUR AND THE LONDON POOR, Henry Mayhew. Earliest (c. 1850) sociological study in English, describing myriad subcultures of London poor. Particularly remarkable for the thousands of pages of direct testimony taken from the lips of London prostitutes, thieves, beggars, street sellers, chimney-sweepers, street-musicians, "mudlarks," "pure-finders," rag-gatherers, "running-patterers," dock laborers, cab-men, and hundreds of others, quoted directly in this massive work. An extraordinarily vital picture of London emerges. 110 illustrations. Total of lxxvi + 1951pp. 6⅝ x 10.
21934-8, 21935-6, 21936-4, 21937-2 Four volumes, Paperbound $14.00

HISTORY OF THE LATER ROMAN EMPIRE, J. B. Bury. Eloquent, detailed reconstruction of Western and Byzantine Roman Empire by a major historian, from the death of Theodosius I (395 A.D.) to the death of Justinian (565). Extensive quotations from contemporary sources; full coverage of important Roman and foreign figures of the time. xxxiv + 965pp. 21829-5 Record, book, album. Monaural. $3.50

AN INTELLECTUAL AND CULTURAL HISTORY OF THE WESTERN WORLD, Harry Elmer Barnes. Monumental study, tracing the development of the accomplishments that make up human culture. Every aspect of man's achievement surveyed from its origins in the Paleolithic to the present day (1964); social structures, ideas, economic systems, art, literature, technology, mathematics, the sciences, medicine, religion, jurisprudence, etc. Evaluations of the contributions of scores of great men. 1964 edition, revised and edited by scholars in the many fields represented. Total of xxix + 1381pp. 21275-0, 21276-9, 21277-7 Three volumes, Paperbound $7.75

MATHEMATICAL PUZZLES FOR BEGINNERS AND ENTHUSIASTS, Geoffrey Mott-Smith. 189 puzzles from easy to difficult—involving arithmetic, logic, algebra, properties of digits, probability, etc.—for enjoyment and mental stimulus. Explanation of mathematical principles behind the puzzles. 135 illustrations. viii + 248pp.
20198-8 Paperbound $1.75

PAPER FOLDING FOR BEGINNERS, William D. Murray and Francis J. Rigney. Easiest book on the market, clearest instructions on making interesting, beautiful origami. Sail boats, cups, roosters, frogs that move legs, bonbon boxes, standing birds, etc. 40 projects; more than 275 diagrams and photographs. 94pp.
20713-7 Paperbound $1.00

TRICKS AND GAMES ON THE POOL TABLE, Fred Herrmann. 79 tricks and games— some solitaires, some for two or more players, some competitive games—to entertain you between formal games. Mystifying shots and throws, unusual caroms, tricks involving such props as cork, coins, a hat, etc. Formerly *Fun on the Pool Table*. 77 figures. 95pp.
21814-7 Paperbound $1.00

HAND SHADOWS TO BE THROWN UPON THE WALL: A SERIES OF NOVEL AND AMUSING FIGURES FORMED BY THE HAND, Henry Bursill. Delightful picturebook from great-grandfather's day shows how to make 18 different hand shadows: a bird that flies, duck that quacks, dog that wags his tail, camel, goose, deer, boy, turtle, etc. Only book of its sort. vi + 33pp. 6½ x 9¼. 21779-5 Paperbound $1.00

WHITTLING AND WOODCARVING, E. J. Tangerman. 18th printing of best book on market. "If you can cut a potato you can carve" toys and puzzles, chains, chessmen, caricatures, masks, frames, woodcut blocks, surface patterns, much more. Information on tools, woods, techniques. Also goes into serious wood sculpture from Middle Ages to present, East and West. 464 photos, figures. x + 293pp.
20965-2 Paperbound $2.00

HISTORY OF PHILOSOPHY, Julián Marias. Possibly the clearest, most easily followed, best planned, most useful one-volume history of philosophy on the market; neither skimpy nor overfull. Full details on system of every major philosopher and dozens of less important thinkers from pre-Socratics up to Existentialism and later. Strong on many European figures usually omitted. Has gone through dozens of editions in Europe. 1966 edition, translated by Stanley Appelbaum and Clarence Strowbridge. xviii + 505pp.
21739-6 Paperbound $3.00

YOGA: A SCIENTIFIC EVALUATION, Kovoor T. Behanan. Scientific but non-technical study of physiological results of yoga exercises; done under auspices of Yale U. Relations to Indian thought, to psychoanalysis, etc. 16 photos. xxiii + 270pp.
20505-3 Paperbound $2.50

Prices subject to change without notice.
Available at your book dealer or write for free catalogue to Dept. GI, Dover Publications, Inc., 180 Varick St., N. Y., N. Y. 10014. Dover publishes more than 150 books each year on science, elementary and advanced mathematics, biology, music, art, literary history, social sciences and other areas.